DEVELOPING CULTUR. ___ ___ ___ ___ ___ ___ ___ ___ IN INTERNATIONAL HIGHER EDUCATION

To function in the diverse world of the twenty-first century requires a crucial ability to navigate its international and interconnected environments effectively. Such a skill may be defined as cultural capability, and developing it is at the forefront of this book, as it guides readers in considering their own experiences of learning and teaching in culturally varied contexts of higher education.

Using information that builds upon data gained from several years of practice, across a range of countries and institutions, the author considers in detail four main themes:

- learning, teaching and assessment as a cultural product of higher education;
- personal and professional interactions between staff and students;
- the political and personal dimensions of the internationalisation of higher education;
- methodological and ethical considerations when conducting research across cultures.

These themes provide for rich opportunities to learn from and about others, about our similarities and differences. In this way, *Developing Cultural Capability* celebrates a world that is multicultural and interdependent, encouraging operation beyond local and national perspectives.

Conducting cross-cultural research is not new, but this book shows how narrative inquiry may be a particularly rich – and sensitive – approach in such research in higher education.

By writing as a practitioner researcher who has reflected, extensively and critically, on her own practice, the author here gathers together empirical research, case studies and personal reflections, beliefs and assumptions into an innovative account of cultural capability. Through these rich accounts, this book stimulates researchers or practitioners grappling with the cultural complexity of higher education today to reflect on their own practices, proposing some ways to create environments that are more inclusive.

Sheila Trahar is Senior Lecturer in Education at the Graduate School of Education, University of Bristol, and Director of the Master in Education taught at the City University of Hong Kong.

DEVELOPING CULTURAL CAPABILITY IN INTERNATIONAL HIGHER EDUCATION

A narrative inquiry

Sheila Trahar

Routledge
Taylor & Francis Group

LONDON AND NEW YORK

First edition published 2011
by Routledge
2 Park Square, Milton Park, Abingdon, Oxon, OX14 4RN

Simultaneously published in the USA and Canada
by Routledge
270 Madison Avenue, New York, NY 10016

Routledge is an imprint of the Taylor & Francis Group, an informa business

Typeset in Bembo by
FiSH Books, Enfield
Printed and bound in Great Britain by
CPI Antony Rowe, Chippenham, Wiltshire

British Library Cataloguing-in-Publication Data
A catalogue record for this book is available from the British Library

Library of Congress Cataloging-in-Publication Data
Trahar, Sheila.
  Developing cultural capability in international higher education : a
narrative inquiry / Sheila Trahar. — 1st ed.
    p. cm.
  Includes bibliographical references and index.
  1. Education, Higher—International cooperation. 2. Education, Higher—
Social aspects. 3. Multicultural education—Cross-cultural studies.
4. Education and globalization. I. Title.
  LC3715.T73 2011
  378'.017—dc22

2010027117

ISBN13: 978-0-415-57238-5 (hbk)
ISBN13: 978-0-415-57239-2 (pbk)
ISBN13: 978-0-203-83400-8 (ebk)

CONTENTS

PREFACE

We live in a world that is interconnected and interdependent, where higher education with its increasingly diverse populations offers rich potential to develop a sense of global responsibility and citizenship. The diverse populations of higher education, brought about primarily by globalisation, are at the heart of this book, which has two, interrelated aims. The first is to illustrate how higher education can effect greater understanding between people from different contexts and academic traditions; the second is to show how narrative inquiry and autoethnography can be used to enable such understanding through illuminating some lived experiences of the 'core players in the process' (Teekens, 2000: 26) of learning and teaching in higher education – students and academics. Such everyday stories that express the multilayered complexities of the 'deeply embedded values, cultures and traditions' (Stenasker et al., 2008: 2) of learning and teaching are often absent from the higher education literature, yet students and academics are the people who constitute those values, cultures and traditions that need to be articulated if we are to understand them. Given that there are relatively few in-depth investigations of the interactions between international students, local students and academics (Brunner, 2006), especially in the UK, it may be naïve to assume that continued growth in the sector is sustainable, unless we can enable alignment between policies, resources and people's commitment.

The book tells a story of a journey. Through its reflexive account of my experiences and encounters as a practitioner researcher in higher education, it aims to promote critical reflection on learning and teaching in higher education environments that are significantly more diverse than they were even ten years ago. I shall be drawing on my more recent experiences as an academic in the Graduate School of Education at the University of Bristol, UK, and, in particular my teaching on our Master of Education (MEd), Doctor of Education (EdD) and Master of Science (MSc) in Educational Research programmes. I also teach on the MEd and

EdD in Hong Kong, and so will be informed by my work in that context as well. Thus the focus is on postgraduate rather than undergraduate experiences, although the academics featured in Chapter 7 teach both undergraduates and postgraduates and demonstrate that similar principles apply across the two levels and across disciplines, even if practices may, of necessity, differ. Throughout the book, there will be glimpses of many of my 'identities' including learner, teacher and counsellor. In fact, it was the teaching of counselling that prompted me to embark on the journey recounted here.

But what title do I give to a book such as this? I wanted to call it *Fellow Travellers*, to reflect that it is an account of many journeys – journeys that were taken – and continue to be taken – by many fellow travellers. Such a title communicates only one of the book's dimensions; an important one but, nonetheless, only one. I then mused on a title that included 'intercultural', 'transcultural' or 'cross-cultural', seeking to choose the term that would best accompany 'communication' in 21st-century higher education. Having worked in a higher education environment that is completely international, certainly in so far as the student constituency is concerned, for more than ten years, I have tussled at various times with each of those terms in my speaking and writing, adopting particular ones for what have been legitimate reasons. In the beginning I was seduced by cultural synergy, a concept that appeared to encapsulate what I was seeking to do – to learn from people from a range of 'cultures'. I was attracted to cultural synergy because it implies a fusion of cultural and academic traditions. Transculturalism was a term that I encountered in the writing of Salvadori (1997). Similar to cultural synergy, transculturalism refers to the creative new knowledge that can be formed through exploring cultural possibilities. I liked intercultural because it felt equitable – 'between cultures'; 'cross-cultural' was a term that occurred in particular in the methodological literature to refer to research that was conducted 'across cultures', which described what I was doing – learning, teaching and researching 'across cultures', in many senses of the words. I have also tangled with 'multicultural' and 'multiculturalism', opting for 'multicultural' in the literal sense of 'many cultures', rather than the more political multiculturalism, which conveys different meanings in different contexts. I then went through a phase of rejecting all of this vocabulary, as it seemed to position 'culture' as something immutable rather than fluid and developing. Not only did these words make uneasy bedfellows for my more postmodern, even occasionally post structuralist selves, but they also seemed to overlook that all communication between people may be regarded as 'cultural' as we are constantly negotiating different identities in our interactions with each other (Holliday *et al.*, 2004). Finally, I decided to use each expression in the book but to call it *Developing Cultural Capability* because I believe that all of us are shaped by values and systems that have different consequences for some people and societies, often resulting in social division. Being 'culturally capable' means understanding what those values and systems are and challenging one's own thinking and behaviour about them. In addition, because I believe that as a higher education practitioner I have a responsibility to do so, it can entail challenging some of the thinking and behaviour of others, in particular where it results in exclusionary practices.

I have listened to enough stories as a counsellor to have learned that narratives are not linear; most, if not all of us, when we are telling stories to others will move back and forth in time (Clandinin and Connelly, 2000). This book is a story that moves back and forth in time, yet its presentation could disguise the non-linear and multi-dimensional experience of its production. I want to make such temporality transparent, to show that the journey, its faint paths and my unsound footing, are as important for me as the outcome, the destination. It is my hope that, in sharing these processes transparently you the reader may be stirred into thinking about your own experiences, values, beliefs and, indeed, academic practices, a little differently.

Every chapter of the book is thus a blend of theoretical and methodological concepts; conversations and interviews with many postgraduate students and academics; discussions with colleagues; email correspondence; reflections on my professional experience; personal memories and reflections – in fact, the 'actions, doings and happenings' (Clandinin and Connelly, 2000: 79) that play such a signif-icant role in informing practitioner research, especially as the research becomes inseparable from 'life in its broadest sense on the landscape' (ibid.). In writing narra-tive inquiry, it is common to use various voices to retell stories gathered. Sometimes I am a storyteller, and so use a chatty, familiar voice; sometimes I use a more authoritative voice, as I interact with theoretical concepts and literature; at other times, I use a supportive voice to enable some other voices to be heard. Through writing in the different voices I hope to:

> Let readers experience with you your search for understanding, the questions you ask . . . what their answers open up for you, new questions that arise and how you interpret their stories . . . You might end up by showing how your stories compare and finally how your story changed as you took in and inter-acted with the other . . . stories.
>
> *(Ellis and Bochner, 2000: 757)*

As the words of Carl Leggo ring in my ears:

> There is no separating the personal from the professional. As a teacher I do not leave my home and family experiences behind me . . . when I enter the classroom. And I do not leave my past either. I am the person I am because of the experiences and people and places that comprise my life and living.
>
> *(Leggo, 2008: 91)*

You are about to read of some of the experiences, people and places that comprise the lives and living of many people who happen to have met in what can often be strange and unfamiliar landscapes of higher education and to 'act and to re-act upon each other' (Chapter 9). Here is an outline of the different ways in which you will meet them:

The **Prologue** and **Chapter 1** tell how the story began. Here I recall my first encounters with students from many places, describing how these experiences led to my embarking on a study into those students' perceptions and experiences of learning and teaching. This chapter introduces Cheng-tsung Lee, a Taiwanese postgraduate who makes many appearances throughout the book. In The First Letter to Cheng-tsung, I make some effort to define the word 'culture' and to establish the book's core themes.

Chapter 2 describes a landscape of higher education in the UK in the early part of the 21st century. In this chapter, I begin to make connections between the personal experiences described in the previous chapter and broader conceptualisations of internationalisation and globalisation as they relate to higher education.

Chapter 3 focuses on learning and teaching in higher education. Following a brief review of some of the key concepts that inform learning and teaching in higher education, the chapter is a journey through a critical consideration of the philosophical roots of my own pedagogical approach. In this chapter, I review some literature of learning and teaching in different contexts as well as drawing on conversations between several people to illustrate how learning and teaching are culturally mediated activities.

Chapter 4 addresses the methodological elements that need to be taken into account when conducting studies with people from diverse backgrounds and academic traditions. It tells the story of how I came to be a narrative inquirer and explains the reflexive and autoethnographical dimensions of practitioner research. I became aware that it was disingenuous to be writing about the influences of culture on others' learning and teaching experiences without interrogating my own, hence the turn to autoethnography.

Chapter 5 is presented as a series of letters to Cheng-tsung Lee, the Taiwanese postgraduate student. The collaboratively constructed stories that are told in the letters illuminate not only cultural influences on learning and teaching but also more fundamental ways in which we learned to communicate with each other. It thus demonstrates and illustrates the possibilities of working through what can be barriers of unfamiliarity, to greater understanding of diversity in and out of the 'classroom'.

In **Chapter 6,** we encounter some 'local' students through the medium of a television documentary. As European societies become increasingly multicultural, there is, of course, enormous potential for developing cultural capability 'at home', yet the experiences of 'local' students in international higher education environments are sometimes neglected. The concept of 'internationalisation at home' acknowledges that the majority of people are not mobile, and thus exposure to cultural difference will not be gained from studying or working in another country. In this chapter, the conversations with 'local' students will illustrate some strategies for enabling students 'at home' to benefit from the diversity of higher education communities.

Chapter 7 is derived from conversations with academics working in the UK. In this chapter, academics tell of their encounters in higher education landscapes, focusing in particular on the ways in which they experience diversity and how they seek to ensure that their teaching is inclusive.

In **Chapter 8** I attempt to engage with my 'whiteness' – a concept that does not have a 'clearly definable cultural terrain nor for many a desirable one' (Frankenburg, 1993: 205), to demonstrate how I might, unwittingly, in the past, have been 'a pawn in a game' of exclusionary practices. I realised that, while I was attributing responses and behaviours of people with cultural backgrounds that differed from my own to their cultural background, I overlooked that my attitudes and behaviours are as related to my culture/ethnicity as are other people's.

Chapter 9 uses the device of fictionalised representation (Clough, 2002) to orchestrate together words from conversations with my own words, memories and reflections, to tell different stories/stories differently. This chapter draws on myriad conversations I had with people, juxtaposing their words with mine so that they are all speaking directly with each other rather than just with me. By using this device to create what is, at times, an uncomfortable and confrontational dialogue, I am able to move beyond 'othering' and to communicate attitudes and behaviours in a creative way.

Chapter 10 summaries how researching my own practice has generated insights into, and effected changes in, my learning and teaching approaches. I reflect on the value of narrative inquiry and autoethnography in conducting research 'across cultures' and offer some ways of developing cultural capability in international higher education. These strategies are scattered throughout the book but are gathered together here to provide a final summary.

A note on ethical issues and other terms used

In Chapter 9 I discuss ethical complexities of narrative inquiry and autoethnography. The names that are given to the people who appear in this book are the names that they have either asked me to use or have agreed to my using. The only person whose given name is used is Cheng-tsung Lee, at his specific request, because he wanted his stories to be heard by others and for them to know that these were his stories.

The term 'international students' is used to refer to those students from outside the European Union (EU) who are studying in UK universities. In the UK, students from the other countries of the EU are regarded as 'local' students for fee purposes; however, they are often positioned as 'international students', usually because many do not have English as their first language. I use the terms 'local', 'host' and 'home' students when referring to those students who are resident in the UK and have been educated there. None of these terms is intended as a signifier of homogeneous groups, nor as a pejorative term. I use them merely, for ease of description.

ACKNOWLEDGEMENTS

So many people have contributed to this book that it is impossible to thank them all personally. There are, however, some that I would like to mention in particular. Thank you to those postgraduates that I met on that bleak November night in 1999; your stories started this journey for me, in many ways. Thank you to my colleagues and students in the Graduate School of Education at the University of Bristol and at City University, Hong Kong; conversations with you continue to inform, challenge and enrich. Very special thanks to Cheng-tsung Lee; your stories continue to move many people to reflect on their own in rather different ways. Thank you to Catherine Montgomery for her very constructive comments on several of the chapters and to Fiona Hyland whose appreciation and feedback was so encouraging and important to me. Thank you to Michael Crossley who read an earlier iteration of parts of this book and who is also a Bob Dylan fan. Many thanks to Philip Mudd at Routledge for his support and to Charles Haynes – also at Routledge and also a Bob Dylan fan – for his prompt, friendly and helpful responses to my many questions.

Finally, as always, special thanks to Barry, Peter and Jessica for being there.

Some material in Chapter 3 has appeared in Trahar (2008) and in Trahar (2007). Some material in Chapters 5 and 8 appeared in Trahar (2006).

In memory of my father, whose belief in education sent me travelling along many roads.

How to encompass in our minds the complexity of some lived moments in life? How to embody in language the mix of heightened awareness and felt experience?...You don't do that with theories. You don't do that with a system of ideas. You do it with a story.

(Coles, 1989: 128)

PROLOGUE

Beginning tales

All research beyond the banal begins in uncertainty, where action is unanticipated and anticipations are unrequited. We enter *slippery, uncertain ground*. *Paths* grow faint, the *footing* unsound. In real beginnings, we nearly always lose our confidence *or our way* some of the time. This awkwardness seems unsightly and unprofessional, so we rarely tell beginning tales.

(Charmaz and Mitchell, 1997: 209, my emphases)

November 1999

I have been asked by a colleague to teach two sessions of a Master of Education (MEd) course, 'Guidance and Counselling in Education', while she is away. I have agreed to teach the second part of this course next term and she believes that teaching these two sessions will be a good opportunity for me to meet the students.

I plan the sessions carefully, combining a range of experiential activities with input from me. That evening it is already dusk as I walk round the Georgian square to the building where the class will take place. The rain is falling steadily. The teaching room is on the third floor of the building. It is a dismal, ugly room containing grubby, orange, polypropylene chairs placed behind tables. It reminds me of a school classroom. A cursory scan suggests that it is not going to be easy to get rid of the tables to form my usual semicircle of chairs. I decide to leave the layout as it is. As the students start to drift in, I notice I am the only local person in the room. I ask everyone to introduce themselves – Evodia from Lesotho, Marilyn from Anguilla, Julian from Argentina, Rosanna from Hong Kong, Jasmine from St Vincent, Eva from Portugal, Sofia from Cyprus. There are others whose names I have forgotten. I am overcome with feelings that I do not recognise but which I know are uncomfortable.

The story never really begins nor ends, even though there is a beginning and an end to every story, just as there is a beginning and an end to every teller... The story never stops beginning or ending. It appears headless and bottomless for it is built on differences. Its (in) finitude subverts every notion of completeness and its frame remains a non-totalizable one.

(*Trinh, 1989: 1–2*)

The stories in this book are built on differences – or, perhaps more accurately, they reflect processes of 'continuously decomposing, reproducing and multiplying' (Gannon, 2009: 69) differences. They are, therefore, headless and bottomless, with uncertain beginnings and endings. This book tells some of these stories.

1

INTRODUCTION

The story never stops beginning ... but the journey starts

It may be that stories never stop beginning or ending, but this is where I pause, take a breather and surrender the stories gathered from learning and teaching encounters in an international higher education context to a wider audience. Sufficient ground has now been covered, albeit much of it very slippery and uncertain, to provoke other conversations with you, the reader.

The incident described in the Prologue was the symbolic beginning of the study upon which this book is based. As a practitioner researcher, teaching and research are iterative processes for me. Because I cannot extricate my identity as a researcher from that of a teacher, the book offers a series of 'nuanced accounts of the intricacies of everyday life' (Malcolm and Zukas, 2009: 499) in a higher education landscape, accounts that seek to communicate the 'felt modalities' (Gannon, 2009: 71) of diversity rather than translations of them within what can be limiting theoretical frameworks.

The event, described in the Prologue, and the uncomfortable thoughts and feelings that were generated, helped me to realise that I had embarked on a journey, a journey that continues, taking me backwards and forwards in time, a journey more important than any destination (Ellis and Bochner, 2000). This chapter marks the beginning of that journey. Here I recall how, in those first encounters with students whose backgrounds I perceived to be very different from mine, I developed a research study. I tell how the study looked in those early days. Then, through The First Letter to Cheng-tsung, I indicate some of its twists and turns and other questions that were raised. Thus, in this introductory chapter, the central themes of the book are established.

Setting foot on the journey: the back story

My burgeoning curiosity about the kaleidoscope of emotions I experienced when working with student groups whose constituency was increasingly diverse initiated the reflexive practitioner research that I write about in this book. My conscious encounters with 'reflection' began much earlier, however, in 1990, when I began my professional training as a counsellor. The concept of 'self-reflection' was crucial in the type of training that I did, even if, as I now realise, seldom problematised. Learning to use my 'self' had become such an intrinsic dimension of my work that, for me, the notion of 'reflective practice' was second-nature. I was always reflecting on what I did, seeking ways to be more effective as a teacher in higher education. As a practitioner researcher, it seemed logical, therefore, that 'reflecting' on my practice would enable me to research a range of experiences of learning and teaching in a multicultural higher education context; those of others as well as my own:

> Reflexivity is . . . an ability to notice our responses to the world around us, other people and events, and to use that knowledge to inform our actions, communications and understandings. To be reflexive we need to be aware of our personal responses and to be able to make choices about how to use them. We also need to be aware of the personal, social and cultural contexts in which we live and work and to understand how these impact on the ways we interpret our world.
>
> *(Etherington, 2004: 19)*

I am now more critical about this apparently unproblematised notion of reflexivity – as I comment on later in this chapter; but when I embarked on the study, I believed that by being reflexive I had the potential to develop significantly greater and more sensitive awareness of the 'personal, social and cultural contexts' in which I lived and worked. In doing so, I hoped to make a somewhat different contribution to the growing debate on internationalisation/diversity in higher education and, more practically, to develop and share strategies for developing 'cultural capability' in that context.

The 'globalisation' and 'pedagogy' themes

> One paradoxical consequence of the process of globalisation, the awareness of the finitude and boundedness of the plane of humanity, is not to produce homogeneity but to familiarise us with greater diversity, the extensive range of local cultures.
>
> *(Featherstone, 1993: 169)*

The original aim of the study was to explore the 'greater diversity', 'the extensive range of local cultures', with respect to learning and teaching in higher education and its increasing numbers of international students. I planned that the study would build upon a critical review of the literature relating to cultural influences on learning and the experiences of international students studying in a foreign country, and would engage with an interrogation of dominant andragogical theories. Methodologically and epistemologically, the study would be located broadly within interpretivist paradigms and would owe much to the spirit of collaborative research.

The study was designed to advance theoretical understanding of the cross-cultural complexities and dilemmas encountered in learning and teaching in higher education. Its dominant aim was to examine how bridges of intercultural learning might be developed so that all the 'hybrid identities' (Marginson and Mollis, 2001: 596) engaged in higher education teaching and learning in contemporary times might work towards greater 'cultural synergy' (Cortazzi and Jin, 1997: 88). More broadly, I hoped that the study would also prove useful in terms of informing higher education policy and practice, even if only at a local level.

In addition to my interest in understanding more about how international post-graduates studying in the UK experienced learning and teaching in the Graduate School of Education at the University of Bristol, I wanted to challenge the stereo-types of particular cultures that, to my embarrassment, I had become aware of holding. In order to do so, rather than indulge in a 'liberal *disavowal of difference*' that can fail to address 'issues of power, identity and culture' (Manathunga, 2007: 95, original emphasis) I wanted to engage in dialogue with colleagues as well as students, not to gloss over difference but, rather, to learn from it. A central theme of the book is, therefore, an intensive, reflexive questioning of my own pedagogi-cal approach, prompted by the international higher education landscape in which I found myself. This questioning is an extension of earlier, empirical research where I explored co-teaching relationships in higher education and the influences of gender upon such work (Trahar, 1996). Focusing on the relationship between co-tutors, I was able to identify factors that contributed to the effectiveness of working together. One of my conclusions was that both male and female students are less likely to respond to discursive and experiential approaches to learning when the facilitator is a woman. This had a profound effect on me at the time because of the value I placed on those pedagogical approaches. The influence of gender on relationships between students and teachers continues to be important to me; but, because of my more recent experiences of working with international students, I sought to explore other influences and dimensions of those relationships. In doing so, I realised that it might be necessary to problematise those discursive and expe-riential pedagogical practices, rooted as they are in particular 'western' beliefs about learning (see, for example, Gustavsson and Osman, 1997; Watkins, 2000; Sparks and Butterwick, 2004; Brookfield, 2005; Entwistle, 2009) and, indeed, the very notions of 'reflection', 'reflective practice' and 'reflexivity', which as concepts might also be critiqued for their 'dualistic, Cartesian worldview' (Erlandson, 2005: 662).

> Globalisation produces two contradictory phenomena: standardisation and diversification... diversification strives to preserve the multiple facets of society by promoting access to the diverse features of world heritage.
>
> *(Hallak, 2000: 25)*

These 'diverse features' fascinated me, yet it seemed that by striving towards 'diversification' I became more aware of an apparent desire for 'standardisation', by which I mean homogenisation rather than a more nuanced response. I acknowledge this as my perception, but it seemed to manifest itself in the structural systems within which my encounters with students occurred. In the local context of my university department we have developed a series of strategies designed to support all students in their 'return to learning'. These strategies include an Orientation Week, a Learning Skills programme designed to help students with studying and writing assignments, and a structured system of personal tutoring. The intention behind the provision of such support, particularly the learning skills seminars, is admirable, as the latter enable international students to become familiar with UK academic conventions (De Vita, 2001, 2002). The activities are well-received and valued by students. But I continue to muse on whether these strategies are attempts at 'standardisation', further examples of the transfer of educational theories, policies and innovations – and pedagogical practices – 'uncritically' (Crossley, 1984, 2000) across international borders, rather than celebrations of diversity. Are they, rather, forms of cultural imperialism that devalue alternative pedagogies and cultural values? On a more personal level, I began to question whether I really wanted to preserve the multiple dimensions of conceptualisations of learning or whether I, too, was seeking to standardise, to assimilate.

I am wary of the neocolonial connotations of the term 'assimilation', but find the notion of a 'transformational ideal of assimilation' (Young, 2001: 208) attractive. This concept signifies a level of assimilation that recognises that, although institutions may express the perspectives of the dominant group, specific ways of working and even policies can be implemented that can be transformative. I believed that the increase in international student mobility carried a moral and ethical obligation on me as an educator and a critical pedagogue (Ippolito, 2007) to work towards a similar ideal. This may be a Sisyphean task, but 'a journey of a thousand miles begins with a single step' (Lao-tzu, 604–531 BCE). A more accurate translation of the original Chinese is 'The journey of a thousand miles begins beneath one's feet' – an even more apt description for practitioner research. This journey began, in my own context, 'under my own feet'; it would be an iterative journey that, in its early stages, perhaps somewhat ambitiously, I hoped might bridge theory, policy and practice.

I recognised at an early phase of the study that I was moving towards a more critical postmodern approach to adult learning theory, where the relationship between the individual and society is both recognised and celebrated. I faced the dilemma that 'the true essence of any teaching/learning exchange emanates from the paradigm established by the prevailing learning theory text' (Flannery, 1995: 152). I expected to take an informed and critical perspective on those theories that continue to be the dominant narratives and to question their relevance in a multicultural environment. I did not anticipate that my research would lead to a new theory of andragogy; but by subjecting different perspectives on learning to critical analysis, I envisaged developing pedagogical approaches that were more culturally inclusive.

Policy themes

Preparation for teaching in higher education in the UK has gained prominence since the 1997 Dearing Report. This report recommended that all new full-time academic staff with teaching responsibilities should have access to programmes to support them in their teaching and should be encouraged to become members of the Institute for Teaching and Learning in Higher Education, now the Higher Education Academy. In January 2003, the UK White Paper 'The Future of Higher Education' was published. One of the aims of this was to create a new unitary body, a 'teaching quality academy', to help develop policy on teaching and learning to conduct research and to establish new national standards for teaching in higher education as the basis of accredited training for all staff. My involvement in Higher Education Academy accredited programmes for new academic staff, such as the one offered at the University of Bristol, offered an important vehicle for dialogue about my research. I was in a position to embed critical discussion of the multicultural classroom into this programme, to draw attention to some of the tensions of working in such an environment and to the importance of being sensitive to diverse approaches to learning.

This was the design of the study when I began in 2001. I now move on to show how, through the process of the research, the original aims remained but metamorphosed into other important questions that I strive to address throughout this book. I have chosen to introduce these changes by means of a letter to Cheng-tsung Lee, a student from Taiwan, who became one of the most significant research participants. His influence is visible throughout this book, although in some ways a similar letter might have been written to many people that I have encountered since that November evening in 1999. Indeed, I might even have addressed it to myself, as it articulates more of the 'research puzzles' that I still strive to disentangle.

The first letter to Cheng-tsung

Dear Cheng-tsung,
There are many stories to be told in this book; stories from conversations that I have had with you and with others. In this letter I want to acknowledge the major part that you played in my learning; learning about the many issues that we discussed, learning about myself, as well as to articulate the major themes of the book that those conversations generated. When we first met, I was beginning to question the philosophical assumptions embedded in Western theoretical approaches to counselling, provoking similar, critical discussions in teaching sessions. In our conversations, I shared with you my subsequent, similar probing of learning and teaching in higher education and of the apparent Eurocentricity of the underlying epistemologies of many research methodologies.

I have sought to relate the stories that we shared to the ways in which learning is conceptualised in different cultures and to my experiences as a learner in my context. I hope you will feel that I have been true to my stated desire to give equality of utterance to the characters – you and others – and narrator – me, and that my own voice has not become more authoritative (Vice, 1997). In *all* the conversations I strove to work to a fundamental principle of narrative inquiry [Chapter 4], that of inviting people to tell stories that were meaningful, rather than assume that they had answers to questions that I might pose (Chase, 2005). So, in Chapter 5, I have re-presented parts of our conversations as a series of stories that emerged. Retaining parts of our dialogue, together with reflections on our responses, demonstrates the interactive subjectivity of narrative inquiry. It is a form of dialogic/performance analysis (Riessman, 2008) – and such analysis is performed in different voices in Chapters 6 and 7. Thus, I have shared the ways in which stories resonate with me, using 'sameness and difference . . . each to interrogate the other, constantly moving between them' (Marginson and Mollis, 2001: 588), and to illustrate how meanings are influenced by our connections between past and present experiences and between self and other.

By articulating these interactions in as transparent a way as possible, I sought to challenge the criticism that because I was an academic conducting research with students, you and others would feel coerced into participating (Merriam *et al.*, 2001). I did not want us to be constrained by such essentialised notions of power that conceptualise research participants such as you as needing to be empowered (Mishler, 1986) and researchers, in particular white researchers, such as me, as powerful. I wanted to be mindful of the power and of the privilege ascribed to my position as a white academic, but reconceptualising power as uncontrollable and constantly shifting can: 'Open up multiple spaces in which interview interactions can be conducted and represented, ways that engage the indeterminate ambiguity of interviewing, practices that transgress and exceed a knowable order' (Scheurich, 1997: 75). The themes of power and of insider/outsider emerged at different stages of the study and are woven throughout the book.

The theme of language

In the first session of the MEd course, Guidance and Counselling in Education, I remember you said that you hoped people would excuse your English. I felt that that was a very brave comment to make that evening. My clumsy response, 'I hope that you will excuse mine', was intended to communicate to you and to others my awareness that I might sometimes use words that were unfamiliar to you. If I did use such words, I hoped you would ask me to explain them. I discovered, subsequently, that some of the difficulties in communication between those who speak English as their first language and those for whom it is an additional language are well known (see, for example, Jones, 2001; Wright and Lander, 2003; Hellsten and Prescott, 2004; Prescott and Hellsten, 2005; Henderson, 2009). The barriers to communication that can be experienced are explored and even decomposed, reproduced and multiplied (Gannon, 2009) in parts of our conversation in Chapter 5. Such barriers also emerge in Chapters 6 and 7 and are dissolved in different ways in Chapter 9, which gathers together fellow travellers' stories.

The cultural theme

'Culture is not what some group has; it's what happens to you when you encounter difference' (Agar, 1994: 22). I like that statement. It resonates with me and reflects the experience I described in the Prologue, that of my first encounter with international students. It challenges the notion that 'culture' is about 'other people' but recognises, in a pragmatic way, that many of us do not think of ourselves as being 'different' until we encounter someone who we position as different or who positions us as different. 'Defining culture is a tricky business in our contemporary society' (Chang, 2008: 16). It certainly is. In the preface to this book, I discussed a range of terms that are used to denote encounters between people whose cultural backgrounds appear to be different. Even though I accept that all communication is 'intercultural' as we always have to negotiate different identities that are performed in our interactions with others (Holliday *et al.*, 2004); nonetheless, in a book entitled *Developing Cultural Capability in International Higher Education* I feel that I must attempt to give the word culture some meaning, so that when I use it, the meaning of the discourse will be clear.

I shall settle for 'Culture is . . . the sum of stories we tell ourselves about who we are and want to be, individually and collectively' (Maxwell, 2001: 1) as well as 'The knowledge people use to generate and interpret social behaviour' (Ryen, 2000: 221). Those definitions are straightforward and describe what others and I do on a daily basis. I will also be mindful of Chang's (2008) 'work-in-progress concept of culture' (p. 21) as this resonates with what I write in Chapter 8 about 'being in progress'. I shall endeavour not to use the terms 'ethnicity' and 'culture' interchangeably, but there may be moments when I do so, mainly because, in those moments, I am influenced by the work of writers who themselves use one term when they seem to be referring to the other.

Being pragmatic, however, I quote Brah's words: 'Studies from various parts of the globe show that two groups sharing a broadly similar cultural space may construct themselves as ethnically distinct; conversely, culturally distinct groups may assert a common ethnicity' (1996: 238) to draw to your attention that cultural specificities themselves are not that important. In my view it is important to recognise and learn about these specificities; but more important is 'The meaning attributed to them, and how this meaning is played out in the economic, cultural and political domains, that marks whether or not specificity emerges as a basis of social division' (ibid.: 235).

Such a statement, inevitably, links to the exercise of power: 'The point is that "ethnicity" is no less or more "real" than class or gender or other marker of differentiation. What is at issue is the specificity of power that configures and is exercised in a given articulation of these differentiations' (ibid.: 241).

It is the potential for the exercise of power, together with the registering of my concern 'about the possible shoring up of Eurocentric moves in supposedly progressive fields of scholarship where one should least expect to find these' (ibid.: 220), that is another area of exploration in this book – and another core theme.

The theme of 'othering'

> A conversation of 'us' with 'us' about 'them' is a conversation in which 'them' is silenced. 'Them' always stands on the other side of the hill, naked and speechless, barely present in its absence. Subject of discussion, 'them' is only admitted among 'us', the discussing subjects, when accompanied or introduced by an 'us' member... The conversation... turns out to be rather intimate: a chatty talk, which under cover of cross-cultural communication, simply superposes one system of signs over another.
>
> *(Trinh, 1989: 67–68)*

As you know, this 'othering' that Trinh is referring to here continues to be problematic for me. In order to recognise the 'other', it is of course necessary to recognise ourselves (Stromquist, 2002). I strive to 'recognise myself' throughout this book yet still find it very difficult not to 'other'. You may remember that I shared my consternation with this with a group of academics in Cape Town in 2008 and received what at the time I found to be a challenging yet valuable response: 'Why not say "we"?' If I use 'we', however, I feel that there can then be a danger of the 'liberal *disavowal of difference*' (Manthunga, 2007). In my experience, although we may theorise about shifting identities and cultures and about race and ethnicity as being social constructions rather than 'realities', discriminatory practices – and 'othering' – continue to occur. Could this be because:

> In practice, the problem with such a multicultural attitude is embedded in our limited ability as individual human beings to grasp the other in terms different from our own, and as 'cultural beings' to extend our cultural horizons beyond the boundaries shaped by our

own contextually situated life stories[?]. Understanding the other person's culture demands an extra effort...which is not without risk.

(*Turniansky* et al., *2009: 39–40*)

In this book, I am risking experimenting with ways of talking about diversity that seek to be celebratory and provocative. For example, I have sought to engage, at times, in intimate, chatty talk. Whether I have engaged in that 'under cover of cross-cultural communication', and superposed 'one system of signs over another' (Trinh, 1989: 68) as an exercise of power, will be for you to judge as the book unfolds. In addition, in Chapter 9 I have created a type of fictionalised dialogue in which people speak directly *to* each other rather than *about* each other. This strategy allows me to retell conversations that were uncomfortable – certainly for me – and to show certain discriminatory views and experiences, without betraying the confidentiality of those who shared these views and experiences with me. It also allows me to interject my own thoughts and feelings, and risk 'we'-ing rather than 'you'-ing and 'other'-ing.

As I end the first letter, this seems a fitting point for you to introduce yourself to the reader, as s/he will meet you many times on the journeys narrated in this book:

My upbringing and background illustrate a correspondence with my cultural context. My interpretation of the world is forged by my interactions with objects in my society.

I was born in a middle-class family in Taiwan. My father was born in the south-east of China. He was a colonel and good at Chinese literature and history. Two thirds of his life was spent in the turmoil of his country's war – the invasion by Japan and the communist rebellion. In 1949 he left behind his family and retreated with the nationalist government to Taiwan. His father had established a private primary school in the old China. My mother is an aboriginal woman from a high mountain tribe – Tsou, which is in the central area of Taiwan. Even though my parents came from different ethnic groups, both of my grandparents' families placed importance on education. I was born in 1968, the oldest son of my family. My father passed away when I was ten years old. He never saw his family in China after 1949. I married my wife, who is of Hakka origin, in 1999 and now we have a four-year-old son.

Best wishes,
Sheila.

The first letter to Cheng-tsung is used here to embody the spirit of my work and to provide an introduction to the substantive part of the book you are about to read. It is an illustration of how the themes of the book, such as cultural capability;

culturally mediated approaches to learning and teaching in higher education; and the critical questioning of my own values, beliefs, culture and ethnicity; emerged through various conversations, including 'conversations' with theoretical concepts. 'There is an African saying that "when you are preparing for a journey, you own the journey. Once you've started the journey, the journey owns you"' (Shope, 2006: 165). I ask you, the reader, to accompany me on a journey; a journey whose destination became unknown; a journey that resisted taking the simplest or easiest routes; a journey that began to own me.

The initial focus of the study, the preparation for the journey, as outlined earlier, was the process of learning and teaching and its conceptualisation in different cultures. It may seem, sometimes, as though I wander away from that focus. I do – that is if one defines learning as only occurring in certain contexts and teaching as only being about the transmission of knowledge. I contend that it is because I kept conversations open and fluid so that people felt able to talk about a range of experiences and concerns, as well as to reflect on learning and teaching in higher education and to question me (Chase, 2005), that unanticipated narratives occurred (Cortazzi and Jin, 2006). It was through the sharing of those experiences that I arrived at new understandings – about many of the people that I encounter every day; about learning and teaching in higher education; about methodological perspectives; about myself.

Finally...

> How do we judge the merits of these stories? When do we know they're reliable and telling?

> I think it's the same judgement we make about any author or any character. Is the work honest or dishonest? Does the author take the measure of herself, her limitations, her confusion, ambivalence, mixed feelings? Do you gain a sense of emotional reliability... Does the story enable you to understand and feel the experience it seeks to convey?

> *(Ellis and Bochner, 2000: 749)*

The ways in which I approached the study that informs this book owe much to narrative inquiry and autoethnography, where the primary focus is on engaging reflexively with the participants and with the research process, and struggling to find ways in which to do so. In reading this book, I ask you to consider it using the above questions. Such questions have guided me to report my research experiences in ways that you, the reader, may understand and resonate with them as 'felt modalities' of pedagogical encounters (Gannon, 2009: 71).

> The narrative rises or falls on its own capacity to provoke readers to broaden their horizons, reflect critically on their own experience, enter empathically into worlds of experience different from their own, and actively engage in

dialogue regarding the...different perspectives and standpoints encountered. Invited to take the story in and use it for themselves, readers become coperformers, examining themselves through the evocative power of the narrative text.

(Ellis and Bochner, 2000: 748)

This is one of my aims in what you are about to read.

2

UNEVEN LANDSCAPES OF HIGHER EDUCATION IN THE 21ST CENTURY

In this chapter, I introduce the context of my work as an academic, connecting my experience with broader conceptualisations of internationalisation and globalisation as they relate to higher education. This chapter expands further on the discomfort that I felt on my first encounters with this landscape – alluded to in the Prologue – providing glimpses of the subsequent links I made between that discomfort and issues of colonialism and imperialism (Biggs, 2003; Devos, 2003).

The university: an 'international' institution?

Given the focus of this book, no doubt there will be an expectation that I will use and define terms such as 'internationalisation', 'globalisation', 'cosmopolitanism' and 'glocalisation'. Indeed, that is what I strive to do later in this chapter. Before doing that, though, I consider it important that we remind ourselves about those two words, 'university' and 'international', that are now used together so often that one would imagine that the 'international university' is a new phenomenon, whereas, of course, it is not.

A traditional view of the university is that it has always been a 'universal' institution and that in the age of European empires and of imperial science, it became one of society's most international organisations (Teichler, 2004). Universities existed, of course, long before the age of European empires. The University of Al Karoaouine in Fez, Morocco, for example, can lay claim to being the oldest university in the world, having been created in 859 CE. Most universities, wherever they are, however, are not ancient institutions but creations of the nation-state, often dependent on national governments for their budgets and, in the postcolonial world, often expected to be concerned primarily with nation building (Scott, 1998). If universities are funded to serve their own national purposes, can they really be defined as international? 'Most national governments want to have at least one university considered as an international research university' (Horta, 2009: 397); they are, therefore, both national *and* international (Halliday, 1999). Those universities that 'established themselves earlier in global higher education', usually in countries with 'dominant scientific systems', are considered to be 'world-class' (Horta, 2009: 389) and to have a competitive edge.

If universities have always been 'international', one may muse on why there is currently so much emphasis on 'international higher education', 'internationalisation of higher education', even a book, such as this one, that focuses on 'developing cultural capability in international higher education'. 'Mass higher education has been critical to the global economy... Opportunities to participate and progress through higher education and into postgraduate studies and research are extensive' (David, 2009: 19). I propose that the diversity of the 21st century university, in particular the cultural diversity, brought about as a result of this more extensive participation, can provide rich opportunities for developing 'a more globalized sense of responsibility and citizenship' (Kahane, 2009: 49). It can thus prepare learners for a world that is interdependent and interconnected (OECD, 1999). Such statements may seem altruistic, even sentimental, but diversity, if celebrated, can support academics and indeed all members of higher education communities to operate beyond the local and national perspectives that can dominate two of the core activities of universities – learning and teaching – and enable this greater global understanding. Rizvi (2000: 6) claims that this can only be achieved by 'the creative utilisation of the imagination of all those that make up the university... in ways that are both self-reflexive and critical' – a core theme of this book.

Internationalisation? Globalisation? Cosmopolitanism? Glocalisation?

Terms that describe the changes in higher education brought about as a consequence of globalisation continue to proliferate and to be contested. The term 'globalisation,' in particular, is often used interchangeably with 'internationalisation' yet they are 'different but dynamically linked concepts' (OECD, 1999: 14), inadequately understood, defying simple explanation (Sanderson, 2004). One useful distinction is that internationalisation refers to the 'growth of relations between nations and between national cultures (in that sense internationalisation has a long history)', whereas globalisation is 'reserved for the growing role of world systems. These world systems are situated outside and beyond the nation-state, even while bearing the marks of dominant national cultures, particularly American culture' (Marginson, 2000: 24). More appropriately, given the context and spirit of this book, the 'logic of internationalism' is referred to as 'essentially pro-democratic', standing 'in sharp contrast to the logic of globalisation' (Jones, 1998: 143) and based on 'conscious action... a response to the challenges brought about by globalisation' (Wachter, 2000: 8).

Given the 'centrality of higher education institutions in the globalized world... the relationships between globalization and higher education seem to be acuter, perplexing and open to multiple and divergent accounts' (Vaira, 2004: 484). As I indicated earlier, globalisation undoubtedly provides opportunities for many more people to move to another country for study purposes (Marginson and Mollis, 2001), thus providing the potential to 'internationalise' higher education, but what does 'the internationalisation of higher education' mean? Does it mean the integration of an international/intercultural dimension into all of the activities of a university, including the teaching, research and service functions (OECD, 1999)? Is the aim of such integration to achieve mutual understanding through dialogue with people in other countries (Yang, 2002)? More simplistically, does the term refer to increased numbers of students, 'sojourners' (Kiley, 2003) from countries other than the host country, who are studying in universities? A cynic might say that 'market-related strategies such as . . . encouraging academics and universities to engage in business and market-like activities to generate revenue' (Mok, 2003: 123), including the recruitment of international students, are designed specifically to reduce the financial burden of the state, as such students can generate high fee income. This income can then be used to shore up crumbling infrastructures, as universities, certainly in many parts of the western world, are increasingly the victims of swingeing cuts in central government funding.

Otten (2003: 13) proposes another dimension of internationalisation and globalisation, that of the 'regional/local level of . . . domestic multiculturalism'. This inclusion of the perspective of the local is sometimes subsumed into the term 'cosmopolitanism' (Caglar, 2006: 40). Similarly – and particularly pertinent within the context of international higher education – Cuccioletta (2001/2002: 4) refers to 'cosmopolitan citizenship . . . that recognizes that each person of that nation-state possesses multiple identities', linking her/him to their own cultural heritage and the culture of the host country. Yet another term, 'glocalisation', 'can be divided into the terms "global" and "localization", a global outlook adapted to local conditions' (Mok and Lee, 2003: 35).

There are many descriptors of 'cross-border' activities. Such descriptors might be added to the list of terms such as intercultural, cross-cultural, transcultural that I discussed in the Preface. Like Kreber (2009), I take the view that the words used as descriptors of these activities are less significant – what is more important is to be clear about the assumptions and motivations mediating efforts – this is what I seek to do in this book. I am settling, therefore, for the term 'internationalisation', associating it 'principally with an ethos of mutuality and practices geared at strengthening cooperation . . . By encouraging greater internationalisation across teaching, research and service activities, the quality of higher education can be enriched' (ibid.: 2–3).

Internationalisation = international students?

Having settled on internationalisation as a preferred term with the aforementioned meaning, I think it important, nonetheless, to reflect on why definitions of internationalisation continue to be so unsettled. One reason is that a nation's history, culture, indigenous population and resources shape, inevitably, its relationships with other countries (Yang, 2005). In the UK, in spite of an increasing amount of research in the field, the meaning of internationalisation still tends to be elided with the increasing numbers of international students. In 2008, for example, I was the project manager of a study funded by the UK Higher Education Academy, charged with investigating 'Perspectives on Internationalising the Curriculum' (Hyland *et al.*, 2008). A question that we posed to all focus group participants – academic staff and students – was, 'What do you understand by the term "internationalisation"'? Most people – and they were from all over the world – made some attempt to offer a definition but very quickly focused on 'international students' in the conversations; thus, by implication, eliding the meanings of the words.

In contrast with the UK, in Australia and Canada, which are also large importers of international students, the meaning of internationalisation is more often linked closely to their domestic multicultural populations. In those contexts, research often moves beyond an examination of the relationship between their own nationals and those from other countries to greater recognition of shifting and multiple identities of all individuals and groups (Yang, 2005). In countries that tend to be exporters, such as Japan, Malaysia and China, internationalisation has still other meanings. In Japan, internationalisation has been embraced as a way of producing graduates capable of explaining their country to the wider world. In Malaysia there has been a push to instil Islamic values in the Malaysian population (Merrick, 2000) as a backlash against internationalisation, regarded as the unidirectional cultural flows from the 'West' to the 'Rest' (Rizvi, 2004). In China, now the third largest recruiter of international students, the term internationalisation tends to refer to China's conformity with what is considered to be 'mainstream', i.e. western international practice. The term *jiegui* – connecting the smaller with the larger – is widely accepted as a crucial facet of internationalisation in higher education in China (Yang, 2002, 2005). Many Chinese academics seem to have sufficient confidence in their traditional culture not to feel threatened by internationalisation (ibid.). This confidence may stem from 'the remarkable capacity of Confucian culture to accommodate other cultures' (Hayhoe, 2005: 582) or it may indicate a naïvety about the effects of outside influences and their hegemonic neoliberalism (Yang, 2005).

Halliday summarises this contentious debate nicely for me when he writes, 'an unconsidered pursuit of the international can lead to a less, rather than a more, effective international contribution' (1999: 99). Higher education discourse is laden with theorising about internationalisation, globalisation, cosmopolitanism and glocalisation. I do not suggest that this discourse is 'unconsidered'. What I do propose, however, is that in spite of claims of vigorous pursuit of revisionist and deconstructive agendas in First World universities to reflect the social and cultural diversity of modern higher education systems (Scott, 1998), there continues to be much less focus on the complexities of intercultural encounters and communication – the lived experiences of the participants – in such environments. The more *considered* voices, the dialogic voices, the polyphonic voices, the critically reflective conversations about personal experiences of daily encounters, through which we might learn about developing cultural capability, are still rarely revealed.

> Intercultural learning is not just a topic to be talked about (thinking and knowing) it is also about caring, acting and connecting...It entails the discovery and transcendence of difference through authentic experiences of cross-cultural interaction that involve real tasks, and emotional as well as intellectual participation.
>
> *(De Vita and Case, 2003: 388)*

Those words 'caring, acting and connecting' resonate with me; they fit with my own desire to challenge the 'talking about', to connect through caring and to act, perhaps differently, through dialogue. But I baulk at the assumptions that are lurking in the second part of the quote – 'transcendence of difference', 'authentic experiences', 'real tasks'. Assumptions of differences that need to be transcended? What would be inauthentic experiences, tasks that were not real? So many culturally loaded statements, each one to be deconstructed throughout this book.

The 'whiteness' of the UK academy?

The questioning of the complexities of multicultural higher education environments has been somewhat less prevalent in the UK, until relatively recently. Clegg *et al.* (2003) suggest that one reason for this lack of work examining the meaning of cultural differences in higher education in the UK is that universities have only recently experienced greater ethnic diversity. By ethnic diversity, they are referring to local students with ethnic minority backgrounds because, as established previously, universities are one of society's most international organisations. Even some 70 years ago, international students made up 10.4 per cent of students in UK universities (Biggs, 2003). In the 21st century, the background of those students has changed, however, with many now originating from Africa and the Middle and Far East (McNamara and Harris, 1997; Biggs, 2003) as opposed to the Anglo-Celtic countries of the Commonwealth, such as Australia and Canada. The 'containment of cultural difference will persist...unless we as practitioners are willing to engage in debate...and challenge the whiteness [of the academy]' (Clegg *et al.*, 2003: 166). The latter research focuses on the attitudes of academic staff towards British black and minority ethnic (BME) students and does not seek to include, as I do, attitudes towards working with postgraduate students who have come to the UK to study. The majority of students that I meet every day are not BME undergraduates; they are professionally experienced postgraduate students from many different countries, including the UK, often learning in a language that is not their first. They bring with them rich and diverse educational traditions and professional experience – and different complexities and opportunities.

'Without reflexive awareness, the 'whiteness' of the academy can go unnoticed and uncommented' (Clegg *et al.*, 2003: 164) is a statement that conveys uncomfortable undercurrents of neocolonialism – particularly when international students may be conceptualised as the 'colonial subjects of our times' (Devos, 2003; 158). It foregrounds institutional racism in higher education. Scheurich (1997: 135) suggests that if a university's 'standard pedagogical method is culturally congruent with the culture of white students but not with the cultures of students of color', this is an example of institutional racism. Clearly, this definition is not unproblematic as it implies a certain boundaried definition of 'white culture' that I have established I am seeking to resist. In addition, 'students of color' is a term particular to the US context. Institutional racism, as defined thus, together with the notion of epistemological racism, discussed in Chapter 4, challenged me to critique, however, not only my own learning and teaching practices, but also what I perceived to be the dominant pedagogy of my own institution and my own 'whiteness' in Chapter 8. I strove to move from 'teaching as assimilation...a kind of colonial phase' (Biggs, 2003: 123–125), towards a diversimilarity paradigm that emphasises 'the appreciation of cultural diversity and cultural similarities' (Ofori-Dankwa and Lane, 2000: 497). Thus, I am not seeking to 'contain cultural difference' but to celebrate it.

As I indicated in Chapter 1, my university department has established a Learning Skills seminar programme as a way of supporting all students in their return to learning. The intention behind this programme is admirable in supporting international students in their efforts to become familiar with UK conventions for studying, writing and producing assignments (De Vita, 2001, 2002); however, such programmes might be based on a premise of 'blame-the-student thinking' (Biggs, 2003: 124) and fail to recognise that international students bring distinctive learning skills. Our own teaching and learning practices are rarely subjected to such critical scrutiny. We seldom question, for example, the validity of taking a 'critical approach' to study:

> This thing we call 'critical thinking' or 'analysis' has strong cultural components...it is a voice, a stance, a relationship with texts and authorities that is taught, both consciously and unconsciously, by family members, teachers, the media, even the history of one's own country...It means...finding words that show exact relationships between ideas, as is required in a low-context culture...It means valuing separateness over harmony.
>
> *(Fox, 1994: 125)*

Even less often do we embrace the experiences of our international students and academic staff and consider how we might learn from them about alternative teaching and learning approaches (Trahar, 2006; Kim, 2009).

'Colonial subjects of our times' (Devos, 2003: 158)?

As I indicated earlier in this chapter, UK universities have attracted students from other countries for many years but the background of those students has changed recently. Many students from Africa and Asia now have to study in the West, for example, as institutions in Eastern Europe and Soviet Russia, which had provided heavily subsidised places to them, now do not do so following the collapse of communism. Student flows may no longer be determined primarily by colonial or postcolonial links, nor be about countries such as Britain importing, and low-income countries exporting (Scott, 1998), but in my own department, we continue to attract students from sub-Saharan Africa, India, Pakistan and the small states of the Caribbean – those countries that were part of the British Empire and whose education systems bear that legacy. Such people encounter, among others, those from Taiwan and China (areas of recent exponential growth in the export of students), increasing numbers from Greece and the newer accessioned European Union (EU) states of Cyprus and Malta, as well as those from the UK. International and EU students account for a high percentage of students on our Masters programmes and have an equally visible presence on our doctoral programmes in the UK.

The UK, as a net importer rather than exporter of international students, is keen, therefore, to retain its fairly consistent 12 per cent share of the market, rendering it second only to the USA in its ability to attract students from other countries. International students made up 11 per cent of all first-degree students in UK higher education in 2006/7, but at postgraduate-level study – the focus of this book – 66 per cent of full-time postgraduates and 42 per cent of all taught postgraduates were defined as international, with 43 per cent of all research postgraduates falling within that category (www.ukcisa.org.uk/about/statistics_he.php). Such students contribute more than £8.5 billion annually to the UK economy.

International students are a market to be exploited, and Tony Blair's Prime Minister's Initiative (PMI), launched in 1999, sought to raise the number of international students in the UK by 50,000 by 2004/5. This target was attained and, in April 2006, Blair launched the second phase of his PMI. The aim of this second phase was to attract more than 100,000 'foreign students' by 2011. One initiative that has emerged from PMI2 is the Teaching International Students (TIS) project. This is a joint initiative of the Higher Education Academy and the United Kingdom Council for International Student Affairs (UKCISA) and is funded by PMI2. In spite of the implications of its title, its aim is to provide guidance for academics on how to meet the diverse learning needs of international students in ways that will benefit all students. But the ways in which increased numbers of international students can 'internationalise' the experience of British students and staff and benefit UK higher education have still not been widely articulated (Merrick, 2000). Indeed, using the definition I have adopted, many would contend that much UK higher education has not been internationalised. Increasing effort has been made to embed an 'international dimension' into the teaching and learning, research, quality assurance and service functions, but there can still be a gulf between the marketing strategies promoting the opportunities for mutual understanding offered by the fresh and enriching perspectives of international students (British Council, 2003) and the experiences of academics and the student community (Turner and Robson, 2006). There can often be a gap between the rhetoric and the engagement of the academics, 'core players in the process' (Teekens, 2000: 26), of higher education, possibly because 'teaching and learning demand more time, energy and patience' (Otten, 2000: 14) in a diverse educational context.

To summarise:

> Globalization is the context of economic and academic trends that are part of the reality of the 21st century. Internationalization includes the policies and practices undertaken by academic systems and institutions – *and even individuals* – to cope with the global academic environment... Globalization may be unalterable but internationalization involves many choices.
>
> *(Altbach and Knight, 2007: 290–291, my emphases)*

'And even individuals' implies, once again, that individuals have a lesser role in the changing nature of higher education, yet it is the individuals who constitute the values, cultures and traditions of higher education that are rarely articulated, made transparent and exposed to critical scrutiny (Turner and Robson, 2008; Trahar, 2010). It is these more neglected areas that are explored in this book.

Personal musings

> The 'real life' experience of cultural diversity is without doubt the most involving form of learning. On the other hand the contact-hypothesis (inter-cultural learning will occur automatically whenever people meet long and intensely enough) has been proved to be wrong in many cases. The personal experience of an intercultural encounter does not automatically initiate intercultural learning.
>
> *(Otten, 2000: 15)*

When I first began contributing to the Bristol MEd programme in 1999, I brought a wealth of experience of working as an adult educator with people who are often defined as 'non-traditional' students. Those who fall within that category are mature students, part-time students combining study with work and family respon-sibilities, and those with very little post-compulsory education. What we had in common, these students and I, however, was that the majority of us were white and British. Our ethnicity and cultural backgrounds were very similar, and, in some cases, we also shared social and educational backgrounds. It was extremely rare for me to encounter students who were culturally different and who did not have English as their first language. The dis-ease, therefore, that I experienced when I first worked with a group of international students (Trahar, 2002a, 2002b) reflected this new experience for me, but also, I realised in hindsight, I was very uncom-fortable with the issues of colonisation implicit in the 'transfer of skills and knowledge from the university sector to the broader community' when 'this broader community is in Asia, Africa or the Middle East' (Cadman, 2000: 476). I feared that I was being 'pseudo-etic' (Biggs, 2001b: 293), especially as in my first encounter with international students, I had planned a session on rational-emotive behaviour therapy (REBT), an approach to counselling developed by Albert Ellis, a white, male North American. Such disquiet reflects Crossley's (1984, 2000) iden-tification of the potential problems arising from the uncritical transfer of educational theories, policies and innovations across international boundaries and a concern that internationalisation should not become a 'cover for creeping Westernisation' (Merrick, 2000: xii). I have therefore been provoked to explore ways in which I might unwittingly continue to 'uncritically transfer' my own atti-tudes and practices of learning and teaching, developed and grounded in particular western cultures when working with people who bring different traditions and values.

I am aware that the western academy can be seen as a colonising institution (Cary, 2004), especially in its subtle treatment of those who do not belong to its dominant culture. There are those (such as Cadman, 2000; Asmar, 2003, 2005; De Vita and Case, 2003) who share my concerns and dis-ease at the apparent lack of consideration of ethical issues – such as inadequate infrastructural support – inher-ent in the growth in aggressive marketing of postgraduate programmes. 'The institutionalisation of power favours the dominant group, local students, and labels international students as the "Other"' (Hellmundt and Fox, 2003: 34). International students can be scapegoated as the source of increased pressure by dissatisfied academics who can be reduced to marginalising and infantilising them (Devos, 2003). A university can be seen as a safe place from which to call for change, and unless I, as a white practitioner, am willing to 'challenge the white-ness [of the academy] . . . containment of cultural difference will persist' (Clegg *et al.*, 2003: 166). By problematising my own 'whiteness', that 'set of cultural prac-tices that are usually unmarked and unnamed' (Frankenberg, 1993: 1), dislodging it from 'its central unmarked and undefined position' (Watson and Scraton, 2001: 273), I am seeking to make transparent not only the problems but also the poten-tial in cross-cultural interactions. In doing so, I am striving to recognise how my ethnicity and cultural affiliations serve as constructions of my identities as learner, as teacher and as human being. 'Before we can recognise the "Other", we have to know ourselves well. This requires a position of ethics, not just being bystanders of external developments' (Stromquist, 2002: 93). I do not want to be a bystander, hovering in the wings of internationalisation, therefore I seek to recognise the 'other' through critiquing my 'self'.

Appadurai's (2001) notion of weak and strong internationalisation is used to reconceptualise the meaning of becoming internationalised, defining it as a 'personal journey of deconstruction and reconstruction' (Sanderson, 2004: 16). Such a personal journey is a kind of bottom-up internationalisation that, while it may not resolve the great imbalances of power in the world, might help level the playing field (Appadurai, 2001: 20). It may also help:

> To show the extent and manner in which globalising processes are mediated on the ground, in the flesh and 'inside the head' . . . paying attention to diverse peoples and places, and their complex and contradictory experiences

of, reactions to, and engagements with various aspects of globalisation as these intersect with their lives and identities.

(Kenway and Fahey, 2006: 267)

I invite you to step into the landscape I have sketched out and join others and me on our journeys of deconstruction and reconstruction, in the flesh and in the head. Perhaps, in doing so, you will embark on a journey of your own. Perhaps, together, we can help to level the playing field.

3
LEARNING AND TEACHING IN HIGHER EDUCATION

In a book such as this, including a chapter that engages with the theoretical literature of learning and teaching in higher education would seem to be imperative, but seeking to disentangle theoretical frameworks of pedagogy from my everyday practice so that they can be examined meticulously and articulated clearly feels somewhat disingenuous and inconsistent with the journeying metaphor that I have established. I have realised, however, that if I eschew a discussion on learning and teaching in higher education, I may, legitimately, be accused of demonstrating a lack of awareness of the silent assertion of 'a model of HE practice that is enculturated rather than culturally problematised' (Turner and Robson, 2008: 20). I have been 'problematising' my model of higher education practice for the past ten years. In this chapter, therefore, I intertwine the intersubjective voices of students' and academics' experiences of internationalisation with more conceptual discussions of learning and teaching.

By now it must be clear to the reader that it is important for my own integrity to be transparent about my own espoused practices and to reveal through dialogue of different kinds how I began to interrogate the philosophical underpinnings of my understandings about learning and teaching. My aim is to offer a short synthesis of the major theoretical concepts that have contributed to and inform learning and teaching in higher education, rather than a very detailed discussion of them. I shall then move on to show how these ideas informed – and inform – my own practices using reading, reflections and research conversations – both face-to-face and 'virtual' – with students and academics to illustrate how I began to question my own values, beliefs and, ultimately, pedagogical positioning. In addition – and this is the more intrinsically fascinating part for me – I shall show, through my engagement with ways in which learning and teaching are conceptualised in some different contexts, how these ideas are culturally mediated and, therefore, need to be considered cautiously in the 21st century higher education landscape.

Those interested and engaged with the scholarship of learning and teaching in higher education will be familiar with the debates presented here; those less familiar – and tempted by my taster – may choose to seek out the work of those such as Prosser and Trigwell (1999), Biggs and Tang (2007) and Entwistle (2009) in order to develop their insights.

A quick romp through the concepts

> Much of the research into student learning and university teaching has followed a research approach that is both cognitive and social, focusing on learning within specific academic contexts, as it has tried to understand the differences in how students tackle their academic work and the reasons for those differences.
>
> *(Entwistle, 2009: 22)*

Entwistle is highlighting here that the major influences on learning and teaching in higher education are psychological and sociological – as one might expect. He continues by reminding us that:

> Research into student learning changed in the mid-1970s...introduced a broader perspective on learning, one that saw individuals as having their own intentions and seeking to make sense of their world for themselves within a social setting. This approach relied much less on the concepts and categories developed by theorists from other disciplines and, instead, sought explanations from the experiences of students. (p. 28)

I have explained that it was the interactions with postgraduates from different parts of the world that started me on the journey of wanting to investigate 'the explanations from the experiences of students' of learning and teaching in an international higher education landscape. Alongside those interactions, however, it was my critical engagement with the literature of learning and teaching approaches in a range of cultures that caused me to recognise the cultural situatedness of my espoused pedagogical principles (Amstutz, 1999) and to start to question my own cultural affiliations. Appreciating that our identities as learners are as shifting and changing as any other identities (Sarup, 1996; Edwards and Usher, 2000; Fox, 2006), I glimpsed the potential for destabilising cultural differences (Gannon, 2009) and for working with my own discomfort to develop new learning (Manathunga, 2007).

Turner and Robson (2008: 11) ask what, for me, is a crucial question 'who shapes the culture of learning and intellectual HE spaces?' If we hold to the view that any teacher is significant in 'mediating knowledge, values and behaviours' (ibid.: 83), then the importance of the problematisation of dominant pedagogical practices is apparent. Problematising this dominance foregrounds the need for those in higher education communities to challenge assimilative notions of diversity and to focus on being open to learning from each other (Trahar, 2007, 2010; Hellsten, 2008).

Recognising that learning, teaching and assessment are constructed and mediated by cultural norms and academic traditions may be seen as a first stage in the process of critiquing the dominant philosophies and practices that underpin learning and teaching in higher education. For example, the striving for self-actualisation and learning autonomy that pervades higher education discourse in the UK context – and in many other 'western' contexts – is often presented unproblematically as if there were shared understanding of the concepts. Such perspectives are based on particular philosophies that favour and privilege individual development:

> In the traditional university disciplines, the ways of thinking are derived, historically, from the underlying philosophy of the Western world, involving causal explanations and critical reasoning, which can then be alien to students coming from very different cultural backgrounds...there needs to be a greater awareness of the ways in which thinking and acting are found in other cultures and the implications these have for university teaching.
>
> *(Entwistle, 2009: 23)*

Surprisingly, there is very little questioning of these 'ways of thinking' in environments that, by their very nature, are about the development and furthering of knowledge. This is somewhat paradoxical – the processes by which we teach and assess learners are grounded in particular knowledges that, as I have indicated, are rarely exposed to critical scrutiny. Ryan and Viete (2009: 305) propose a 'third space pedagogy', a pedagogy that engages us in interrogation of our own beliefs and values to 'help us understand the impact of our positioning as teachers and learners with different linguistic, cultural, disciplinary and experiential knowledge, and on our sense of ourselves in relation to others as writers, knowers, professionals'. I realise that my own autoethnographic explorations could, if one chose to, be positioned within this conceptual framework of third space pedagogy. But I am resistant to being positioned, to allowing the 'clutches' of 'classification...to look down on me' (Trinh, 1989: 48). Unlike Trinh, I am not so dramatically pessimistic as to believe that 'classification' entails 'death', but I am aware that I can enjoy to 'baffle, rather than bring out contours' (ibid.) sometimes, as a way of ensuring that I do not have theoretical labels attached to me that then become very difficult to loosen.

Tennant *et al.* (2010), in their work on higher education research and teaching, make useful reference to Skelton's (2005) four discourses that he proposes inform the everyday teaching practices of academics. These are: the traditional liberal; the psychologised; performative understanding; and critical understandings. Such perspectives are drawn from Skelton's interviews with holders of the National Teaching Fellowships (NTF) in the UK. Of intrinsic interest and value in offering a framework within which people teach, it must be remembered, however, that the majority of academic staff in the UK do not hold an NTF. Indeed, research indicates consistently, as I said earlier, that many are unaware of the concepts that inform their teaching approach. In recent conversations with academic staff from three UK universities with growing international student populations (Chapter 7), I asked about the philosophy that informed their teaching. These were people of good hearts and minds who considered teaching to be important and cared about students, yet most were unable to articulate the concepts that informed their teaching other than 'student-centred'. In these conversations, academics were able to describe, eloquently, what they did in the classroom but were less able to provide a rationale for it. They were committed to ensuring that students had positive learning experiences and spoke sympathetically about what they perceived to be particular needs of international students, yet very few could articulate any kind of philosophy. For me, this raises several questions: How important is it to be informed by theoretical knowledge about learning and teaching? Is it sufficient to seek to be effective and sensitive to students' needs? Is that position in itself a 'theoretical perspective'? Yet, in their own areas of research, those same people would pay close attention to the importance of theorising. It is a puzzle to me, and reminds me of when I used to contribute to the various Learning and Teaching programmes offered by the University of Bristol. I recall only too well that, for many participants, 'educational theory' was a 'red rag to a bull'. What they wanted was 'hints and tips'. I am, therefore, heartened by the following words from a physicist:

> I wanted to share with students my realisation that knowledge, even in something as mundane as physics, could be seen as a collection of models of the world, invented by individuals, rather than as solid facts which had to be swallowed so much like castor oil. Thus learning was so much more than gaining knowledge, even understanding how things worked; it was *being a learner* that was important, and for intrinsic rather then merely instrumental reasons.
>
> *(Entwistle and Walker, 2002: 24–28,*
> *cited in Entwistle, 2009: 72, emphasis in original)*

Walker subsequently designed his teaching to be 'multipli-inclusive' (ibid.: 78), a commendable strategy. Teachers who work in this way enable 'students at different levels, and with differing interests and goals, to take something valuable from the experience' (ibid.). This notion of multipli-inclusivity in teaching prompts me to turn to Haigh's (2009) contention that the recognition of multiple modes of *knowledge* represents a considerable intellectual challenge in international higher education, particularly when there is a 'deeply embedded, largely subconscious, cultural preconception that only Western tradition is normal' (ibid.: 280). This challenge is experienced in particular by 'local learners' who, limited by their previous experience with narrow curricula, may feel 'chauvinistic resistance to the intrusion of, if not outside ideas, then outside ways of doing things' (ibid.). So, do we have a conundrum? We have local learners, and indeed academics, for whom multiple ways of 'knowing' may present considerable challenges, and we have international students who may feel alienated when they encounter local ways of learning and teaching. Yet, as I will show in Chapters 6 and 7, if we can rise to these challenges embracing, them as opportunities rather than risks (or at various places along that continuum), then we move beyond this endlessly privileging of 'the West' to creating spaces for dialogue that can lead to new understandings in pedagogy – and, more broadly, to developing cultural capability.

From adult learner to adult educator: a story of learning and teaching

> Nobody embarking on a study of education in countries and cultures other than their own does so (or at least nobody ought to do so) without being acutely aware of how little, despite their best endeavours, they end up knowing... about what is *possibly the most elusive theme of all* (the practice of teaching and learning) and *how such practice relates to the context of culture, structure and policy in which it is embedded.*
>
> *(Alexander, 2000: 3, my emphases)*

I have italicised those particular words because they evoke and capture the essence of my musings on the practices of teaching and learning – elusive. I am a lecturer in higher education. The experiences that so roused my curiosity began in the classroom. Before long it became obvious to me that the ways in which we all – students and academics – experience this educational environment would connect with our previous experiences of learning and academic traditions and relate to structures and policies in our cultural contexts.

Considering how my own practice had developed, however, I reflected on the situations within which I had been learner and teacher, and the cultural and social contexts that had spawned the development of the philosophical and theoretical principles on which my practice was based. I made connections between those reflections and policies such as the UK's 1944 Education Act and the Robbins Report (1963) that had led to the structures within which I had been educated. I am of the generation of British people who were able to access higher education free of charge – in marked contrast to students of today who leave higher education burdened with debt. My father's influence on my learning and on my education was considerable. It is salutary for me, still, when leading Widening Participation research projects to remember that I carried several Widening Participation 'indicators' as the daughter of a skilled manual worker with no history of university education in the family.

My approach to learning and teaching has developed from being an adult learner and educator with significant experience of working with students who are defined in the UK as non-traditional (Chapter 2). I would not, however, define my earlier experiences of education as learner-centred. It was not until I entered higher education as an undergraduate that I encountered practices that encouraged me to participate in discussion and to debate social and political issues. Through such activities, I recognised the value of *my* experiences and their relationship with the world around me. Following this undergraduate experience, my experience of training to be a counsellor some 15 years ago led me to realise that, in order for learning to be effective, I needed to feel comfortable and emotionally connected, not only with the subject but also with the process of communication of that subject. In this way I came to experience learning as much more than the transmission of a set of facts or body of knowledge. The process of learning effected important changes in the ways in which I viewed myself and the ways in which I behaved towards others. It is not difficult to see, then, why I have been committed, as a practitioner, to implementing student-centred approaches to learning and teaching with their emphasis on discursive and experiential activities. I was involved in counselling training in the UK for a number of years, where these methods were, and still are, predominant. Having moved into other areas of teaching with different student populations, I have remained attached to the view that it is through experiencing a participative approach to learning, where the learner is encouraged to articulate their own needs, which are respected within the learning community, that learning is experienced as a much deeper and more personal process, one that can transform lives.

Active versus passive learning; deep versus surface learning (Marton and Saljo, 1984); formal input versus experiential learning; learning through discussion; learning styles/preferences (Honey and Mumford, 1982); situated learning (Lave and Wenger, 1991); learning as transformation (Mezirow, 1991); student-centred teaching and learning (Rogers, 1994; Knowles, 1990) – each one of these theoretical frameworks has influenced me. It was not until I began to work with people from different parts of the world that I began to question, at a deeper philosophical level, what I did and why I did it. Until then, it had seemed sufficient to be able to be explicit and transparent about the theoretical ideas I was drawing on in designing teaching sessions. Indeed, this was a valuable and intrinsic part of those sessions I mentioned earlier, which I ran on the University of Bristol's Learning and Teaching programme for academics and postgraduates, because I demonstrated how 'theory' supported pedagogical practices in the same way that 'theory' supported research (and practice) in participants' own discipline (Brawn and Trahar, 2003). I received excellent feedback on my teaching. Most people liked the way I worked, appreciating the amount of preparation in the planning of creative and stimulating sessions. If my approach worked well, why question it and seek to change it? The answer is: Because I became conscious that there might be a lack of sensitivity to diversity in my approach, wary that this might be symptomatic of an underlying cultural imperialism.

The practices that I espoused are grounded firmly in Knowles' (1990) guiding principles of adult learning; acknowledge Freire's (1972) conceptualisation of learning and teaching as internally related processes, and Mezirow's (1991) notion of perspective transformation. Knowles' (1990) principles are learner-centred and are informed by humanistic philosophy, in particular the work of Carl Rogers (1951, 1994). They have always seemed to me to be sound principles, reflecting my own experience by advocating that learning is most effective when people feel valued and respected for the experiences they bring to the learning environment and are supported to develop as autonomous learners. 'The underlying epistemological and pedagogical values beneath routine practices remained both implicit and culturally inviolate... people... remained indelibly linked to a locally articulated knowledge tradition fixed in its socio-historic context' (Turner and Robson, 2006: 26).

Resistant as I am to labels, I determined that those of 'implicit values' and 'culturally inviolate' would not be attached to me, that I would be aware of the dangers of 'false universalism' of 'adopting... practices across cultures without recognising the distinctive historical and cultural dimensions' (Phuong-Mai *et al.*, 2006: 4).

> Few academics are... closet essentialists, or Platonists... but sound as if they are when one questions the founding definitions and assumptions that... they may not even be aware of holding... they can create particularly painful dilemmas for students from differing backgrounds, of differing turns of mind whose identities and loyalties are cast as liabilities from which they should liberate themselves.
>
> *(Minnich, 2005: 161)*

Some of these pedagogical 'definitions and assumptions' are articulated further in conversations with Cheng-tsung in Chapter 5, but those such as Sparks (2002), Ladson-Billings (1995, 2000), hooks (1989, 1994, 2003) and Jarvis *et al.* (2003) challenged me to consider the ethnocentricity of much of the theorising to which I was attached. The research, from which the theorising was derived had often been conducted by and with white North-American men, yet universal applicability was claimed for it. Knowles, for example, neglected to consider the educational experiences of women and of ethnic minorities (Sparks, 2002). Even Carol Gilligan (1982), whose work I admired and who challenged the androcentrism of much lifespan developmental psychology, neglected to include non-white women in her earlier investigations.

It may be impractical to become familiar with the pedagogical traditions of every student and to 'teach' to all individual cultural preferences (Biggs, 2001b, 2003); yet: 'An understanding of culturally distinct values may promote *learning* from ways unlike one's own, and... differences *between* cultures may highlight important but previously unrecognised differences *within* cultures' (Tweed and Lehman, 2002: 90, my emphases).

I now recognise that these principles, to which I have been so attached, are located within a particular view of the world, within societies where individual fulfilment is paramount. Such cultural traditions of individualism, which place the individual firmly at the centre of the teaching and learning exchange, may explain the earlier emphasis on psychological rather than social explanations for educational phenomena and behaviours and the 'absence of the learner as a social being' (Malcolm and Zukas, 2001: 38). I continue to question, therefore, the extent to which a set of principles located in such cultural traditions may be relevant when working with students who come from rather more collectivist cultures, where more emphasis is placed on group rather than individual good and where success may involve significant others, the family, peers and society as a whole (Salili, 2001).

I then became concerned that I might, albeit unintentionally, be implying that students needed to 'liberate themselves' from their 'identities and loyalties' (Minnich, 2005: 161) if I were to continue with pedagogical practices that were unexamined for their cultural influences (McCoy, 2000). In order to examine some of these cultural influences, I asked two colleagues, Maroussia and Angeline, to observe a learning and teaching session on the MEd Guidance and Counselling course and to then have a conversation with each other to discuss what they saw. In the following section, I invite you to eavesdrop on their conversation.

A pedagogical conversation across cultures?

Maroussia is Irish-French and was educated in Belfast until the age of 9, completing her education in France. Angeline is British. I gave them no specific areas to focus on, as they observed the learning and teaching session, leaving it to them to decide how they would manage the observation and subsequent conversation. My only request was that they record the latter so that I could listen to it. I had been influenced by the work of Carola Conle (1999), who, in seeking to gain a better understanding of her teaching in order to discover if there were problems that she did not see in her multicultural higher education environment, asked observers into her classroom. After each observation the observers had a conversation about what they had witnessed. Each person interpreted the event differently. Conle suggests that this interpretation was shaped by their personal, social and cultural biographies. Their conversation begins:

Maroussia: Well, they certainly...more generally, seemed very much at ease with one another within the group. There was some talking right across the room at the beginning so it wasn't just chatting in pairs or in small groups; it was also broader group; and also very much at ease with Sheila. There was no feeling of tension that I could detect. There were some people who were more withdrawn than others but I didn't see that as anything to do with the class; just more generally something personal about the way they were. I thought that was nice...and this...openness...and it was interesting that both the doors were open as if Sheila was trying to reject anything, you know, that was, like, very formal classrooms, so the use of the doors, her own not being too dominant and being seated in the circle without tables. I was wondering actually about that...about there not being any tables because, well it's not very convenient when you're taking notes and they were expected to take notes at some point when there were the three models of...

Angeline: And they wanted to take notes.

Maroussia: . . . Yes, they were also meant to take notes during the video and so I was wondering whether it was, if that kind of, um . . .

Angeline: This kind of blurred boundary between the kind of . . . I think when you have . . . perhaps when . . . it is something peculiar to teaching counselling. They've got what would be a kind of group set-up in the counselling situation where you are all looking at each other, and then because it's still a teaching situation, there's still the need to somehow write one's notes and things like that . . . the kind of tension between that . . .

Maroussia: . . . Which was also visible in the interactions because a circle in the room suggests some kind of interactions, that don't have a focus on the tutor but will just be completely symmetrical among all the participants.

Angeline: But is . . . and there is also, um, a transparent arrangement. I mean you can very much see who's talking to who, which can inhibit some other interaction.

Maroussia: Um, that's true. So there was a feeling of wanting to create an atmosphere, which was very informal, chatty, which may correspond more to the type of atmosphere Sheila wants to create than to the need at some point in the teaching situation . . . the need to take notes.

Maroussia and Angeline focus on the layout of the room, both speculating about why I have laid it out in such a way. For Angeline, it links with her understanding of 'teaching counselling'; Maroussia assumes I want to create a particular atmosphere, one that is 'informal' and 'chatty'.

I am reminded of the old joke: 'How do you recognise a counsellor at a party? She's the one moving the chairs into a circle.' The circle is 'so sacred and reified in adult education as to be an unchallengeable sign of practitioners' democratic purity and learner-centeredness' (Brookfield, 2005: 131). I have moved away from this reifying of the circle, but I confess that I still prefer seating to be arranged, without tables, so that group members can see each others's faces. One reason for this arrangement is pragmatic; I continue to favour a discursive, experiential approach and tables can be barriers to such interaction between students, and between students and me. I have been challenged to question, however, whether there is a 'more troubling and ambivalent reality . . . beneath the circle's democratic veneer' (ibid.). Rearranging the chairs into a circle may not 'do away with power . . . [but] displace it and reconfigure it in different ways' (Usher and Edwards, 1994: 91). It may, as Angeline says, 'inhibit some interaction' and have the potential to be painful and humiliating for those students who may be conscious of their linguistic ability, their accent, their 'difference'. Is this assumption of displacement and reconfiguration of power a consequence of Foucauldian influences in the West? Is it another example of how we appropriate an indigenous practice, the native American 'talking circle', used as an indisputably democratic method of involving all members of the community in decision-making (Bohanon, 2006), and contaminate it (Trinh, 1989)?

Angeline and Maroussia had a conversation across their many 'cultures'. This was prompted by observing a learning and teaching session with a group of men and women from Greece, Taiwan, Kenya, Cyprus, the USA and the UK. Here is an example of multilayered complexity. Making explicit cultural influences that might be at work in the learning environment makes possible all sorts of conversations. Such conversations inform, and are embedded in, the writing of this book — as above! Extended extracts from other conversations — those between Cheng-tsung and me in Chapter 5, and in Chapters 6 and 7 — might even capture some of those most elusive themes of practices of teaching and learning (Alexander, 2000) in higher education.

East and West … and the rest?

I once began a piece of writing with the Socratic quote, 'I shall not teach him, only ask him, and he shall share the enquiry with me' (Socrates 469–399 BCE). I used these words as the basis for a convincing set of arguments for my espoused andragogical theories, showing how they informed my practice. 'There's nothing so practical as a good theory' (Lewin, 1951: 169), and, as I embarked on this journey, I began to get beneath the surface of this Socratic questioning approach to teaching that I had long valued — and, to some extent, still do.

Socrates is considered by many to be the father of western philosophy (Tweed and Lehman, 2002, 2003). He alleged that learning, and thus knowledge, progressed through his own and others' questioning of held beliefs, hence the term 'Socratic questioning'. This term is used to support a pedagogical practice that is common in the West, that of posing questions or problems to students and facilitating them to construct responses from their interactions with each other (Watkins, 2000). Such a practice relies heavily on the learners' willingness and ability to interact with each other in a purposeful way. It positions the teacher/lecturer not so much as an expert but as someone who needs expertise to facilitate an intrapersonal learning process.

Socratic philosophy has been embedded into a rationale for learning through activity and discussion so favoured by Rogers (1994) and Knowles (1990), and reflected vividly by Kolb (1984, 1999) in his experiential learning cycle. It emphasises the importance of the teacher/lecturer in creating a classroom atmosphere within which such learning can progress, and has become subsumed into a set of andragogical principles. Learning is considered to be most effective when people are encouraged to identify their learning expectations and needs, to negotiate the ways in which their learning will take place and to regard the teacher/lecturer as a resource rather than a didactic expert whose role it is to transmit knowledge and 'truth' (Knowles, 1990; Rogers, 1994). Those who favour these approaches to learning are often critical of more formal learning, usually in the form of the traditional lecture, and rote learning, believing that such practices constitute a 'surface approach' (Marton and Saljo, 1984). Experiential learning, 'deep learning', is thus privileged.

Some theoretical comparisons 'across' cultures

Several writers (including Hofstede, 1980, 1986, Volet, 1999, Watkins, 2000, Kember, 2001, Kennedy, 2002, Ng *et al.*, 2002) conclude that in Chinese culture there is a high level of collectivism, a strong sense of belonging to a social group and a preference for working together in groups to solve problems. Such conclusions do not sit easily with stereotypes of the Chinese learner as being passive, reticent and reluctant to participate in group discussion (Kember and Gow, 1991; Turner and Acker, 2002). Perhaps I am slipping into the dualities that I am dogged with throughout this book; 'Chinese learners', a term that once again assumes homogeneity, being regarded as *either* passive *or* active, when, of course, 'they' can be both.

Confucian philosophy on learning reveals some similarities with the Socratic approach. Confucius employed dialogical methods, was informal in his relationships with students and believed that they would be transformed by the knowledge they acquired. One element of Confucianism that has had significant influence on my own pedagogical approach is the encouragement of questioning and discussion, but *after* the learner has focused on understanding and acquiring concepts (Pratt *et al.*, 1999; Watkins, 2000). Here is another challenge to the stereotype of the 'Chinese learner' as shy and reluctant to participate in discussion. Welikala and Watkins (2008: 9) suggest that 'to be vocally and critically interactive for the purpose of learning...can relate to other important cultural scripts' and is less beneficial to higher levels of thinking and to deepening understanding (Webb, 1996; Jones, 1999; Teekens, 2000; Brookfield, 2005) than remaining silent. Thus, an apparent reluctance to participate *may* be related to language difficulties or to a lack of understanding of the non-verbal cues that are an intrinsic part of communication (Jones, 1999). It may not be reluctance at all, however, but may be due to a belief that learning does not occur *through* discussion but *by* discussion following acquisition of 'knowledge'. Silence, rather than being a lack of engagement in the process of learning, is thus an active process and socially positive in contrast to what may be seen to be confronting others, in the encouragement to be 'critical', which pervades many western discourses of learning. The following email, which I received from a Korean doctoral student, illustrates this latter concept. She emailed me immediately after a seminar in which I had shared my initial discomfort with some students' positioning of me as an expert. Seeking to be congruent with my student-centred beliefs, I viewed myself as a resource, a person with expertise. Rather than resisting this label of 'expert', I was striving now to embrace it, having learned that, for many students, it was important:

> I thank you for your sharing of your experience in the seminar. I hope you do not mind sharing of my experience and thoughts during the seminar.
>
> First of all, I thank you for your kind acceptance of my question. Even though I was/am a strong-headed woman, I noticed the feeling of guilty within me because I asked you a question (challenged you) at that time. Strange, isn't it?

I also noticed that you were trying not to take the title, an expert (but you admitted you had many expertise). Some Korean students (I believe this can be similar to any Asian students) unconsciously expect (sometimes strongly demand) you to take the role, an expert; because you have the expertise. This mean that they expect (or demand) you to tell them about your expertise with authority. Most students are ready not to argue or discuss but to absorb your expertise. Some students, of course, ask their teachers some questions.

Another issue was that keeping quiet was seen as a virtue in Korea: meaning behaving well. If a student asks questions often, they might be told off; because they tended to interrupt teachers' pace of teaching. A way of learning knowledge in Korea was traditionally reflecting, like Buddhist monks did/do: keeping on thinking with one clue until getting awareness (or an answer).

I must also admit that the seminar encouraged me to reflect and think more and further and deeper.

I remember that seminar so vividly; I remember her question; I remember how I felt when I received the email. Reading it now I notice that the sender is also slipping into 'generalisations' – 'Korean students'; 'Asian students', 'most students'. Yet it had, and continues to have, a profound effect on me. For example, recognising that some students consider that it is rude to ask questions of the 'teacher' based on ignorance (Jin and Cortazzi, 1998), and the notion that 'keeping quiet' is a 'virtue' are both beliefs that I strive to remember in teaching.

'When an elder dies in Africa, it is a library that burns' (West African proverb, Ki-Zerbo, 1990)

The layers of complexity of many different cultures in the higher education landscape are rarely considered in the literature, rather the focus of research tends towards comparisons of students from 'one culture' with another, often the 'host culture'. Later in this chapter, extracts from conversations with Dau from Kenya, and with students from Taiwan and China, provide practical illustrations of this complexity. I have found it particularly difficult, for example, to locate literature on theoretical frameworks of learning in African contexts. Fasokun *et al.* (2005) suggest that this paucity of literature on indigenous ideas on learning in Africa is due to the oral traditions in documenting ideas as opposed to writing them. I learned that the precolonial scheme of linkages is crucial to the understanding of ways in which learning is conceptualised and 'theorised' in Africa: 'A linkage between general knowledge and practical life. The normal method for the transmission of knowledge was a series of practical exercises ... Education was linked to culture through the incorporation of cultural practices like games, dancing, music and sports' (Brock-Utne, 2002: 238). Knowledge is transmitted orally from one generation to another and by practical example; learning through experience is therefore important. The predominance of oral traditions means that different knowledges are transmitted in a variety of oral ways – such as poetry, storytelling, folklore and riddles – and rote learning is an important learning strategy in those parts of Africa where there may be few books and other resources. Magical under-standing and interpretation of the 'truth' is widely accepted and connected to the ways in which people 'know', thus somewhat different from much western conceptualisation where 'truth is neither presented by authority figures nor socially negotiated. Rather it is found by the self' (Tweed and Lehman, 2002: 91). The interpersonal relationships between teacher and student are emphasised, together with the former's responsibility for minimising the anxiety in the learner, very similar to my own beliefs in the importance of establishing learning environments within which people feel supported and encouraged to take risks. In addition, facilitators are not the only ones with knowledge (Fasokun *et al.*, 2005).

It is important to be reminded that there is no single African culture, just as there is no single Chinese culture and no single western culture; there can be as many differences within those cultures as there are between them. I was intrigued, however, by reading about a stereotype of the female African learner in an article by Maundeni (1999). Unaccustomed to being vocal or assertive in the classroom, she consequently experiences difficulties with learning that is more 'participative' (ibid.). The following extract from a conversation with Dau, a student from Kenya, followed by extracts from conversations with students from Taiwan and China, challenge such stereotyping.

'She can express herself without fear.'

Dau is a Kenyan woman. I became curious about my observations that those students who were not first-language English speakers – in this group they were Chinese speakers – positioned Dau quite carefully. They would often look to her for an alternative English word in order to help them understand a concept, using her as a kind of cultural informant. Gradually, I, too, began to position her in a similar way; I would look to her if I felt that students were puzzled by a word that I had used. I was interested to discover whether my perceptions and experiences were shared by her and by others, and asked her about this in one of our conversations:

Dau: The other thing, of course, is that they kept on telling me that my English is very good. So, it's like, you know, for them, OK, I'm an African which they have not met any other African, this is their first experience. And they do not expect us to talk that kind of English. Because, of course, as much as we have been colonised, they imagine we should be having our own language, we have our own language, which is not the case anyway – our academic work is all in English, everything is in English. So that is the only advantage. But to them they say, like, I am bright, you know that kind of thing. So they expected me to be in their situation. Let's assume Swahili is my day-to-day speaking language. So I should be having difficulties in the speaking English. So now that I can speak fluently and express myself they imagine I am exceptionally good. Do you get what I mean? Which is not the situation. Some of the other students come to me asking me how long it takes to write an essay or to read for the essay. And they get surprised when I tell them that it really takes time and effort to put it on the paper. They imagine that this woman is intelligent, this lady is intelligent. English is not her language and she can speak so fluently, she can express herself without fear.

In conversations with Yi-Ju from Taiwan, and Ying from China, I asked them about their relationship with Dau:

Yi-Ju: Well, she is really kind . . . whenever I talk with her I really learn a lot from her. I really like to talk to her. Even if some other classmates they think maybe her accent is quite difficult to understand. But it's getting better and better for me, so now I can communicate with her much better than before . . . I think, maybe she doesn't meet so many difficulties in writing assignments, doing the homework assignments. And she gets used to this environment very well . . . she really knows much about the systems.

Ying: And in the class we like to be with Dau and I think she knew that. Because her English is good so if we are in the same group with her we feel safe. Because Dau will speak out on behalf of us. And she was happy to do that.

Mindful of my desire that my voice should not take precedence over the voices of others, I ascribe, tentatively, some meanings to the above conversation extracts. Those students with Mandarin as their first language are assuming a level of both linguistic ability *and* conceptual understanding in Dau (Prescott and Hellsten, 2005). Dau, aware of their positioning of her, is wary of it, sharing with me that her colleagues are surprised when she tells them how long it takes her to produce her assignments. Rather than encountering difficulties in a system that is perceived as emphasising participation (Maundeni, 1999), Dau becomes the spokesperson for the Chinese-speaking students, speaking out on behalf of them, expressing herself without fear.

Learning and Islam

I owe much of my limited but growing knowledge about Islam to students from Malaysia, Saudi Arabia, Syria and Lebanon. Two particularly pertinent Islamic principles are those of *ummatism* (the concept of Islamic community and nations) and *tawhid* (God as the One and Absolute being and the only source of truth and knowledge). The former is especially related to *values* – holding that 'no value . . . is merely personal, pertinent to the individual alone' (Al Faruqi and Nasseef, 1981, cited in Al Zeera, 2001: 63), and the latter is reflected in the Muslim obligation to bring unity and harmony to their lives through *tawhid*. Al Zeera (2001: 60) is deeply critical of what she terms the Aristotelian principle of '"either or" . . . which holds that every proposition must be true or false' – an insight that reflects my oft-stated discomfort with dualisms. Muslims do not hold with either/or schools of thought but are trained to be integrated human beings and to learn to tolerate and accept differences rather pursuing homogeneity. I have learned that a teacher/lecturer is expected to have an ethical involvement with her students and to model certain values. She is regarded as a mu'addib – a person who is responsible for the 'inculcation of adab which is the discipline of mind, body and soul' (Tamuri, 2007: 376). One student wrote eloquently about his engagement with person-centred principles, but that he would be unable to advise a person who had approached him for help in ways that were counter to his Muslim faith. He believed Rogers' (1951) emphasis on the development of the internal 'locus of evaluation' to be contradictory to the Muslim tradition of looking outside of oneself – to the community – for direction (*ummatism*). But Islam is not a monotheist faith and, inevitably, I have encountered divergent views. Another student, for example, an Ismaeli Muslim, informed me that the similarities between the principles of her faith and those of humanistic philosophy had drawn her to person-centred practices, both as a counsellor and as a teacher.

Going round in circles?

In examining some of the learning and teaching concepts prevalent in some other cultural traditions, I conclude that definitions of learning, as an individual process, a collective experience, led by an expert, or facilitated by a person with expertise, are not as precise as I once thought. I can extrapolate elements that resonate with my own preferred practices – such as the importance of respect for diverse ways of constructing knowledge and conceptualising truth and the relationship between teacher and student – and those that challenge me – such as the recognition that silence can be an important part of the process of learning and understanding, and the need to claim my own authority and expertise.

But what is more important is that such questioning has shifted me from a liberal humanist position towards a more critical postmodern approach to adult learning theory, where the relationship between the individual and society is recognised and celebrated. This 'continual working tension between the similarities and differences of individuals, of cultures and of learners' (Flannery, 1995: 155) needs to include considerations of the socialisation of people and an understanding of the institutions in which learning often takes place, and their relationships to individuals and cultures. Taking account of this situatedness 'would make research in teaching and learning more complex, less generalisable' (Malcolm and Zukas, 2001: 39). My research and practice have evolved – and continue to do so – from teaching and learning experiences in higher education environments, which *are* complex, and are connecting with experiences in other 'institutions' and contexts. I never sought, however, to produce results that are generalisable; rather to generate discussion from the voices of the participants and from my own to stimulate a more critical consideration of a dominant pedagogy so that students and teachers can learn from each other – one of the earlier aims of the study that I described in

Chapter 1. Nonetheless, I do believe that it is I, as the lecturer, who is a 'core player in the process' (Teekens, 2000: 26). I say that not to proselytise about my own importance and influence, but to acknowledge an ethical responsibility, as an educator and a critical pedagogue, to foster intercultural communication and learning and discover ways to develop cultural capability. I cannot assume that it will just happen, and I need to involve all students 'in order to create more sensitivity and awareness for the various opportunities for personal development afforded by internationalisation' (Otten, 2000: 15).

In this chapter, I have shared a journey that has meandered through some theoretical frameworks of learning and teaching in higher education, taking many different paths, in an attempt to position myself and to illustrate the perspectives that have influenced me. Becoming more aware of the culturally mediated philosophies of these perspectives changed the way I approached the planning and delivery of my teaching, my attitude towards learning and the way I related to people. In the next chapter, I ask you to accompany me on my methodological journeys, similarly contingent upon unexamined beliefs when I embarked on them. As we embark on these journeys, you will see traces of familiar footsteps as I wrestle with methodological literature and the '-ologies'. Try not to tire; my interactions with others infuse my writing and each of these elements shifts my perspectives and understanding – as they may do yours – if only a little.

4
RESEARCHING ACROSS CULTURES
The case for narrative inquiry and autoethnography

In this chapter, I tell the story of how I became a narrative inquirer, offering a rationale for that methodological approach as congruent and suitable for researching 'across cultures'. The chapter is presented as a series of phases, mainly chronological stopping points on a methodological journey. It reveals my engagement with philosophical concepts and methodological frameworks as well as connections with earlier, personal experiences of learning that were remembered throughout the process of reading and writing. The chapter provides some working definitions of cross-cultural research and engages at greater depth with reflexivity and autoethnography in order to explain the role of these perspectives in practitioner research.

My experience of research is that, like life, it cannot be parcelled up into neat little chunks, each phase done and stored away. Life does not stand still, it is 'always getting in the way, always making what may appear static and not changing into a shifting, moving, interacting complexity' (Clandinin and Connelly, 2000: 125) – an apt description for practitioner research. It was – and is – not at all static; it continues to be a shifting, moving, interacting, multilayered complexity. This account of my encounters with research methodology seeks to peel back some of the layers of that complexity, to make them transparent and, in doing so, to elucidate and to extrapolate some clarity and rationale for using narrative inquiry and autoethnography.

A suggestion that I give to students when they are starting to develop their research, whether at Masters or doctoral level, is to consider the methodological approaches used in other research on their topic of interest. Such a strategy can help them to decide whether they are attracted to certain methodological approaches, whether studies in their field tend to adopt similar approaches that they might use or whether they might select a methodology that is completely different in order to research the topic in an alternative way. In my case, however, there were few studies similar to mine. There was a burgeoning body of research on 'international students', but much of it, as I indicated earlier, was comparative; few people in this field were engaged in researching their own practice reflexively; therefore, methodologically, there were few comparisons to be made. It felt, therefore, in the earlier phases of the study, as if I were learning to read all over again.

Phase one: learning to read

The story of the Kitty card

In searching and re-searching for 'a research methodology', I realised that the process reflected how I approach 'learning', and of learning to read as a little girl. Even at the age of 4 I had high expectations of myself, wanting to have a new 'Kitty card' – a card with simple words on it used in learning to read – every day, because I was eager to move on to a book. I was racing through the cards, able to have a new one daily, until one day I was told by Miss Jackson, my teacher, that I had to take the same card home again to read with my mother. In reading it aloud to Miss Jackson, I read one word incorrectly. I burst into tears, tears of frustration at not getting the word right first time. I felt that same frustration as I struggled with finding an appropriate methodology for conducting research across cultures. I wanted to be a 'methodologically self-conscious researcher' (Clough and Nutbrown, 2007: 31), articulating transparently the iterative relationship between research and practice. Each element, therefore, needed to be connected methodologically through a kind of symbiotic process.

But reading literature on research methodologies and social science philosophy, I find some of the words/language impenetrable. 'Reminds me of how so many of our texts argue in postmodern abstract jargon for greater accessibility and experimental forms,' said Carolyn Ellis in conversation with her partner, Art, when he 'quickly fell into the handbook genre to argue against writing in the handbook genre' (Ellis and Bochner, 2000: 735). Like Ellis, I, too, reflect on why many people write in ways that are impenetrable, particularly when they seem to be reporting research that claims to be emancipatory. Why write in a language that is exclusive? At least I feel excluded by it – surely others must do so too.

A learning strategy that I developed for myself when I was small was to take a word and speak it to myself in different sentences on my way to school in order to determine its meaning. The word I remember, in particular, is 'exceedingly'. This was not a word that either of my parents would have used in everyday conversation, and so where I heard it remains a mystery to me. I must have heard it somewhere, however, as I spoke it to myself and then used it and was praised by my teacher for using such a long and complex word correctly. It occurs to me that I continue to adopt similar strategies, even if they are slightly more sophisticated, when I bump up against new ideas that I find 'exceedingly hard'. I realise that in order to ensure that I can communicate a complex concept to others, I need to find ways of understanding it myself. The way I have developed of doing this is to read, to translate into simpler language, to relate the concept to my own experience and then to communicate it to others using my own words and anecdotal examples. Teaching research methodology has given me more opportunities to share this strategy. Many of the concepts of social science research methodology are alien to the students; particularly, but not exclusively, to those for whom English is not their first language. Producing my own summaries of the salient points of the texts in accessible language. and using illustrative examples from everyday life, helps students not only with their conceptual understanding but also with their ability to apply theoretical ideas to their own experience and practice. They begin to see research as embodying natural curiosity – as do I – and thus to visualise themselves as researchers.

Phase two: qualitative meandering

Simply put, qualitative research examines 'what things "exist" rather than determines . . . how many such things there are' (Walker 1985: 3). I wanted to explore what was happening in the 'classroom', what people were doing and experiencing, what I was doing and experiencing, and the meanings we ascribed to those events. I never considered any approach, therefore, that presumed a single, absolute truth in human reality, nor one that assumed a correct reading or interpretation of an event. I was not concerned with measuring or pursuing patterns of cause and effect. I was not setting out to make claims of universality.

The clear differentiation between the human and natural sciences articulated in the later part of the 19th century was mainly due to interpretive understanding, the shared ways in which human beings make sense of their world. Additionally, the linguistic philosophy of Wittgenstein (1953) proposed that language serves a number of functions, is itself a social function governed by a set of rules, and that it was therefore crucial to understand the way that language is used within communities. This importance placed on language was elaborated on by Winch (1958), who claimed that it was not only the social representations inherent in language, but also *all* human activities that are embedded social practices that can only be understood and interpreted by observing the local rules that guide the customs – the contextualised shared meanings. As I propose throughout this book, culture exerts a powerful influence on the way we live our lives and create meanings, but it is possible to create and recreate culture (Sparks, 2002), to bridge and dissolve such boundaries as there might be between cultures (Crossley, 2000; Fox, 2006), and to choose not to dissolve any boundaries but instead to celebrate them in mutual enrichment (Bakhtin, 1986; Speedy, 2006; Trahar, 2006).

> We have the capacity and the power to create and recreate culture to respond to contemporary times, to new and expanded understandings. We make choices about how we will engage with others and who we will be in those interactions . . . All cultural voices are multisubjective, contingent, power-laden, incongruent and offer political solutions to everyday negotiated

realities . . . out of our particular history and set of experiences we know only 'positioned utterances' and must negotiate meaning with others who speak with 'positioned utterances'.

(Sparks, 2002: 116)

I wanted to move to a place where greater understanding of those 'positioned utterances' might contribute to different approaches to learning and teaching, approaches that were more cognisant of a broader range of academic and cultural traditions, but I needed to discover appropriate ways, methodologically, to do so.

In Chapter 1, I wrote about my growing sense of frustration at what could seem to be a rather disingenuous valuing of greater diversity. Similar frustrations exercised me on the methodological journey, provoking me into questioning the underlying philosophical assumptions of the methodologies that I was considering. This then took me into investigating the power exercised in particular discourses (Foucault, 1980). For example, I revisited feminism, but this time recognising what it might have to say about the deligitimisation of the so-called cultural 'other' as well as the gendered 'other'. In much earlier research (Trahar, 1996), I had investigated the influences of gender on the co-teaching/team-teaching relationship and how tutors and students experienced that relationship. Now here I was, again, using feminism to explore 'otherness', but this time 'cultural otherness' to critique the western philosophical tradition, a philosophical tradition that obliterates not only differences of gender but also delegitimises the presence of otherness and difference (Benhabib, 1992).

From this revisiting of feminism as a way of conceptualising the gendered basis of power, it was a natural step to investigate how western philosophical traditions can delegitimise the so-called cultural 'other'. There are those such as Helu-Thaman (1999), Tuhiwai Smith (1999), Hickling-Hudson *et al.* (2004), Bishop (2005), Muthayan (2005) and Dunbar (2008), who seek to dismantle the 'unrecognised' cultural domination of the traditional methodologies and to encourage the development of indigenous research methodologies. I acknowledge also that 'westernness' is itself a construct, and that western forms of knowledge and 'civilisation' are directly indebted to older, non-European forms (Bernal, 1987). At this stage, however, it was 'epistemological racism' (Scheurich, 1997: 132) – the claim that the fundamental influence of ethnicity in shaping interpretations of reality is ignored, or given only minimal attention in the dominant epistemologies – that disrupted my thinking.

Epistemological racism

Stanfield (1993a, 1994) and other 'scholars of color' (his phrase) have argued that the traditional epistemologies – not our use of them, but the epistemologies themselves – are racially biased ways of knowing, and that the fundamental influences of ethnicity in shaping the way we each interpret reality are either ignored or given only minimal attention in these epistemologies. The claim is that the lack of response to the idea of 'epistemological racism' is evidence of a lack of understanding among researchers as to how race is a critically significant epistemological problem in educational research. Stanfield was writing almost 20 years ago and was critical of the then dearth of methodological literature that sought to de-Europeanise approaches to issues concerning 'people of color' by introducing more indigenous approaches. Clearly, the work of those scholars cited earlier now rises to meet Stanfield's challenge, but it was my encounters with such ideas (including other postcolonial perspectives, such as Trinh, 1989; Tikly, 1999; Morrow and Torres, 2003 and Swadener and Mutua, 2008) that challenged me to scrutinise my somewhat glib methodological strategising. I began to examine the roots of a range of methodological frameworks to ascertain for myself the extent to which they were Eurocentric ways of constructing knowledge. Crucially, I believed that in seeking to hear how people from cultural backgrounds that differed from my own experienced learning and the multicultural environment of the University of Bristol's Graduate School of Education, I needed to attend to such methodological complexities. I deemed it necessary to locate any claims that I made within appropriate frameworks. I reached a stage of feeling that I needed to find a methodology that was *not* underpinned by Eurocentric ways of knowing; since to work within a framework that was conceptualised in such ways would be a compromise of my espoused values of transparency and respect for difference.

Phase three: researching across cultures?

I then began to consider much more critically the conducting of research across cultures. One definition of cross-cultural research is that of research across cultural borders, where data, through observations, interviews or documents obtained, are seen through the researcher's 'cultural eyes' (Ryen, 2000: 228). Conducting cross-cultural research is not new, but what is newer is the 'growing acknowledgement of the perils of crossing cultures unconsciously' (Sparks, 2002: 116). Thus, by under-estimating or ignoring cross-cultural dimensions, research may once again become colonial (Ryen, 2000; Swadener and Mutua, 2008). I found many well-rehearsed arguments in the research literature to indicate that only 'minority group researchers' can produce knowledge about 'minority groups' (Stanfield, 1993a & b, 1994; Anderson, 1993), but I resisted those critics who issued various injunctions such as the impossibility for students to talk 'honestly' with me because of the power imbalance, or that doing research with students from cultures that differed from my own, as a white British academic, was another form of colonialism. I rejected these notions of immutable boundaries between cultures as they seemed to leave no space for dialogue, no potential to effect deeper understanding.

Andersen (1993), however, suggests that academics can learn to read their personal and cultural biographies as significant sources of knowledge. Those she refers to as 'majority group scholars' can develop and utilise tension in their own cultural identities to enable them to see different aspects of minority group experiences, to examine critically majority experiences and beliefs, and to examine self-consciously the influences of institutional racism. White feminist scholars can transform their teaching and thinking through developing research practices that acknowledge and take as central the class, race and gender relations in which researchers and research participants are situated (Andersen, ibid.). Further, hooks (1989) suggests that it is not that white researchers should not write about or attempt to learn about the experience of minority group students, but that their interpretations should not be taken to be the most authoritative. This latter point supports my earlier problematisation of reflexivity, expanded on later in this chapter. Claims of reflexivity may marginalise already marginalised voices.

My meandering thus far had led me to critique the epistemological and onto-logical assumptions informing many traditional methodological approaches, to grapple with ideas of indigenous methodologies, and had raised the issue of power in particular discourses. The next layer of complexity was the relationship between me and the people with whom I was interacting.

Phase four: unwinding the relationship between researcher and researched

It is now common for many researchers to redefine their relationships with their 'subjects' and to strive to work within methodological frameworks that are less hierarchical, making explicit the social, gender and cultural differences in research processes. However, untangling the gender and ethnic attributes of the historical formation of dominant patterns of research in the social sciences is complex, neces-sitating 'radical efforts', not only to critique but also to 'revise the paradigms underlying qualitative research strategies', creating and legitimising new ones (Stanfield, 1994: 183).

One solution might be a multicultural philosophy of social science (Fay, 1996); dialectical thinking that acknowledges the fluidity and openness of many cate-gories. This fluidity and openness is denied by the 'either/or' mentality provoked by the oppositional categories of much social thought. 'Beware of dichotomies. Avoid pernicious dualisms. Think dialectically' (ibid.: 241). I began to muse on some apparent dichotomies and dualisms, focusing especially on the relevance of terms such as 'universalism' and 'particularism' when conducting research across cultures. I began to develop an idea that, although a polarising of these terms is generally unhelpful, there are times when holding one position against another may be advantageous. Thus, dislodging and problematising my own 'culture', my own 'whiteness' (foregrounded throughout the book but especially in Chapter 8), is an example of how a holding of that position may be a way of 'seeing' more clearly my own and others' 'culture(s)'.

Fay (1996) proposes that assimilation (in which differences are obliterated and the universally human is instigated) and separatism (in which differences are emphasised and maintained and the particular is highlighted) are alternative ways of conceptualising universalism and particularism, but are similarly 'false choices'. I was attracted to this notion of 'false choice' between apparent dichotomies. At the same time – as I indicated earlier – I recognised that particularism may be a valuable standpoint in situations where differences are obliterated to such an extent that the result is enforced homogeneity.

Movements of the oppressed have questioned the 'assimilationist ideal' (Young, 2001: 208), the idea of a universal humanity that denies natural differences. Self-organisation and the assertion of a positive group cultural identity is a more effective strategy for achieving power and participation in dominant groups and institutions. Young (ibid.) cites examples of African-Americans in the USA, the women's movements and, more recently, the movements for gay rights. Each of these groups began to look for recognition by adopting a distinctly assimilationist and universalist orientation, seeking in their different ways to show that they were 'no different' from anyone else. They subsequently rejected this assimilationist ideal, by refusing to accept and adopt identities that were not theirs but those of the dominant group. Thus, blindness to difference, often expressed in the assimilationist ideal, disadvantages groups whose experience, culture and socialised capacities differ from those of privileged groups.

Shifting to a more post structuralist perspective, I prefer the metaphor of cultural traffic that moves ambivalently between poles and transgresses borders, dissolving them on the way. I like Giroux's (1992) notion of 'border crossings' – deconstructing the notion of borders to look for cultural specificity among diverse groups in order to find commonalities among differences.

Such musing led me to social constructionism. The products of research – the social constructions of reality – are not facts or findings that reflect an objective reality but versions of the life-world constructed by the researcher, or co-constructed between researcher and participants (Gergen, 1985, 1999). Then I discovered that the word 'autonomy', which is so often used in conjunction with the word 'self', as in the 'autonomous self', the 'autonomous learner', is etymologically related to the Greek *nome*, meaning pasturage, grazing; and *nomas*, wandering in search of pasture. So the self only comes into being as it wanders in search of others; reflection and dialogue are movements of opening towards otherness (Maranhao, 1991). Now I was starting to get somewhere. As a practitioner researcher, I did not enter the field to gather research data; I was – and am – in the field, 'a member of the landscape' (Clandinin and Connelly, 2000: 63), in relationships with students, towards whom I wander(ed) in conducting the study.

Phase five: to be or not to be reflexive? More dualities?

In Chapter 1, I indicated that my study was reflexive. Positioning myself within a reflexive paradigm was potentially problematic, however, because of the unsettled definitions of reflexivity. I understood reflexivity to be a process in which the researcher was continuously reflecting upon herself, sharing with the reader and the research participants the effect that the latter's stories and the research experience was having upon her. From this reflexive process, stories can be co-constructed, offering potential for other, alternative, preferred stories to emerge.

'To be reflexive is to have an ongoing conversation about experience while living in the moment' (Hertz, 1997: viii). It is important for the researcher to locate herself within 'power hierarchies and within a constellation of gender, race, class and citizenship' (ibid.) and to acknowledge how her own positions and interests are imposed at all stages of the research process. As researchers, in order to make sense of what others are telling us, we need to draw on our own histories, especially when what we are hearing resonates with our own lives. By including her own voice, the audience is more able to 'situate' the researcher, and so is more able to understand her perspective. In my experience, it is still rare for researchers in the field of internationalisation in higher education to reveal to their audience how their lives may have paralleled those of respondents. I cannot do research without being part of it. I *am* a reflective practitioner. Hertz's (ibid.) further suggestion that anyone engaged in the exploration of human beings should have undertaken a great deal of self-exploration reflected the journeying towards greater self-awareness that was an integral part of my counselling training. It continues to help me make other discoveries about myself. Working at relational depth with my participants, engaging in authentic conversations to appreciate my own and others' cultures of learning, involves and, indeed, I propose, *necessitates* appropriate self-disclosure.

The aim of reflexivity is to make explicit the social organisation and cognitive structures of the social field of social scientific knowledge. Hall (1999), however, contends that social constructionists have not found it easy to move beyond general claims to describe the specific cultural rationales that inform alternative constructions of knowledge. He proposes a 'Third Path' as a way of understanding inquiries in cultural terms, as structured practices with roots in shared discursive resources that facilitate communication about the sociohistorical world. I like the way he defines inquiry as 'a bit messy, resistant to thoroughgoing rationalisation and open to challenge from other cultural standpoints' (ibid.: 8). Meanings are central to my study, as is the importance of describing what I bring to the research endeavour. But, the meanings that will be exposed can only ever be the meanings consciously attributed by narrator and listener. Although reflexivity positions itself as a way of uncovering and making visible the social and cultural positioning of researcher and participants, it is not sufficient to understand all of the complexities of difference. We can only 'explicate the processes and positions we are aware of being caught up in. Some of the influences arising from aspects of social identity remain beyond the reflexive grasp' (Reay, 1996: 443). I can only do what I can do; reflect on what I am aware of. I shall share, then, some more . . .

Angst about the 'self'

Making one's self more apparent as the 'translator', via reflexivity, carries with it a danger, in that one risks making one's self even more central to the discourse, pushing other voices out to the edge (Edwards and Ribben, 1998). Such is another example of oppositional categorising of social thought – either one is central or one is absent. Yet another 'opposition' is that the concept of reflexivity is contingent on a particular cultural construction of self. Anthropologists who have studied representations of the individual, the self, in 'other' cultures have not been able to find the same importance that the 'western' tradition has attributed to self-reflection since the Enlightenment (Maranhao, 1991). In much Chinese research, for example, this interest in the self has been lacking, perhaps because of the perceived unhealthy alliance between self and individualism in the many Chinese cultures. The topic of the self becomes even more fascinating in a collectivist culture, where there is much emphasis on self-effacement (Bond, 1986) and concern with the self is often ridiculed and played down in favour of group considerations.

If the concept of the reflexive inner self as a coherent unity is a specific historical production developed in western societies and produced through particular methodologies (Skeggs, 2002), where does this leave me? In seeking to be reflexive, to what extent am I indulging in yet another Eurocentric methodological tradition that may seem, at best, unfamiliar to my research participants, and, at worst, another form of epistemological racism? Am I ignoring the notion that 'reflection' is also a 'matter of discourse' (Erlandson, 2005: 662), and that by reflecting on my own practice I am contributing to an 'epistemology of practitioners', enabling my 'discursive captors' to compare the 'everyday doing of . . . [my] situated practice . . . with others and with a norm' (ibid.: 668)? But the value of practitioner research is that it can generate 'insightful accounts of processes which go beyond the particular story itself' (Pring, 1999: 6). By striving to think and to write dialectically, in order to recognise the fluidity and openness of a range of perspectives on reflexivity, I seek to afford other practitioners opportunities to compare their practice with mine. My 'discursive captors' might even learn something!

Phase six: a narrative inquirer emerges

'What *does* narrative inquiry help us to learn about our phenomenon that other theories or methods do not' (Clandinin and Connelly, 2000: 123, original emphasis)? This is a good question. A quality of narrative inquiry that differentiates it from many other qualitative methodological approaches is that experience, rather than theoretically informed research questions about that experience, is the starting point (Phillion and He, 2008). I have written in this chapter about philosophical perspectives that were influencing me, in particular interpretivism and social constructionism, but narrative inquiry also 'bumps up against post-positivism, Marxism and post-structuralism' (Clandinin and Rosiek, 2007: 59). I found myself in the 'borderlands', a metaphor used to explain the ways in which 'narrative inquirers frequently find themselves crossing cultural discourses, ideologies and institutional boundaries' (ibid.), which is what, indeed, I was doing.

Broadly speaking, narrative inquiry, focuses on the meanings that people ascribe to their experiences, seeking to provide 'insight that [befits] the complexity of human lives' (Josselson, 2006: 4), human lives that are even more complex in societies that are increasingly diverse (Phillion and He, 2008). I turned to narrative as a mode of inquiry, 'persuaded that social science texts needed to construct a different relationship between researchers and subjects and between authors and readers' (Ellis and Bochner, 2000: 744–5), which is what I was seeking to do.

The initial focus of my study was student learning experiences in a multicultural higher education environment. I was curious about what happened in the 'classroom' and the meanings of what happened for the people involved in the learning and teaching 'events'. In narrative inquiry, however, what is apparent – what can be seen and observed – is not all there is to say. What is also important are the ways in which people interpret the social world and their place within it. Andrews (2007: 489) advocates narrative inquiry as particularly appropriate in cross-cultural research because the importance of 'being able to imagine a world other than the one we know. . . the seeing of difference' is crucial. I found it challenging, however, to imagine worlds other than those that I believed I knew through my encounters with 'difference'; such imagining eventually became more possible through the autoethnographic dimensions of the study.

Narrative inquirers can be resistant to more globalised meanings being derived from their work (Fox, 2008). I was wary of 'generalising' from qualitative research of this kind; indeed, as I indicated earlier in this book, I was not seeking to make generalisable claims from my research, rather to provide rich stories of learning. I realised, however, that it was disingenuous and inconsistent with my avowed epistemological and ontological position if I were to regard each story as unique, only telling me about that person's experiences.

> What close narrative study of a single case can add is displaying how larger social structures insinuate their way into individual consciousness and identity, and how these socially constructed 'selves' are then performed for (and with) an audience, in this case the listener/interpreter.
>
> *(Riessman, 2008: 115–116)*

In order to make such claims, though, the researcher has to provide information not only about her narrators but also about herself, and to provide sufficient information about the context within which the conversations have taken place, when, and the relationship between narrator and listener. Using narrative inquiry – because of its positioning of both researcher and participant – we are able to glimpse – and sometimes more than glimpse – the larger historical, social and cultural stories within which we all dwell, and which inform the stories that we tell and how we tell them. 'Stories don't fall from the sky (or emerge from the innermost 'self'), they are composed and received in contexts – interactional, historical, institutional and discursive, to name a few' (ibid.: 105). So, for example, the extracts from the stories throughout this book, told in conversation with me, can never be only participants', or my unmediated story or stories that were created through our interaction in a particular context and relationship; they are stories formed and informed by the wider historical, social and cultural contexts. Thus, although my original intention was to investigate the learning experiences of a group of postgraduate students, hearing their stories of learning challenged me to reflect on my own, to afford me insight into the broader 'cultures' from within which 'we' were speaking and positioning ourselves and how our learning experiences were shaped by those cultures.

'*To experience an experience* – that is, to do research into an experience – is to experience it simultaneously in these four ways' – inward and outward, backward and forward (Clandinin and Connelly, 2000: 50, original emphasis). Looking at our diverse experiences of learning through individual and collective narratives allows me to understand how learning and teaching knowledge is 'narratively composed, embodied in people and expressed in practice' (ibid.: 124). I can think of no better way to illustrate this latter point than to tell a story.

I had two teachers with the surname Jackson. Miss Jackson, she of the Kitty card, was young and pretty. Mrs Jackson was older, plumper and motherly. I started school when I was four-years-old. That first day, it was dark, there was snow on the ground and my mother had given me a huge piece of Christmas cake to eat at break-time. The cake was so big that I could not eat it in the time allotted for the break, so rather than throw it away, I wrapped up the remaining piece and took it home.

Why have I chosen that particular story to tell? (Mishler, 2004). What does it tell me about myself? How does the reader interpret it? I am that tiny four-year-old girl again. I am back in that classroom on that dark January morning. Frightened, yet eager to please and excited about learning. 'The cake was so big' could be a metaphor for much of my work. Sometimes I wish I could just 'throw it away' rather than wrap it up, take it home and continue to work on it:

> The causal linkage of events in a narrative is often known only retrospectively within the context of the total episode. The significance and contribution of particular happenings and actions are not finally evident until the denouement of the episode and the understanding of the new action can draw upon previous understanding while being open to the specific and unique elements that make the new episode different from all that have gone before.
>
> *(Polkinghorne, 1995: 8)*

Writing the 'Christmas cake' story now, I can recall the 'event' and remember vividly how I felt; but the meaning I am attributing to the story is retrospective. Thus, within the 'context of the total episode', the contribution of this story and my understanding of it help me to understand 'the new episode' (my experiences as a practitioner researcher in my current environment). Continuing to follow this train of thought, I can claim, legitimately, that the significance and contribution of particular happenings and actions in my study may not become evident until its *denouement* – perhaps the final chapter of this book – and may not be evident even then. That will be an ending to this particular story but, on the other hand, it will only be an ending to a chapter of other stories. 'The story', or some versions of it, will continue, both in my life and, I imagine, in the lives of the people who have been involved in it. One of my family narratives is that, as a child, I was always writing stories. Mrs Jackson, of whom I spoke earlier, used to take these stories home to show her husband. I cannot remember the content of those stories but I can remember the 'action', 'the 'happenings' and the 'significance' of them in my family and my subsequent lifelong love of stories – reading them, listening to them and, now, writing them again.

> Narrative inquirers tend to begin with experience as lived and told stories...
> Narrative inquiry characteristically begins with the researcher's autobiographically oriented narrative associated with the *research puzzle* (called by some the research problem or research question).
> *(Clandinin and Connolly, 2000: 40, original emphasis)*

The first story of the beginning of this narrative inquiry was of an encounter with a group of 'international students' one miserable night in November 1999. It is, however, through the process of writing that I have been able to uncover a range of different, earlier, beginnings to my 'autobiographically oriented narrative associated with the research puzzle', some of which are shared in this book.

Narrative inquiry does not depend on the gathering of one form of 'data'. I invited students and, subsequently, other academics to have conversations with me that were recorded, transcribed and 'analysed', but 'interviews' are often less important than the noting of events, feelings, hunches and conversations in the corridor (Clandinin and Connolly, 2000; Clough, 2002). Such 'other data' were captured by means of the maintenance of a reflective journal, and were explored, subsequently, in research conversations. But 'talk' is never simple. I came to realise that when students 'talked' with me about their experiences of learning, 'structures of inequality and power – class, gender and race/ethnicity – work their way into what appears to be "simply" talk about a life' (Riessman, 2008: 115). In listening to them talk about their experiences of learning, if I were to be an 'active participant' rather than a 'detached observer' (Phillion and He, 2008: 6), sharing my own resonances, perceptions, experiences, through narrative interviewing, then what might emerge would be richer stories that said much about the cultural, historical and social influences on our learning – and on teaching.

Narrative interviewing

Some time ago a visiting scholar from Spain asked me to explain a narrative interview to her. It is difficult to find a simple definition. There is an assumption, particularly in feminist standpoints and epistemologies, that more egalitarian relationships can be achieved through reciprocity and the sharing of emotional responses in interviews (Atkinson and Silverman, 1997). There is also a belief that being empathic can enable us to be more understanding of the meanings that others attribute to their lives, and that these meanings can be communicated through a narrative interview (Josselson, 1996). Bauer (1996: 2) defines the 'basic idea' of a narrative interview as being to 'reconstruct social events from the perspective of informants as direct [sic] as possible'. Riessman (2004: 709) defines the narrative interview as a 'discursive accomplishment' in which two active participants together produce meaning. Josselson and Lieblich (2003: 269–270), claiming that narrative research interviewing is 'different both from traditional research interviews and clinical interviews', define it as requiring the: 'Interviewer [to] keep her research aims and personal interests in mind, while leaving enough space for the conversation to develop into a meaningful narrative. It has to procure "stories", namely concrete examples, episodes or memories from the teller's life.'

From these definitions, then, we may infer that a narrative interview is a conversation between, usually, two people for the purposes of the research of one of them, and that sometimes the narrator and listener will work together to produce the narratives. The extent to which the interviewer will share aspects of her own life and experiences is contingent upon the extent to which she sees herself and her own stories as contributing to the development, the 'thickening' of others' stories. I invited participants to have conversations with me that were recorded. I regarded these as 'open' conversations, in that I did not have a set of questions to ask; but it would be disingenuous of me to pretend that I did not have an agenda. Without doubt, I had an agenda; I was a researcher and I wanted to have conversations with people in order to explore some of the areas about which I was curious. The conversations were open in the sense that I usually began by inviting the participant to talk about their experiences. Sometimes I prompted participants a little, to gather from them not only their experiences as a learner/teacher, but also other experiences that they considered to be relevant. Listening to the conversations, I can hear how many of my memories were triggered within the conversation. These were memories of 'shared events' and were also memories from my own early experiences of learning as well as more intimate memories about other parts of my life. I shared them with the participant, eager to gain their perspective. Such sharing of memories causes me, when I listen to some of the conversations, to feel discomfited. This discomfort mirrors my concerns about reflexivity and the danger inherent in the centrality of the researcher's voice. I was concerned that I was putting my self 'so deeply back into the text that it completely dominates' (Lincoln and Denzin, 1994: 578), but, at the same time, being reflexive *in* the interviews, the conversations 'evoke stories that create meaning as they are told' (Etherington, 2004: 39) – as I hope is illustrated in the Letters to Cheng-tsung in the next chapter.

One criticism of narrative inquiry is that, 'If you are a storyteller rather than a story analyst then your goal becomes therapeutic rather than analytic' (Ellis and Bochner, 2000: 745). But this is slipping into dualities again: I must be either a storyteller or a story analyst, when I am both. I am telling my own stories, telling others' stories as I heard them, and engaging in some re-presentation of those stories. Yet, again, it seems impossible not to think dualistically. I privilege representational social science or I 'privilege certain kinds and occasions of narrative performance' (Atkinson, 1997, cited in Ellis and Bochner, 2000: 745) when I am free to do both, provided that I articulate that that is what I am doing. Here is another mirroring of my own struggle: I am resistant to being labelled and putting labels on myself, as I say throughout this book; I do not like gossip, yet like the idea of my study as 'gossip on a grand scale' (Clandinin and Connelly, 2000: xxii). I know that sometimes I position myself deliberately as an outsider in this academic landscape that I have stumbled into so that I do not become gathered up into some collective 'academic' identity. I can often feel like an outsider but I imagine that I am perceived, certainly by students, as an insider. I pointed out earlier, that as a lecturer engaging in research with students, I cannot escape from this being a relationship in which certain 'powers' are ascribed to me. Yet again, I recognise the dualistic notion of this 'either an insider or an outsider' position, and am grateful to Naples' (1997: 71) feminist re-reading of the insider/outsider debate that claims insider/outsider as a 'bipolar construction'. This perspective neglects the interactive processes through which 'insiderness and outsiderness' are constructed, defining them as fluid rather than fixed positions; researcher and researched are thus constantly shifting relationships and moving between them.

Phase seven: the autoethnographic turn

Delamont (2009: 51) positions autoethnography as a 'cultural *cul de sac*'. I have some sympathy with this perspective, in particular with her assertion that 'retreat into autoethnography is an abrogation of the honourable trade of the scholar' (ibid.: 61). Yet Delamont is distinguishing between what she defines as autoethnography where the *only* object of study is the researcher and 'reflexive autobiographical writing', which she proposes to have 'analytic and pedagogic power' (ibid.: 61). Muncey's (2010: 2) experience of autoethnography emerging 'out of the iterative process of doing research, while engaging in the process of living a life', most definitely resonates with me, hence I strive to ensure that 'analytic and pedagogic power' is displayed through my autoethnographic writing.

The dis-ease about the positioning of my own voice continued, however. I was concerned that I might be accused of being 'self-indulgent rather than self-knowing, self-respectful . . . or self-luminous' (Sparkes, 2002: 214). As a practitioner researcher, I wanted to go beyond 'self-indulgent exercises to provide . . . deliberation and critique that will generate guideposts for future practitioner research' (Brooker and Macpherson, 1999: 219). I wanted my research to make a difference to me, to my participants, to my practice and to those who read it. And then I recognised that once again I was being dominated by this dualistic mentality; either it had to be autoethnographic and neglect the voices of others, thus making my own voice louder, or my own voice – with all the questions about my identities, cultural and otherwise, raised by the research – had to be silenced. The definition of autoethnography as an:

> Autobiographical genre of writing and research that displays multiple layers of consciousness, connecting the personal to the cultural. Back and forth autoethnographers gaze, first through an ethnographic wide-angle lens, focusing outward on social and cultural aspects of the personal experience; then they look inward, exposing a vulnerable self that is moved by and may move through, refract and resist cultural interpretations.
>
> *(Ellis and Bochner, 2000: 739)*

decided me that my study *is* autoethnographic. It is through being immersed in it that the social and cultural aspects of my own life have been exposed. This is a testament to my earlier statement about the roots of the word 'autonomy' – that the self comes into being through reflection and dialogue with *others*.

Finally, this chapter is 'a kind of conversation between theory and life, or at least between theory and the stories of life contained in the inquiry' (Claninin and Connelly, 2000: 41). By tracing my journey towards finding an appropriate methodology(ies), I have presented it as conversations between 'theory' and some of the 'stories of life' being told, wrestling openly with the tensions that have arisen for me. Through the writing I have identified some strong themes and influences such as feminism, reflexivity, epistemological racism and autoethnography. It strikes me how much the process of writing reflects the ambivalence I feel and have sought to make explicit (Richardson, 1994, 2000). I have gone back and forth many times, so that the end-product – this chapter – does not appear in anything like the order in which I encountered the ideas or wrote about them. This experience embodies the narrative inquiry process. It does not move in a unilinear fashion from past to present to future (Polkinghorne, 1995) but is like a prism catching the light and randomly illuminating the surfaces. In the next chapter, I put this metaphor to the test. Hopefully, some other surfaces will be illuminated further by showing how narrative inquiry informed conversations with Cheng-tsung.

5
LETTERS TO CHENG-TSUNG

Letters are written to someone with the expectation of a response. In letters, we try to give an account of ourselves, make meaning of our experiences, and attempt to establish and maintain relationships... one of the merits of letters is the equality established, the give-and-take of conversation.

(Clandinin and Connelly, 2000: 106)

This chapter is written as a series of 'letters to Cheng-tsung', the postgraduate student in Chapter 1. In each letter, I have used dialogic/performance analysis to 'story' extracts from our many conversations held while he was a student in Bristol. Each story reflects core elements of learning and teaching experiences in an international higher education landscape as well as myriad other subjects such as emotion, emotion in learning, conflict, and complexities of language. Telling the stories through the letters affords me the opportunity to give an account of myself, to continue to question and to make meaning of experiences, and to illustrate the give-and-take of our conversations. In the first letter I 'wrote' to Cheng-tsung (Chapter 1), I described how the themes that had guided the study initially changed, and other questions and themes emerged. These subsequent letters pick up on those questions and themes and develop them.

The second letter to Cheng-tsung

Dear Cheng-tsung,

I began our first 'narrative interview' by telling you that I was intrigued by your email to me in which you said that you wanted to write an essay about 'the self-concept between the two cultures'.

Cheng-tsung: Okay. Don't expect too much. [LAUGHTER]

Sheila: I just think it's really, you know, interesting that you've come up with that idea.

Cheng-tsung: Because maybe I have some experiences that in my past experience, especially when I come to England I found there is some difference between the two cultures. So I think it's very interesting between the two cultures to see the human being, to see the self of the person. To some degree I think it is different because you see things different with the... different point of view, and sometimes I think how to solve a problem is very different. So I think maybe there is some basic difference, lots of differences.

My curiosity about your essay title prompted you to talk immediately about 'some difference between the two cultures'. Your words 'between the two cultures to see the human being, to see the self of the person', now seem eerily prescient, given what you subsequently wrote in your dissertation (Lee, 2003 unpublished MEd dissertation – quoted later in this letter). You continue by talking about some of the differences you have noticed between the ways in which people relate to one another in Taiwan and England:

Cheng-tsung: I think the most obvious thing is that the families influence, the key person have a very powerful influence on their behaviour or their behaviour or their thinking, especially on women. So... I mean when I came to England I found it is very different – the people here is more self-oriented, oriented.

Sheila: What is it about us that leads you to say that people are more self-orientated?

Cheng-tsung: I have had some talks with British students here and I found that I told them about my experience about... such as if a boy want to make friends with a girl, he want to be... maybe he likes the girl very much but if his family don't like this girl. So *always* in Taiwan the boy will have some fight to his family to be with that girl. But the same situation here, I think... I mean maybe the parent will have the same attitude as Taiwanese parent, but the behaviour is quite different.

Sheila: So how is it different?

Cheng-tsung: What I understand is that the parent here is not so strong in behaviour against the relationship, against the boy to make friends with the girl. Sometimes parents will control their boy, their boy not to see the girl. Or even more is that they will intrude the relationship directly, they will tell the girl directly.

> Yeah. I mean another point is that sometimes people make some trouble, they were always thinking about themselves, how to handle this problem. Everything is according to his own thinking or consideration, and especially here. But in Taiwan I found that it is very interesting, people don't always think himself or herself's thinking or consideration, they will take other people's opinion into their own consideration.
>
> I cannot make a concrete example now. But my feeling is that in our culture we may pay much more attention on other people's opinion.

I feel pleased that you are having conversations with British students and that your observations about the 'differences between the two cultures' result from those conversations. Pleased, because you are making relationships outside of our teaching sessions, challenging research that concludes that, even when students report favourable experiences in an intercultural learning environment, they will not often seek to interact with students from different cultures (Volet and Ang, 1998; Volet and Tan-Quigley, 1995; Koehne, 2005; Harrison and Peacock, forthcoming).

We continue:

Cheng-tsung: [LAUGHTER] Because in my learning process to be a counsellor, I learn the counselling, everything about counselling, I think theory is all totally come from a book. Especially from the United States, yeah? But we don't put much attention on our own culture's issues. So sometimes I feel it is strange. Such as some kind of approach, especially focused on the emotional reaction, or some therapy is focused on emotion. But in our culture emotion is very repressed. So I think that is it appropriate for a Chinese to confront such a strong feeling or emotional method? Sometimes I doubt is it appropriate. So . . . maybe this is according to my own experience because sometimes I am not used to face such strong feeling or emotion. So I have to find out something that is on the basis of the Chinese culture.

I mean in our culture if we have any method or way of thinking to solve a problem, shall we have to depend on all the helping method or approach from the Western culture? So I also think that before the counselling method passed through to our culture, our ancestors, I mean *how* could they solve their problems without counselling method? [LAUGHTER)]

Sheila: Well . . . they obviously did didn't they?

Cheng-tsung: Yeah. [LAUGHTER] Obviously they solved their problems without counselling methods, but how could they do such things? I mean I am interested or I am curious about what kind of a method or thinking they used to solve their problem.

Sheila: Because I mean you're right, there must have been something, mustn't there? Because I think in all cultures there's always been problems and different ways of . . . well as you were saying, different ways of solving them.

Cheng-tsung: Yeah. Maybe there is one thing is very important, in our learning process, our focus, our learning focus will be more put under I mean Western technology or civilisation. So everything from Western culture is good to some degree. We lose some reflection or the thinking about our own culture. So the first priority to solve a problem always use the Western method, always to think what is the scientific way to solve a problem.

But I think maybe we can use this kind of a method or way of thinking, but for human beings, for people, I don't think it is the best policy to handle problems.

The following year, you wrote in your dissertation:

From the beginning, my learning focus has been on how to consider related counselling issues in indigenous way. As soon as I started studying counselling in Bristol, I became aware of the different effects that diverse cultural contexts could have, and I wondered how I could use a foreign approach to understand Chinese lives. I also started to feel curious about indigenous methods of problem-solving. Then I noticed that the construct of one's self plays a crucial role in using different counselling approaches.

It appears that you had started to question the 'uncritical transfer' of 'western counselling theory' to your own culture when, as you say, your ancestors must have had ways of solving their problems that did not involve such concepts. It seems to be the first time that you have challenged these concepts and you question why you have to depend on 'all the helping method or approach from the western culture'. I like the way you are challenging such dominant narratives of coun-selling. It is subversive and accords with my own desire to subvert and disrupt modernist 'truths'.

The story of authority

You began to speak about your struggle with authority figures, telling me some stories about ways in which power and authority are conceptualised in Taiwan, to explain your struggle to me. I am very uncomfortable with your, and then my, use of the word 'boss'. By saying, 'If I were your boss', which I'm not, but let's imagine I am, 'and if you disagreed with me', I am trying to encourage you to talk more about what you have spoken about earlier: 'We try to avoid every conflict as possible we can.' We move back and forth between talking about your experience as an employee and a subordinate to your boss, and your experiences at school. I have called this 'The story of authority'.

Cheng-tsung: Sometimes I agree with that. In the learning field, I mean in the education field, in our culture the teacher always... I mean... the upper level hierarchy. Students... don't often express their opinion.

Yeah. Even in the postgraduate, the student won't have much opportunity to discuss their lessons or studies with their teachers. So in most case, the learning to some degree is... you are *forced* to do something, to do your learning. You don't have your own idea or opinion, you just obey the teacher's instruction and you can finish your learning.

Sheila: Do you think that that's... I mean you've been through that system... do you think that that's... good, useful, effective... productive?

Cheng-tsung: [LAUGHTER] I mean that depends. It depends on the goal of the learning. Because sometimes a lot of the students in Taiwan don't think learning itself is useful, they just want to get a degree and use this degree to get some job. So the learning is a tool to get good job. You don't have to use your brain. You just depend on her or you just obey the instruction.

Sheila: So in the classroom, then, the teacher talks and you listen... or not listen, of course... but the teacher does most of the talking?

Cheng-tsung: Yeah. [LAUGHTER] I think we always listen yeah... by appearance. [LAUGHTER]

Sheila: Well, that's what I mean. [LAUGHTER] So you give the appearance of listening but you may or may not listen. So I mean, coming here where we put a lot of emphasis on discussion and giving you the opportunity to talk with other people about your opinions on particular concepts, doing, working experientially, that's very different?

Cheng-tsung: Yeah, it's very different, but I like it.

Sheila: You like it?

Cheng-tsung: I wish I could have [LAUGHTER] better communication ability. Maybe it depends on the stage of development because I think maybe every stage will have a different need.

Sheila: Mmm... I wonder if it does. I suppose I'm thinking, you see, when I went to school... the teacher spoke and we listened, or didn't listen. You know, what you're describing isn't actually that different from my experience at school. Until I got into the sixth form – you know the sixth form, when you're about between the ages of 16 and 18?

Cheng-tsung: Ok, that's our senior high school.

Sheila: Where the groups... well certainly in my own school, which was quite small... the groups would be quite small. And I guess we were treated more as adults by the teachers so there were more opportunities for discussion. And then when I was a student I went to a polytechnic and it was *very* interactive and very *good* teaching and... well, it was the late 60s when it was *very* student-centred. I loved it.

Cheng-tsung: I have the same feeling, yeah.

Sheila: But because I *so* enjoyed that way of working with other groups of students, doing things together, debating, didn't matter if we disagreed with the lecturer – so much the better really, being encouraged to have opinions. In fact *really really* being encouraged to have opinions. And...

Cheng-tsung: I think the language is the biggest problem. I'm eager to communicate with all the students or the tutors here... especially focused on my interest in topic... but the language is a big limitation.

Sheila: You perceive that to be a limitation?

Cheng-tsung: Yeah. Because some concept I cannot... describe detailed in English.

You tell me about the place of the teacher in the hierarchy (Cortazzi and Jin, 2001; Ho, 2001) and we move on to discuss our memories of our learning experiences. I want to share my own experiences of being at school and, although certainly not a passive, 'surface' learner (Marton and Saljo, 1984), I want you to know that my own school experiences up until the age of 16 were very much of the transmission model of learning (Jarvis *et al.*, 2003) – the teacher spoke and we listened (or not, of course). I like the way you say, 'I think we always listen... by appearance', and laugh. Why do I like that response? Is it because you are confirming my own view that learning is less effective when students seem to be passive? So in spite of writing in previous chapters that I do not want to engage in the uncritical transfer of pedagogical approaches, do I still believe that in order for learning to be effective we have to be active? By active, I mean participating in activities and discussion, not the 'active' of silent reflection (Webb, 1996; Jones, 1999; Teekens, 2000; Brookfield, 2005; Welikala and Watkins, 2008).

I share with you my very positive experiences of being an undergraduate student. The memories evoked are very vivid. I am back in those seminar groups enjoying the conversation, the debate, and the 'games'. I can see the young management lecturer whose classes were the most lively I can remember. The 'communication games' that he used enabled me to learn the importance of listening closely to what another person is saying:

Sheila: And then when I was a student I went to a polytechnic and it was *very* interactive and very *good* teaching and . . . well, it was the late 60s when it was *very* student centred. I loved it.

Cheng-tsung: I have the same feeling, yeah.

I have repeated this extract to emphasise the important beliefs that I reveal. I tell you how much I loved the interactive teaching approach, but then justify this by my words 'Well it was the late 60s' and '*very* student-centred'. I had never heard of Carl Rogers (1994) or the phrase 'student-centred' at that time, but I felt as if what I had to say was important, or at least as important as what others had to say. I am applying that knowledge retrospectively, recognising the personal value and effectiveness of this learning approach. Sharing these memories with you, you express similar feelings. This is (for me) an unexpected connection, made by keeping the conversation open (Riessman, 2004, Shope, 2006).

The story of the pantomime

You tell me 'The story of the pantomime', after we had discussed some of your difficulties with speaking in English. You disrupted the conversation by saying 'I think the cultural context is very important' followed by your reference to 'kind of a feeling of distance'. I am struggling to understand what you mean by this feeling of distance. You tell a story about a pantomime, an alien concept for you, to explain to me:

Cheng-tsung: I think the cultural context is very important. Because another thing I don't understand about this society, you know this culture, it's always kind of . . . I don't know how to say . . . kind of a feeling of distance. Because I cannot fully understand what is going on here, you know, so sometimes it is difficult to really understand.

Sheila: Because of this distance?

Cheng-tsung: Distance. I mean the depth of the understanding because some, cultural issue operate. Underneath meaning or something like that, I could not understand fully, so I always have limitation to understand about the concept or the theory or something like that. And another thing is I have to take more time to transform what I have learned here into my cultural context or my experience. I want to integrate them and try to find some new idea

Sheila:	And you said that sometimes what that means is or what you feel that means is you don't really grasp the depth of a concept because of this cultural distance.
Cheng-tsung:	Yeah. I can make an example of that. Just as there will be a play, panto, in Christmas time. [LAUGHTER] I am very curious about what is the panto. You know, Dione has told me something about a panto, I can imagine, but I cannot catch the real feeling or the meaning of panto.
Sheila:	How could you catch it then? Can you imagine how you could?
Cheng-tsung:	I just imagine the . . . scenario, the people they will do, you know in the theatre.
Sheila:	So if you went to watch one . . .
Cheng-tsung:	Yeah. I think I will. [LAUGHTER] Yeah.
Sheila:	If you went to watch one that would help you to understand?
Cheng-tsung:	To some degree I think it will. But two weeks ago I go to see *The Hobbit* in the Hippodrome and I borrowed the book *The Hobbit* from the library, and after doing that I still feel I have some kind of . . . some feeling of distance.
Sheila:	Yeah, cos you don't really . . . yeah, I'm not sure I would understand *The Hobbit* either . . .
Cheng-tsung:	[LAUGHTER]
Sheila:	. . . but that's probably because I don't like those kind of fantasy things. But this distance is . . .
Cheng-tsung:	Because I can understand the story . . .
Sheila:	You can understand the story . . .
Cheng-tsung:	. . . but I can't catch the essence of the play or the meaning of that.
Sheila:	But there's something, there's something missing.
Cheng-tsung:	Yeah. I don't feel it is enough for me to . . . I still think . . . they still have something more I can understand. So I'm not satisfied. [LAUGHTER]
Sheila:	So, it's the something that you feel . . . you're missing and that leaves you with this feeling of not being satisfied.

Dione, a student from Malta, has told you about pantomime and its role in English culture at Christmas. In trying to imagine what happens in a pantomime, you cannot 'catch the real feeling or the meaning of a panto' from Dione's description. I suggest that you might be able to do so were you to go and watch a pantomime. You appear to agree, but then tell me that when you went to see *The Hobbit*, even though you borrowed the book to read, you still had 'some feeling of distance'. I tell you of my dislike for 'fantasy things', to reassure you that I, too, would probably not understand *The Hobbit*. Is this another way of communicating to you our similarity, neither of us understand 'fantasy things'? Do I want to reassure you that we are not really that different? Writing it now, it seems that what was a well-intentioned and genuine comment (I do *not* like 'fantasy things') is rather obsequious. Thankfully, you choose to ignore it, and to continue with your own train of thought. What was missing from your experience of going to see *The Hobbit*? What were you trying to tell me? What did *I* miss? Was the 'something missing' your feeling that, because of the cultural distance, you could not connect with me, and those who share a similar cultural background, on a deeper, emotional level?

Finally...

In this letter, note how much we talked about in that conversation. I learn about the difficulties in dealing with conflict and the avoidance of it, in your Taiwanese culture. We share some of our earlier learning experiences; you talk about your struggle with authority, with language, and we both seem to feel that understanding the spoken and written word is not sufficient without an emotional connection to a subject. You and I were telling many stories in that conversation, each using a story to explain to the other what we mean. Are we co-constructing some stories, so that alternative stories emerge? This conversation was not a therapeutic one; I was not your 'therapist', nor were you mine, but I believe that had I kept a tight focus on learning and teaching issues, such connections might not have been made. I have gained much from the conversation that I can use in my teaching. I have become more aware of different approaches to the expression of emotion and to authority. I learn that I can theorise about the importance of balancing idiographic and nomothetic concepts in communication 'across our cultures' but the experiences I have sought to describe here are, for me, testimony to those words that I quoted in Chapter 2:

> Intercultural learning is not just a topic to be talked about (thinking and knowing) it is also about caring, acting and connecting...It entails the discovery and transcendence of difference through authentic experiences of cross-cultural interaction that involve real tasks, and emotional as well as intellectual participation.
>
> *(De Vita and Case, 2003: 388)*

I have re-presented our conversation, together with my reflections in this letter, to show how we were, perhaps, transcending difference, through emotional and intellectual participation. In my next letter, I will share stories that we told to each other some months later, when you had begun to write your dissertation.

Best wishes,
Sheila.

The third letter to Cheng-tsung

Dear Cheng-tsung,

The story of being mild

This story was told in a conversation we had about eight months after the first recorded conversation. The taught part of the MEd had ended, and by now you were working on your dissertation. I had started to become a little concerned about you, as our contact had been less regular. I had become mindful that it might be more difficult for students from Confucian-heritage cultures to ask for help (Wu, 2002). Aware that this was yet another stereotype that I needed to be wary of, nonetheless I was emailing you intermittently to reassure you of my willingness to meet. By this stage in the year, I felt that we had developed an open and trusting relationship. I was familiar with your written work, I knew something about your family, and I was aware of the high regard that other students had for you. Before you came along that day, I had read through the transcript of our last conversation, not because I wanted to preempt *this* conversation, but to remind myself of the main themes.

I had read your dissertation in draft form prior to our meeting and been intensely affected by it, by the power of the writing, by the sadness of some of the stories, but also by the way in which 'you' were emerging from the nightmares you described. You had given your consent for me to use any material from our conversations together, but it was at this point that I asked you if I could also use parts of your own writing. You were 'honoured' by this request. The following words are some of those that provoked particularly powerful responses in me:

> My teacher often punished me for my poor maths record in front of the whole class. I felt humiliated, ashamed, guilty, resentful, worthless and that I was stupid. Every day I lived in fear of being beaten or slapped. I could not imagine that one day I would be successful. Under such 'duck filling', corporal punishment and trampling of my human dignity, I never learned maths well and became very passive in learning.

You then continue by telling a story about how you decided to study abroad after a period in hospital:

> In my mid-thirties, suddenly I found that I was at a developmental crossroads in my life. I could lead my life as usual or make some changes. But, I was not sure of the opportunities. Nevertheless, the thought of obtaining a degree was an instinctive response. But if I went back to the education system, it also means that there is no escape of facing my 'learning trauma' again. I remembered how hard it was to survive my academic nightmare and was I choosing to go through all the torture again? I think I got 'PTSD' for learning! I

laughed to myself bitterly; at least, perhaps, I have found the quickest, but not the best, way to view my obscure future.

Then you describe your early learning experiences in Bristol:

> I still remember the first time I saw my personal tutor in class, a warm, mild and middle-age white woman. As soon as I saw her, half of my uneasiness was cast away because I felt that she is the person I could communicate with. Her speed of speaking, the attitude of willing to understand and sincerity made me feel that *I could be myself*. I never expected that a learning experience could be so different. I like to be respected as a learner; I thought to myself that if I had been taught this way all along then what would have been different? It seemed not bad to me that the 'ground' impression was inspiring.

Mild, middle age, white

It was difficult to read the words 'mild, middle-age white woman'. I am white, I am middle-aged, and I am a woman; but 'mild' was not a word that I would use to describe myself, nor was it a word that others had attributed to me. 'Mild', to me, suggested lukewarm, lacking in charisma, passive, introvert. Because this word leapt off the page – inaccurate, from my perspective – I was consumed by a need to understand the meaning that you attributed to it.

We had had many discussions about the differences between Chinese and English. You had told me of your struggle to find the 'right' English word to explain what you wanted to say. In the first few minutes of the conversation, I asked you about your use of that word:

Sheila: Is this me you're describing in here? Is this... when you say you first met your tutor, is that me?

Cheng-tsung: Yeah. [LAUGHTER]

Sheila: When I read it, it was a very interesting... it was really interesting for me to read it.

Cheng-tsung: Why? [LAUGHTER]

Sheila: Well... because, because you know it's very interesting to read a description of yourself written... particularly when you say 'white'. I mean you know of course I *am* white.

Cheng-tsung: Okay.

Sheila: ... but to see it... and in the context of the kind of research I'm trying to do... you know there is... I talked to you about this before... there's a lot of stuff written about whether it's possible or ethical to do research with people you know from different cultural backgrounds, particularly *being white*.

Cheng-tsung: Yeah.

Sheila: So when I saw this it was just very interesting to have that, and I've actually used it in the paper. The word I wanted to ask you about was this word 'mild'.

Cheng-tsung: [LAUGHTER] Mmm...

Sheila: I really wanted to ask you what you meant by the word 'mild'.

Cheng-tsung: I don't know. I just used my understanding about this kind of word to express my feeling at that time. I don't know... maybe I don't know exactly what 'mild' means. But the meaning of the 'mild' for me is a very gentle or very... I don't know how to describe it exactly... it's very... I mean I don't have to worry my pace, I don't have to adjust my pace to somebody else's pace.

Sheila: You don't have to?

Cheng-tsung: Yeah because sometimes I feel I have to adjust my pacing to somebody else's pacing. Yeah.

Sheila: Are you talking about pacing, pacing of speaking or pacing of...?

Cheng-tsung: Not really the speed of speaking. I use the word 'channel' yeah [LAUGHTER] I think maybe to some extent we are in the same 'channel', so I don't have to worry other things about our communication.

Sheila: Right. So you felt, then... maybe you felt that we were on the same wavelength.

Cheng-tsung: Wavelength?

Sheila: Wavelength. Do you know that expression?

Cheng-tsung: No.

Sheila: Um, a wavelength. It would be like... how can I explain it? You know like a radio, you're listening to the radio... you have to get the right wavelength or the radio crackles.

Cheng-tsung: Yeah, that's right; yeah, wavelength.

Sheila: So we have this expression for people who are thinking, maybe, thinking in the same way, communicating well. We say that they are on the same wavelength.

Cheng-tsung: Yeah, yeah.

Sheila: Because there's no crackle! [LAUGHTER]

Cheng-tsung: Yeah, yeah, that's what I feel.

Sheila: So that's what you felt?

Cheng-tsung: Yeah. Because I think myself, I think myself, I'm a mild person, so I think ... I mean the wavelength is the same, yeah.

Sheila: So that was what you meant by the word 'mild'.

Cheng-tsung: Yeah. [LAUGHTER] Always have good temper or something like that.

At the beginning of the conversation I am musing on the word 'white', but then I do not pursue this with you. You define me as 'white', and, of course, I am white, but like many other white people I had never stopped to think of myself as a 'colour' (Frankenberg, 1993, 2004). It is as if, because I *am* white, there can be no more to say about it. You know that I have decided to write a chapter in this book (Chapter 8) about my whiteness. Some of the responses I have had to this decision are similar to those Bonnett (2000) received when he spoke to people about his undertaking to write a book about white identities, '"I know about that already," I have been informed on more than one occasion, with the added explanation "I *am* white, so what's to know?"' (ibid., 2000: 1, original emphasis).

'I *am* white, so what's to know?' caused me to overlook that opportunity to discuss my whiteness with you, but the event stayed in my mind; a seed had been planted. I had talked about 'problematising my whiteness', but I was not really clear what that meant, nor how I was going to 'problematise' it, other than by defining myself as a white woman, to locate myself in the study (Hertz, 1997). Eventually, I realised that it was completely disingenuous to be researching the influences of culture on learning and teaching, without including an exploration of the influences of my own culture, my own ethnicity.

Writing this now, I am aware of how dismissive I am of another word that you use, the word 'channel'. I did not want to accept 'mild' as one of your definitions of me, and now I seem to want to coerce you into using a word, 'wavelength', that I have chosen. Another reading of those few lines might be that we are both struggling to understand the other, but I am the one who questions your use of particular words, assuming that, unless we use the same word, we might not understand each other.

I listen to the recorded conversations and can feel great warmth towards you when hearing your voice, marvelling at the similarity of our sense of humour. I can congratulate myself smugly on how, as we become closer, you become much braver and more able to be critical of your experiences in the UK. 'The story of the rotten shrimp', told in a later letter is a good example. I can claim that, because of my counselling background, I have an ability to empathise with you. Empathy is, as you know, one of the core conditions of the person–centred approach to counselling (Rogers, 1951), but it is criticised as 'romantic illusion' by Gunaratnam (2003: 102). Caruth and Keenan (1995: 264) are even more critical: 'Empathy is about sameness ... Something is not confronted there, when you think you're understanding or empathising in a certain way.'

For me empathy is not about sameness; it is about striving to imagine another's world in the way that they themselves see it (Andrews, 2007). This does not mean that I understand or know it, rather that through trying to see their perspective, I am more able to question my own. 'Rather than . . . erase the complexities of difference and powered relations in the interview, there is much to be achieved by distrusting any neatness, and actively searching out and valuing the complexity and richness that comes with the mess' (Gunaratnam, 2003: 104). This extract of conversation was triggered by my curiosity about your use of certain words. One of my readings of that conversation now is that I was colonising your use of language (Trinh, 1989; Rassool, 2004; Shope, 2006), perhaps seeking neatness, using my perceived power, rather than hoping that ours was a symmetrical relationship. Yet, for you, being 'mild' was a similarity between us. We uncovered a connection and, as a result, I was better able to understand how you had positioned me. This process of 'uncovering and discovering' could be interpreted as a 'getting closer to' position (as I discuss more fully in Chapter 8), but I feel it took us to another level of understanding.

I am fortunate that my relationship with you, as with many other students, has continued and, of course, we met in Taipei recently when you arranged a reunion. Remember, though, that I had reconsidered the way I re-presented this conversation many times and sent that section of the chapter to you to read. Here is a reminder of the email that you sent to me:

> Frankly speaking, the reason why I mentioned your whiteness is perhaps my 'yellowness'. For me, I never thought that my best learning experience should have happened with a 'foreigner'. My assumption was a British teacher could never better understand what I need in learning than a Chinese teacher because of different languages. The truth told me I was wrong. I have learned that there are something could go beyond the boundary between languages. Real listening and cherish my 'being' as a learner is far more precious than limited languages.

I suggest that we are engaging in a:

> Complex interaction – the intersubjectivity – between researchers and narrators' voices . . . These researchers examine *their* voices – their subject positions, social locations, interpretations and personal experiences – through the refracted medium of narrators' voices.
>
> *(Chase, 2005: 666, original emphasis)*

As I end this letter, I hope that you will recognise how your refracted voice enabled me, as always, to examine mine.

Best wishes,
Sheila.

The fourth letter to Cheng-tsung

Dear Cheng-tsung,

The language of emotions story

Following on from our conversation about the word 'mild', you began to recall the problems you had to find 'the right word'. In our earlier recorded conversation, you alluded to this difficulty, but now give me specific examples. For the first time, I begin to understand how you must have struggled. People whose first language is English can feel that they have to use particular vocabulary and spend too much time explaining technical terms to those who have English as an additional language. The latter claim that the former speak too quickly and use jargon, thus they can feel excluded from conversations. Such experiences of being spoken to, by both students and lecturers, in the diminutive voice can lead students to feel diminished and marginalised (Hellsten and Prescott, 2004). Many other conversations that I have had support such findings. Wan Yi, from Taiwan, acknowledged that those students whose first language was English were trying to help her to contribute to discussion by waiting for her reply. She felt that they assumed this was putting added pressure on her and so would move quickly on to the next point. She found this experience diminishing. Mei, also from Taiwan, commented, 'They assume that Chinese people don't have opinions.'

Cheng-tsung: Because I am in such a situation, I found a similar situation happened in the autumn term. Because we would have to practise some skills, counselling skills. I felt it was very difficult for me to use a proper word about emotions, or feeling adjective. I found that I always used the, I mean, the wrong words.

Sheila: The wrong words?

Cheng-tsung: I mean not exactly what my client felt...Yeah. So I always feel that it's very difficult to...I mean, to correspond to my client correctly, because I cannot use the proper words to reflect his or her feeling or emotions. So for me, I felt that it's a split experience. Because when I was in Taiwan I can do my empathy...very good. But here I cannot use my...such kind of a word to convey my concern or idea exactly.

Sheila: Exactly?

Cheng-tsung: Yeah. So I felt it's a gap between I mean the two experiences – between Taiwan and Bristol. So from that time I found that I'm very anxious [LAUGHTER] or worried to use what is the proper word to express or reflect the exact feeling or emotion somebody has felt. Or I myself I feel

Sheila: So with the person you were speaking to, you were listening to, were they ever correcting you? Did they ever say, 'No it isn't that' or 'Yes it is that'?

Cheng-tsung: Um ... sometimes I found that my client will respond me with some ... you know the gesture or their appearance ... I would know that I used, I used an improper word.

Sheila: And then what would happen? How would you manage to find ... as you say ... the right word?

Cheng-tsung: So I ... I mean I go to the library [LAUGHTER] to find some other books about the emotions following the counselling training, pamphlet or something like that, and I found there are some emotional terms or this kind of terms listed in the book. So I try to find them again under special meaning of this kind of a word, how to use them, in what kind of circumstances I can use this kind of term. So I found some new vocabulary or new terms that I'm not so familiar before. So I try to find this vocabulary, try to remember those words, yeah.

Sheila: It must be difficult

Cheng-tsung: Mmm, yeah, because the English I found that the emotional terms is large.

Sheila: You mean we have a lot of different words?

Cheng-tsung: Yeah. For me, I mean for a Mandarin Chinese speaker I have, I have to use the very exact term to describe some kind of emotion or feelings. Yeah. We don't have so specific words or terms to clearly describe the emotion or the feeling in Chinese.

Sheila: Can you give me an example?

Cheng-tsung: Such as 'mild'. [LAUGHTER]

Sheila: Mild.

Cheng-tsung: Yeah. Because for me 'mild' in some way is not specific or not a, a very clear term. In my view really it's little about considerate or good-tempered, or very warm. All this kind of meanings. I mean all this is included in the meaning of mild.

It is not only a difficulty with the language; it is also that English has so many words to describe similar emotions. You seem more confident to talk to me about this difficulty. Has my sharing with you my response to the word 'mild' helped you to formulate your own different meanings? I am struggling to understand:

Cheng-tsung: Yeah. But this is the same situation that I remember that I started my counselling training. I always try to reflect somebody else or my client's feeling or emotion. But I found one thing is very difficult because in the daily life, Chinese-speaking, we are not often use this kind of emotional term. So I mean the client, he or herself, is not used to listening to this kind of emotional term. So sometimes if I use a more unusual term to reflect his or her feelings I mean the way it links [LAUGHTER] will be...we cannot connect each other.

Sheila: Because you would use a word seeking to reflect how that person seemed to be feeling?

Cheng-tsung: Yeah. Or this kind of word just can appear in the...I mean not in the verbal pattern or verbal form, it may be just used in the written form. But some specific feeling, if I felt I can reflect I will link it to the written form. Because for me that would be more accurate. Yeah. But for my clients sometimes I found it is difficult for him or for her to perceive I mean this kind of term.

Sheila: So say somebody's...I'm trying to picture it...say somebody is...very upset...say they're crying and they're obviously very upset. I mean, presumably you would...oh I don't know, can't presume it...I would say, 'You're obviously very upset'...or, 'You're obviously very distressed'.

Cheng-tsung: Mmm...distressed...but in Chinese I think there's one word, we say that, we say if you're very 'nanguo'.

Sheila: 'Nanguo'?

Cheng-tsung: 'Nanguo', yeah. But 'nanguo' means...it's more wide meaning compared to English. Because 'nanguo', I mean nanguo means...means, it include upset and distress. Yeah. So I think just use 'nanguo' to reflect this kind of feeling. I don't have to distinguish specifically what's the difference between the uneasiness or distress or...

Sheila: That would say it all.

Cheng-tsung: Yeah, if you say 'I feel distress' for me my interpretation is that 'nanguo'

Sheila: 'Nanguo'.

Cheng-tsung: Yeah. I cannot distinguish between upset or distress. But I can distinguish the angry end of the upset.

Sheila: That would be a different word.

Cheng-tsung: That would be different.

Each time I read and listen to this part of the conversation, I am embarrassed by how tortuous it seems. We have circled around and return to discussing language and meaning. You use the word 'mild' again, but this time we use it as a vehicle to explore words that describe emotions. I am curious to understand how you would reflect different levels of distress in another person, and you introduce me to the word 'nanguo'. I find it difficult to pronounce and need to hear it several times before I can pronounce it correctly.

Following this conversation, I bumped into you in the library and asked you how to spell 'nanguo', as I had realised its symbolic significance for me; it was important that in any writing or retelling of that story, I re-presented that word correctly. On receiving the transcript of this conversation, I immediately corrected the spelling.

Our discussion of emotional language leads me to want to share with you Maroussia's comment about my use of the 'language of emotion' (this occurred in the conversation that appears in Chapter 3). I want to hear your views on this. You have explained to me how difficult it is for Chinese people to show and express their emotions. Maroussia assumed that my use of the 'language of emotion' would be confusing, and possibly alienating, for people who did not associate learning with emotion (see, for example, Claxton, 1996). Cultural influences on emotion in learning continue to be an under-researched area (Li, 2002), yet *hao-xue-xin*, the 'heart and mind' for wanting to learn is a key dimension in seeking knowledge in Confucian-heritage cultures (Kennedy, 2002). Did you feel confused and alienated?

Cheng-tsung: [LAUGHTER] I mean maybe this is what . . . I mean the wavelengths is the same. Because, personally, I think that emotion plays a very important role in my learning.

I notice that you return to the word 'wavelength', which seems, in spite of my subsequent turmoil, that I was colonising your language, to have been a useful word for you to tell me that emotion plays a very important role in your learning. This statement is borne out in your dissertation, where you describe your painful experiences of learning. My teaching approach is familiar to you because you have the same *belief* that learning is an emotional experience. This is a challenge to my assumption that my approach to learning and teaching might be alienating and threatening for those students whose previous learning experiences have been in more formal contexts, where the 'teacher' is the imparter of knowledge and where 'emotions are still treated as interruptions to learning rather than resources for learning' (Claxton, 1996: 53). You then tell me, however, that other students, your colleagues, are not familiar with this kind of learning:

Cheng-tsung: So I'm very like your way in the classroom. I have the same belief in learning. So I'm very used to this kind of a learning, learning pattern. Yeah. Somebody can take care of my emotional feeling. But I *know* indeed there are some other students, my colleagues, they are not used to this kind of, this kind of way of learning. Yeah, because I mean, traditionally, especially, such as in Taiwan, if a student go to the classroom they would expect that the teacher, 'You just tell me something that I should *learn*'.

So I mean the only thing happens, should be happening in the classroom is that teacher teaches his knowledge to the students, they won't mind any other things. I mean this kind of atmosphere in our learning circumstance or environment. And so if the teacher who in classroom he or she teaches students, I mean she specially concerned about the student's feeling or emotion, they will feel weird . . . or very strange, because they are not used to take care in this way.

Sheila: So the teacher wouldn't be interested – the teacher or the lecturer or the tutor wouldn't be *interested* in how you felt?

Cheng-tsung: Mmm, I think most of the teachers weren't concerned about my, our, feeling or emotion in the classroom. Mmm, I think maybe I mean the reality . . . maybe they would like to concern about our emotional feeling, but the reality is that the environment force them to do in this way. Because we have 40, 40 to 50 students in one classroom. So maybe for some teachers it is very difficult to handle such so much students in one classroom take care of their emotional feelings separately. This is one reason. Another reason is the content of the teaching required by the authority, I mean the curriculum is very intense. So I mean most of the time they are considering how to finish their teaching job, to teach their materials to the students regardless of the students are emotional.

Sheila: So it's very much content, content-driven.

Cheng-tsung: Yeah. And I found since I received the counselling training, I found I liked this kind of learning very much because it can take care of my emotional feelings. Yeah. So compared to the past learning experience, I thought, yes, this is what I want.

Sheila: So I guess that was something else, was it, that helped you to feel on the same wavelength? (that word again). The one thing I can't imagine changing is that belief that if learning is going to be effective, then I do actually believe that people . . . well certainly I need to be emotionally involved in it. So, in other words, I need to *feel* that the learning is . . . the actual *learning*, that it's useful, that it's enjoyable. Yeah, that you know I like . . . it's a place I like being.

Having established that we share similar views in relation to the role of emotion in learning, we move on to discuss ways in which I might be more sensitive towards students who perhaps feel less confident to share opinions and feelings with others:

Sheila: And yet one of the things that's been suggested to me is that in the beginning it might be easier if you actually had people have discussions with people who speak the same language as them, so that they can become a little bit more familiar with talking about themselves in their own language.

Cheng-tsung: Yeah.

Sheila: And a little bit more confident to, you know, kind of put together an idea or their ideas in their own language. And then perhaps to develop more confidence to then work in small groups with people who are from... well, who speak other languages. So what do you think about that idea?

Cheng-tsung: Yeah, I think this is a very good idea.

Sheila: Yeah. I suppose because I've been so eager to... you know mix people up...

Cheng-tsung: Yeah.

Sheila: ...um, that hadn't occurred to me, that actually that very mixing up of people at a very early stage might actually be quite frightening...

Cheng-tsung: Yeah.

Sheila: ...you know, for some people, first of all who aren't used to being asked to talk about themselves and to express their opinions and to express how they *feel* about something.

Cheng-tsung: Yeah. But you know, I mean most Taiwanese students they would like to be in the group which is organised by especially differently... they come from different countries. Because we also... I mean we've all thought about if we go abroad for study we have to... I mean contact with foreigners as possible as we can. So we all have these kind of sense. So if we go abroad for study and we found that we don't have so much opportunity for contact with the foreigners, to some extent, we will disappoint.

Sheila: Yes, I've heard that before. And I suppose I think that's a really difficult one because it is something I'm aware of particularly where there are so many Taiwanese students. And I certainly have had other people say to me that they have been *disappointed* by their experiences here because they haven't *met* people that they thought they would meet.

Cheng-tsung: Yeah.

Sheila: And so I don't know whether there are things you think that we could be doing, you know to, to change that.

Cheng-tsung: [long pause] I don't know. At the moment, the only way I think... I mean the solution is that... I mean don't recruit so many Taiwanese. [LAUGHTER]

I am sharing with you the idea of inviting students to work together with others who speak their language, especially at the beginning of the course, when most people are anxious. I want to know what you think of this suggestion. I respect and value your opinion, and if you think it is a good idea, then I shall try it. I had been reading Cadman's (2000) article at the time. Cadman believes that it is vital to recognise that international postgraduates are steeped in their own academic traditions when they arrive in another country to study. Those experiences are an overlooked resource. They could help the host institution to understand learning practices in other cultures and to critique their own approaches to teaching, learning and assessment. I was much influenced by this article, not only because Cadman shared my interest in exploring postgraduate experiences, but also because it introduced me to the work of Helen Fox (1994) and challenged me to reconsider the concept of 'criticality' and 'critical thinking' in the western academic tradition.

You knew that I was questioning the cultural situatedness of my approaches to teaching and learning. Crossley's (1984, 2000) work, had alerted me to the dangers of the uncritical transfer of educational policies and innovations across international boundaries and had challenged me to apply similar principles to my teaching and learning approach. I want to hear your perspective on these issues that were salient to me. I really liked Cadman's conclusion that, 'Valid "transcultural" education requires that the values of western academic tradition be critiqued through the perceptions and experiences of international scholars' (Cadman, 2000: 475).

I want to know what *you* think about this statement. I am still not sure whether you feel that you have been afforded opportunities to critique the western academic tradition. Perhaps you feel you have, given what you wrote in your dissertation, quoted by me on page 63?

Best wishes,
Sheila.

The fifth letter to Cheng-tsung

Dear Cheng-tsung,

The story of the rotten shrimp

The story of the rotten shrimp is another example of an unanticipated narrative (Cortazzi and Jin, 2006). This story seemed to emerge from my desire to share with you my feelings about the '"whiteness" of the academy that seemed to go unnoticed and uncommented' (Clegg et al., 2003: 164). The concept of institutional racism (Scheurich, 1997) was challenging me to interrogate not only my own teaching and learning practices, but also to investigate more critically the dominant pedagogy of the institution and of my department. I was keen to move from 'teaching as assimilation...a kind of colonial phase' (Biggs, 2003: 123) towards a transformational ideal of assimilation (Young, 2001). I wanted to share some of these reflections with you, to gain your perspective:

Sheila:	And what we don't do enough of... and I feel very strongly about this... is this, what we're doing now, is to talk to you about your experiences and to use those experiences to inform and to look more critically at what we do. So I kind of wondered... I'm interested in how you feel about that.
Cheng-tsung:	Personally, I think that... I mean the support from the university, especially Education School, I think it is enough for me personally.

This is not the response I was expecting. I anticipated that you would agree with my statement, but your response is that you have felt supported. You then disrupt the conversation to tell me some different stories, stories about specific experiences from your life in the UK. You might be said to be radically transgressing from the 'knowable order' of the 'interview', providing an example of 'the indeterminate ambiguity of interviewing' (Scheurich, 1997: 75).

Cheng-tsung:	But I mean the whole learning environment, because we are not only I mean, staying in Education School, we have to go out and meet with somebody else, some other part of Bristol. Yeah. I mean in the university I think this is a friendly environment, but outside the university I don't think it is. I don't think it is so friendly as I thought.
Sheila:	You don't think England is as friendly as you thought it would be?
Cheng-tsung:	Yeah, personally, yeah I think some part of England or outside the university, that image is, I mean... is different from I thought before. Yeah. I thought I mean British should be a very polite country. [LAUGHTER] According to my image that this is a very clean place or something like that. But some image is contrary to my past imagination.
Sheila:	You thought we were polite and you thought we were clean?
Cheng-tsung:	Yeah [LAUGHTER]
Sheila:	And you don't think we are?

Cheng-tsung:	At the moment, yeah. [LAUGHTER]
Sheila:	You don't think we are polite?
Cheng-tsung:	I mean outside university. I mean some people are really rude, yeah.
Sheila:	In what way? Can you give me an example?
Cheng-tsung:	Because . . . such as 2 weeks ago, I went to the airport to receive my family and I went to the bus station and I tried to get on, get on the coach. And the coach is delivered from the bus station to the airport every half-hour. But when I get there in time the coach driver told me, told me that he won't drive this time because he said that the traffic is so bad. But there is no previous information about cancelling this bus service.
Sheila:	So he just cancelled it?
Cheng-tsung:	He just cancelled. Nobody told me that, nobody told me this kind of a . . . this cancellation.
Sheila:	Yeah.
Cheng-tsung:	And he didn't, I mean, apologise to me.
Sheila:	Right.
Cheng-tsung:	And the coach station, they didn't say anything about this kind of . . . such kind . . .
Sheila:	So that would be an example of how you don't think that we're particularly polite
Cheng-tsung:	Yeah. But I found it is usual in this place, yeah? It's not so I mean . . . strict, strict on the regulation all the time. I found this interesting, it's very interesting. [LAUGHTER] Yeah, so maybe in this way. And some feeling is very subtle, because I found sometimes you're, you're communicating with some businessmen or . . . if you go shopping sometimes, I found the feeling . . . that made me feel I am not respected. Yeah. But I think maybe it is the reason maybe I don't use the very fluent English. So maybe I misunderstand this meaning or meaning yeah. So maybe this is part of the language difficulty.
Sheila:	But what it makes you feel is not respected.
Cheng-tsung:	Yeah.
Sheila:	I think that's really important.

You then continue to illustrate further your feelings about not being respected by telling me the story that I have titled 'The story of the rotten shrimp':

Cheng-tsung: I remember that one of my colleagues in TEFL pathway, once she was going to a noodle bar, yeah, and she ordered a bowl of noodles. And she found something in her bowl, I mean a shrimp or something like prawn or something like that, is rotten. And they called the waiter to complain about this situation. But they found that the attitude of this waiter is very bad. Yeah? But I mean maybe we are afraid of, I mean, the language, how to communicate well or maybe we are so worried about we are so rude in some way, so...

Sheila: Oh so you think *you* might be being rude?

Cheng-tsung: Yeah, yeah. So we force ourselves not to complain more, even if we feel we are not...uncomfortable. So the thing is...I mean is over without any further, any further solution...even if they still feel unsatisfied.

Sheila: That's really difficult, isn't it? Because you don't know why that is, do you? What you're saying is you don't know...the waiter was *rude* and you don't know whether the waiter was rude because you complained...

Cheng-tsung: Yeah.

Sheila: ...or because of the *way* you complained, because of the *language* that you used.

Cheng-tsung: Yeah.

Sheila: And because you don't *know*, you don't know why he was responding to you in that way, you then don't do anything, you're left not doing anything.

Cheng-tsung: Yeah. [LAUGHTER] I mean in that kind of a situation we don't have enough words to complain properly.

Sheila: Yeah.

Cheng-tsung: So most of the time we will...I mean...constrain.

Sheila: Constrain yourself.

You told me in an earlier conversation that Chinese people constrain themselves and avoid confrontation. I feel you have now given me permission to probe a little more about your difficulties with making a complaint. I want to find out how to encourage students to express any dissatisfaction they may feel with their learning experiences. It is difficult to imagine that students are completely satisfied. I want to respect the importance of face (Bond, 1986, 1991), to be mindful of the author-ity invested in the 'teacher' figure (Pratt *et al.*, 1999), and yet I still want to hear about their dissatisfactions. I use the 'rotten shrimp' as a metaphor, which you immediately respond to with laughter. I sense that you like it; you are sharing my attempt at humour:

Sheila: So would that happen here? Thinking in the department, you know if there was something you weren't happy with, I mean say something like the rotten shrimp...

Cheng-tsung: [LAUGHTER]

Sheila: ...in a bowl of noodles, what would you do about that?

Cheng-tsung: You mean in education school?

Sheila: Yes, yes.

Cheng-tsung: I feel that I am very relaxed if this kind of situation happened, because I know you are here and I know you are very supportive. So if something happened I am not satisfied, I will tell you.

Sheila: Right, yeah. So you would have been happy to do that.

Cheng-tsung: So I'm very relaxed here, because I have a very strong support behind my learning. So I don't have to worry...I mean I always have enough support, so I can relax in my learning.

Sheila: But so...okay, so what you're saying then is that's very important, that's been important, to feel that you've got that support. So that if you were not happy about something you could have come and spoken to me about it.

Cheng-tsung: Yeah, that's right. Yeah, the point is some colleagues of mine, I mean...a Taiwanese student, they are no, they are not quite satisfied with their learning here.

Sheila: Right.

Cheng-tsung: I think maybe the main reason is that they don't have sufficient support from their tutor.

I change the direction of the conversation at this point. I have obtained from you some expression of the dissatisfaction I was searching for, even if, as you say, it was not dissatisfaction with me but with others. You tell the two stories, both of which seem to be about rudeness and finding it difficult to complain. I take the opportunity to use the metaphor of the rotten shrimp to explore with you how you would complain about situations with which you were unhappy in the learning environment. Your response is to tell me that you would have been able to come and talk to me, because you had enough support and can feel relaxed in your learning. This is in marked contrast to our earlier conversation, where you told me that you would find it very difficult to complain to me. But I choose not to pursue the line of conversation. Listening to the recording, this change in direction is pronounced. Is it that you were about to discuss colleagues, and I am concerned about the ethicality of this, undoubtedly a concern in narrative inquiry and explored in Chapter 9? Or am I more interested to obtain more feedback from you on my own practice?

The story of the personal tutorial

I move on to share with you another factor that has emerged from my reading – the role of the teacher. We had discussed this in an earlier conversation, but I had read more about it subsequently:

Cheng-tsung: And this makes me think about that many Taiwanese students imagine British education, higher education, especially is one thing – which is tutorial. So some students come from Taiwan, they find that they are not... I mean once they found that the tutorial is not so familiar, so similar with they have imagined it, they feel disappointed in some way.

Yeah. But some students I mean they don't think they get enough, some support from this kind of a tutorial. And they worry that their English is so poor they cannot communicate well with their tutor. They even think that they will bring some trouble for tutor. [LAUGHTER] So they don't want to attend the tutorial. Yeah. So this is kind of a double bind.

Maybe I mean the basic thing for him them is to... I mean for them is to build their basic relationship with you. I don't know maybe for Taiwanese, if the relationship was established everything is...

Sheila: Yeah. So if they feel that they've got that relationship, or they're getting that kind of relationship with different people, with different tutors, particularly their personal tutor, but also the person who's teaching the class...

Cheng-tsung: Yeah, that's right.

Sheila: ...then that may well help them to feel more...

Cheng-tsung: More valued or more respected.

Sheila: more valued, more respected, yeah. Yeah that's a really important thing, yeah.

And so we talk about the value of the personal tutorial. You inform me that Taiwanese students really like the idea of the personal tutorial. Many of them are, however, disappointed. They feel that they cannot make full use of this precious, individual attention because of their lack of language ability and will bring 'some trouble' for the tutor. What do you mean by this? Do you mean that it will be troublesome for the tutor, because communicating what they need from the tutorial will take more time? Do you mean that if the tutor believes that students are struggling, that will be a loss of face for her/him?

I learn much from this part of our conversation and it influences me to make changes to my teaching and learning practice. You persuade me of the need to direct students to have a tutorial with me. You tell me that relationships are important for Taiwanese people. You know how important they are for me, too, but you also know that, for me, they are founded on principles of autonomy and encouraging self-responsibility (Rogers, 1951). I make myself available, but deem it the responsibility of the student to contact me should they need help or want to meet. I determine to myself that I need to take more 'pedagogic control' and to question my 'local culture' (Wu, 2002: 389) of belief in learner autonomy. Rather than contain cultural difference, I need to use it and be more directive and proactive in enabling students to ask for support.

Josselson (1996) suggests that narrative inquiry should be mutual and collaborative, within a relationship that is being established over time, which allows for the telling and retelling of stories. In *this* conversation, held at a later stage in our relationship, you retell stories told in the earlier conversation. You disagree with me. It is easy for you to suggest different teaching practices that I might adopt. You continue to 'disrupt', determined to let me know the lack of support felt by some of your colleagues. At the end of this extract, you also reinforce the importance of feeling respected and valued. Thus the conclusion here is that we agree that this is important, but that the ways in which respect and valuing are demonstrated are different in our respective cultures. You have challenged my perceived authority. Perhaps the 'feeling of distance' you expressed in 'The story of the pantomime' has been bridged?

It is fitting that the final words of these letters are yours, as, after all, 'letters are written to someone with the expectation of a response' (Clandinin and Connelly, 2000: 106). Here is a reminder of the email that you sent to me after I asked you to comment on this storying of our conversations:

> Reading your paper is always an enjoyable experience for me. I read it repeatedly and feel that how much I wish I could communicate all my inspired idea with you on person...Maybe next time you may go to Hong Kong 'by way of'' Taipei, so I can show you another different 'travelling narratives'.

All my best wishes,
Cheng-tsung.

And of course...in 2007, I did.

6

DEVELOPING CULTURAL CAPABILITY IN INTERNATIONAL HIGHER EDUCATION

The local student perspective

In this chapter, I draw on conversations with several 'local' UK students conducted for various research projects, including one that was an investigation into potential barriers to postgraduate education as perceived – and/or experienced – by British minority ethnic postgraduates. I have decided to include the latter in order to explore the possible intersection between different agendas in higher education, influenced by the Equality Challenge Unit (ECU (2009)) report mentioned below. I am extrapolating selected extracts from longer conversations so that it appears as if the participants are speaking to one another in a television documentary programme. In this way, I am using a form of performative analysis (Riessman, 2008) through my 'voiceovers' as the presenter of the programme.

The ECU's 2009 study, *Internationalising Equality, Equalising Internationalisation*, focused on the intersection between equality and diversity in the higher education sector, identifying opportunities for synergy between broader equality and diversity agendas and internationalisation, particularly in learning and teaching practices. The study cites internationalisation at home, which has at its heart the commitment to ensure that local communities – of academics and students – benefit from the opportunities brought about by greater diversity in higher education. This is the 'perspective of the local' that I referred to in Chapter 2. In this chapter, therefore, I discuss internationalisation at home in more detail.

'Local' students are defined as those who were either born and/or educated in the UK and who are, therefore, studying and working in a context with which they are familiar. I remind you, the reader, of my desire to reject fixed notions of culture and ethnicity, yet in much research conducted into the 'local' student experiences and perceptions, participants 'articulated perceived differences between themselves and their international peers that relate to various dimensions of cultural distance' (Harrison and Peacock, forthcoming).

Harrison and Peacock (2010: 129) draw attention to the 'majority of existing studies that assume homogeneity among the international student population, ignoring important differences in culture, faith and ethnicity, which, in fact, exist across the home/international divide'. In all of my research and practice I have sought to reject the assumed homogeneity of 'international students' and 'home' or 'local' students. So often these 'groups' are positioned as homogeneous in the academic literature and, indeed, in policy discourse at local, national and international level. This chapter does not ignore the differences listed above. The participants in my documentary have a range of backgrounds; they vary in age from 25 to 63, in ethnic backgrounds and in gender and faith, but what they have in common is that they all define themselves as British postgraduates. Some of them refer to their 'differences', others do not. In the 'documentary', however, you may notice that it is the ethnic minority students who cite experiences of being singled out as 'different', whereas the white students focus more on the 'other' students and how they interact – or not – with them in culturally diverse communities.

A few words on widening participation

In the UK, the success in recruiting undergraduate students from black and minority ethnic (BME) backgrounds is widely reported (see, for example, Modood, 2006; Wakeling, 2006). There is, however, little published research focusing on widening participation and postgraduates, and even less that focuses on ethnicity of postgraduates – identified as a potential barrier to participation in postgraduate education. The representation of minority ethnic groups has increased to about 13 per cent compared to 6 per cent of the population (Storan, 2006). In so far as ethnicity is concerned, widening participation strategies may, therefore, be seen as an unqualified success. The minority ethnic population is, of course, not homogeneous. Individual minority ethnic participation rates vary considerably, and representation varies between institutions, subjects, regions and courses. Overall, participation in postgraduate study by UK BME students is high – 16 per cent of the total postgraduate population (Wakeling, 2006). Given that widening participation strategies with regard to BME students may be seen as successful, nonetheless it is important not to become complacent and assume that barriers to participation have been dissolved (Leonard, 2000).

It is important to understand that there may be barriers to participation in learning for any student; after all, 'For most students going to university is a further step on a journey of self-discovery in which they are able to assess themselves and hear themselves being assessed by others in a range of personal, social and academic settings' (Gu *et al.*, 2010: 1). There can, however, be a danger in arguing that the needs of all students are the same, leading to a failure to address important issues of power, identity and culture, and, without any malicious intent, to practices that are exclusionary. Harrison and Peacock's (2010) study indicates a 'limited classroom interaction between home and international students, coupled with a degree of indifference or avoidance' (p. 127). They even use the term 'passive xenophobia' to describe the attitudes of the 'local' undergraduates they interviewed. Haigh (2009: 278) echoes this concept of xenophobia when he says, 'the comments revealed two kinds of xenophobia, with that against the ethos and inclusion of ideas foreign to the discipline being greater than that against ideas foreign to the culture'. Some of the experiences 'performed' in this chapter resonate with those described, yet many do not. This may be because the 'participants' are all postgraduate students and there are indications that age may be a significant factor in people's propensity to recognise the value in greater opportunities to get to know people from a much more diverse range of backgrounds.

The programme begins . . .

Sheila (voiceover):	Tonight's programme is in our series Developing Cultural Capability in International Higher Education. In this programme we are focusing on the 'local' student perspective and, in particular, a concept that has come to be known as 'Internationalisation at Home'. As I have said in previous programmes in this series, 'higher education is swept up in global marketisation' (Marginson and van der Wende, 2007: 7), yet, in the UK, other anglophone countries and many other European countries, the local communities of learners are also increasingly multicultural. Interestingly, Haigh (2009: 272) suggests that 'frequently the cultural gap between a local community and its minorities is greater than that between them and it's "international" learners who often come from other Western nations or Westernised elites'. It may be that, this evening, we shall see this perspective reflected in the studio.

The programme is set within a framework of internationalisation at home, a concept that acknowledges that the majority of students (and staff) in higher education are not mobile, and thus the opportunities for developing cultural capability will not be gained by travelling to other countries for study or work. In addition, internationalisation at home is congruent with the perspectives of those such as Appadurai (2001), Haigh (2008, 2009), Sanderson (2007) and Trahar (2007, 2009) who foreground the importance and value of the personal awareness and reflexivity of academic staff in higher education, especially in encounters with those they may position as 'different' from themselves and, indeed, find themselves differently positioned by.

Teichler (2009), focusing in particular on the internationalisation of higher education in Europe, points to a recent shift in the discourse towards an increasing emphasis on 'internationalisation at home', highlighting that 'efforts to internationalise higher education cannot opt any more for standalone activities, but have to integrate border-crossing activities with some steps towards international convergence and with mainstream activities at home' (p. 105). Further, Turner and Robson (2008: 68) suggest that an 'overall positive climate' can be developed through assisting 'established and new participants' to identify ways in which learning and teaching can be more effective in international higher education institutions. Unfortunately, though, much of the research, as mentioned previously, indicates a tendency for students of diverse cultures to be reluctant to interact both within the classroom and on campus. The comment below made by a local student in research conducted for the Higher Education Academy (2008) supports this perspective:

> It's not about rudeness or about people disliking each other, it's just the natural groups that people tend to form with people from their own countries. Sometimes people prefer to speak in their native tongue as well, which I find quite a lot with the Chinese students. But yeah (I) don't really see much of mixing with international students.

There can be complex reasons for lack of student interaction (Hyland *et al.*, 2008; Montgomery, 2010) including cultural cliques, language, cultural differences in socialising, and institutional and degree course barriers. However, in previous research for this documentary series, it was also evident that for some people, simply taking part in one of our focus groups on internationalisation changed their outlook and awareness of these issues. One group of local students, for example, seemed to reach a consensus that internationalisation was of value, and with just a little effort their own intercultural learning could benefit.

But who are 'local' students? I have gathered together several people in the studio for tonight's programme and will let them introduce themselves.

Rebecca: Good evening, I'm Rebecca and I'm doing a Masters degree. I'm in my 40s and from the UK.

Jan: I'm Jan and, at 63, I think I'm the oldest person here tonight. I was born and brought up in the UK.

Jasbir: I'm Jasbir. My family is from Bangladesh and I came here to the UK as a baby. I'm now 32. I'm a full-time postgraduate student.

Chris: Hi, I'm Chris. I describe myself as a white, middle-aged, northern, working-class male.

Shana: I'm Shana and I'm very proudly Black and Welsh.

Waheeda: Good evening, I'm Waheeda. I've lived in the UK since the 1970s. I came here from Uganda to visit my brother but was never able to return as Idi Amin decided to force all of the Asian population to leave the country.

Diane: Hi, I'm Diane. I'm probably the youngest person here at 25. I'm doing a Masters degree in social work.

David: I'm David. My family came here from the Caribbean but I was born here in England. I'm doing a part-time Masters degree.

John: I'm John. I came here as a refugee from Africa and am doing a Masters degree.

Sheila: Thank you all so much for joining me this evening to share with me your experiences as learners in higher education. As you know, this programme is in a series called Developing Cultural Capability in International Higher Education and so, in particular, I'll be asking you to focus on issues of diversity – in whatever ways you interpret that term. Can we start with you, Chris?

Chris: OK, fine, I'm happy to begin. Well, I'm here doing a doctorate. I'd describe myself as a 'white, middle-aged, northern, working-class, male'. I have worked as a lecturer in higher education in several contexts including the USA and The Netherlands.

Sheila: Maybe you could start, Chris, by telling us about making the transition to being a 'student'. How do you experience the learning environment?

Chris: Well, it seems to me that students construct different spaces in our department. I choose to inhabit a room where students from several different cultures congregate rather than another room peopled by students from one country. This latter room is a multifunctional space where they pray, work and cook food. It feels like a very foreign place and less comfortable than the other rooms. The space has more of a religious overture, and because I find that constraining, I miss out on interaction that could be beneficial. Don't misunderstand me, I'm not offended; you need the freedom to pursue your own way of life. If we're going to make people really welcome then perhaps we should provide separate facilities, but that sets people apart.

Sheila: So this is a community that excludes others?

Chris: Yes, but I absolutely understand why it happens. Is it OK to be alone with a man having an intimate conversation? It would be problematic. I wouldn't want to put people in a position of feeling uncomfortable.

Sheila: I see. It hadn't occurred to me that you might be wary of approaching this particular group of students because of your gender?

Chris: Yes. I have a tendency to greet women by kissing them on the cheek. I wouldn't dream of doing that with these students – they might think that it was completely inappropriate. But perhaps my vision of their faith and culture is more restrictive than it is.

Waheeda: I assume that the women are Muslim, Chris. I'm a Muslim, too, although I choose not to render my faith so visible as the group of women that you describe. I imagine though that you didn't have the experience that I had before I even began my course. When I came for the interview, the question I was asked was 'And what do you think you will be able to give this course as an Asian woman'? And it took me a year into the course to get angry with that and another year to come to terms with it. [laughs] Because it felt almost like I'd been given a place on the course, not because they thought I would be able to do it or I'd be good at it, but because I was an Asian woman who would bring something different to it. Was I filling a quota? I guess that's what I felt as well. It's like when people I know have to visit an Asian doctor or an Asian lawyer or have an Asian teacher, there is a feeling, which I can see in people's eyes, that they're not going to get the same service, perhaps, as they would from someone who was white. Whether there is any truth in that or not, I don't think it matters. I think it's a feeling that people have that they might not get the same, or as good a service, perhaps.

Diane: Yes, I agree. I think being a British ethnic minority is that you grow up getting a feeling for areas . . . So as an ethnic minority, if you walk into a pub and there are no ethnic minorities, you feel it. And you just kind of live with this feeling . . . I mean at university you're not expecting any problems from that but it still doesn't mean there's not a level of discomfort around it . . . It's very easy to be overlooked or ignored or whatever.

Jasbir: I get really fed up, though, of all of this 'political correctness' and 'liberalism'. In fact, probably it's gone the other way in my mind actually. I remember using the word 'foreign students' in the department and I was told off for it. [laughs]

Sheila: Do you know why?

Jasbir: Well . . . they like to call them international students. So my response was, 'Why do you want to call them international students? They are foreigners.' And the tutor said, 'It might be offensive'. So I said, 'But do you know it's offensive? Have you asked anybody?' She said 'No'. This is the kind of liberalism that really gets up my backside, 'cos it means white people are making decisions on behalf of other people about what's right and wrong.

John: Yes, I do wish they were less condescending and patronising, because in being so politically correct you become very patronising.

Sheila: So do you feel patronised being invited to take part in my research project and, subsequently, this programme?

John: Oh no, because I really wanted to come here and say these things.

Sheila: I can see that you want to come in here, David.

David: In some aspects I suppose you know it does matter. I suppose there are a lot of . . . you know friends of my father saying like, 'Oh you know everything's against Black people. And people, you know, struggle to get jobs.' My father said . . . nodding to his friend and agreeing with all this. And I looked at my dad; I'm thinking, 'What's my father on about?' – five children and we all work and we've all got skilled jobs. So . . . if certain groups aren't represented in something, then you have to look at why that is, you know. As I said, some people feel like they're always . . . being Black or something, that they will always be at the bottom of the pile. Well, you know, then you've got the question, well have they got the guile, you know, to challenge those things and say, well, why? you know, and question, Well why is that, can I do something?'

Sheila: So, given that some of you are talking about feeling patronised, how did you all feel when you received my invitation to participate in this documentary?

Shana: I mused on what it would be like to refuse. Could I refuse? Did I feel I could refuse?

(Sheila's voiceover):   Viewers may conclude that Shana's comment might have nothing to do with ethnicity or culture but she made it very clear that it was. Shana and I had met several times when I was doing background research for this programme but when I asked her to participate in it, she said that, although she experienced me as open and willing to discuss contentious issues about ethnicity and culture, nonetheless, her immediate response when the request came was to muse on what it would be like to say 'no'.

Shana: But that did go through my mind . . . what might it be like to say 'No'? Again, power relations, positions of power, you know, you being white and in a position of power.

(Sheila's voiceover):   Shana's comment here attests to perceptions in previous programmes about the importance of recognising and acknowledging the ways in which the effects of race, ethnicity and culture most certainly exist, even though we may consider them as 'deeply unstable social constructs' (Gannon, 2009: 71). In fact, in next week's programme, which we are calling 'Only a Pawn in the Game', at the moment, the 'deeply unstable social construct' of whiteness is investigated.

John: As far as I'm concerned, this documentary is an academic exercise. You do the research for it, you produce a programme, but you don't do much at the grassroots level.

Sheila: Hearing you say that, I'm curious about why you agreed to participate?

John: Because . . . it's like planting seeds, you can't know where a seed will fall. Because, definitely even within the academic world, if you can inform the policy-making body, probably something could work out . . . but there is a need to do more than just these questions. Because even if I say this, if I share with you some of this experience we've gone through, it doesn't seem to have any breakthrough within the system. The system is quite intact.

(Sheila's voiceover): In a previous conversation with me, John was robust in his declaration that, as a white woman, I would never be able to understand him as a Black man. I wanted to be respectful of this viewpoint and the basis and experience from which I imagine it was derived. Nonetheless, I questioned this statement. This led him to tell me that, although he would have liked to have had a Black member of staff in his university department with whom he could relate, what was more important was to have 'someone who is conscious and sensitive about the needs'.

In the 'classroom'

The one situation where home and international students were in a position to spend significant time in contact was within the classroom setting.

(Harrison and Peacock, forthcoming)

Sheila: Can we move on to focusing on your experiences of the 'classroom'?

Chris: They reminded me of my very early experiences of school where you sit next to somebody on the first day and they become your friend. I found myself sitting with a woman who was from the same part of the country as me and with whom I had a great deal in common. But I tried to make sure that I circulated. I like that, I'll always do it. I'm mindful that it's easy to stay with the same people but, when it's a temporary kind of situation, I'll always make an effort. I valued the diversity of the group. I taught in a completely international classroom in The Netherlands and it's such a kick to deal with the different expectations that people have. I can learn things that I can apply later in my teaching. I can learn about myself.

Sheila: Can you tell us what you are learning, about teaching, about yourself?

Chris: Well, firstly, the way that my gender is constructed as a northern, English male. Then, some of the African guys. Learning about the warmth and the laughter, different from dealing with the English. I've also been help-ing one of the Chinese-speaking students with her data-collection. She was clueless about how to ask people to do something in an English university and was sending out emails with 'interviewees wanted' as the subject header. Well, you know what happens, people just bin it. I was able to show her a bit of guile. It's made a big difference to her. She and her husband took my wife and me for dinner. That's nice but I didn't see it as a completely social occasion. The international students assume that I'm cruising along without problems. They don't see my internal angst, that I worry about being able to string a sentence together.

Sheila: I'm encouraged by that story, Chris. You're aware of how you're positioned by some of the students and, although you describe yourself as full of internal angst, clearly you took great pleasure from helping the Chinese-speaking student with her data collection. This is a marked contrast to much research in this field. Indeed, a comment made by an undergraduate student when we were doing background research for this programme was: 'I don't think I'd ever thought about going out of my way to specially help somebody. I mean I do what I can when asked, but beyond that there's not really anything there.'

(Sheila's voiceover):   How typical is Chris? Here is someone who is struggling with his own confidence yet in his encounters with the 'other', clearly values what he is learning about himself. He worries about offending people because he is aware that he holds certain perceptions that may not be accurate. From an internationalisation at home perspective, I suggest that it is crucial to provide opportunities for people like Chris to articulate their perceptions of each other, to ask questions that might be embarrassing. If we do not feel able to ask such questions, we remain cowering behind uncertainty, unsure about whether or not we are being offensive.

Sheila: Can I bring you in here, Jan?

Jan: I found being a doctoral student really really different. The group consisted of all sorts of ages and nationalities and I enjoyed being forced to look outwards, to engage with all sorts of people and to be challenged. This is amazing! I'm interested in what's going on, what people are saying and how they're saying it. I was interested that, very often, although the English was not correct, how they used language to explain things. If I stopped panicking about not understanding, sometimes they put it better than we can. There were certain people who positioned themselves at the top and didn't welcome anyone else. I began to notice how the international students positioned themselves. Because – we talk about 'international students' but that made me very aware of wanting to know who was who, how people positioned themselves. One of my peers referred to one student as 'the little Chinese girl' – I managed to bypass a lot of that. I *felt* the local learner; I didn't feel that put me above everybody else, if anything – less. So I decided that the effort had to come from me. I was not the definitive 'This is how it's got to be'. I'm in a minority; I'm just one student. If I were doing it again, I'd want to become more a part of that community.

Sheila: You would want to find ways to be more present?

Jan: I would want to make an effort to find out how I could have been more involved.

Sheila: I know that you're also doing some teaching – can you tell me about that?

Jan: I find the teaching very challenging. There are so many international students; my biggest problem was remembering their names. I don't make assumptions that I know about their culture and that they don't know about mine. I position myself as both teacher and learner – I have to listen and learn with them. For example, I encourage them to challenge me about 'my culture' and, in doing so, one student said that 'we' think all English people are arrogant. We live in a multicultural world and there are frustrations when a student doesn't catch on, but you have to look at that in context. It's been good for me to get to know them in greater depth. For example, I found one student was very rude and I assumed that this was probably cultural. I discovered that she has very little sight, she doesn't see very well, and this was the reason for her apparent 'rudeness'.

Rebecca: Well, my experiences were somewhat different from yours, Jan. I went to talk to the tutor to express my concerns about the number of 'foreign students' in the group. I felt 'held back' by them and I was 'being less challenged' than I had hoped by the course. On the other hand, I was enjoying the course, I could see that the tutor was attempting to be inclusive but, nonetheless, was disappointed. During this conversation, the tutor asked me to tell her how I would like the course to be and I said that, ideally, there would be fewer foreign students but I recognised that was not going to change. I enjoy writing and so we agreed that I would keep a reflective diary recording my thoughts and feelings. Just before Christmas, I emailed the tutor to ask whether she thought that it would be OK if I were to bring in some mince pies for our final meeting. She welcomed this gesture, aware that I was making an effort for people to get to know me. I was concerned that my reactions might be racist. For this reason I made mince pies for the last session before Christmas. This was a kind of atonement. I know that I often use food in this way to atone for behaviour of which I'm not proud; I also deliberately chose a kind of food which was emblematic of Britishness as I worried that the foreign students would think that my unwelcoming behaviour was typical of British people in general.

Sheila's (summary at the end of the programme): And so, with those rather provocative words from Rebecca, it is time to draw the programme to a close. What are we to make of what we've heard this evening from this diverse group of British post-graduate students? As you might expect, it's difficult to draw firm conclusions. Rebecca and Jasbir position international students rather negatively; others, such as Chris and Jan, are much more positive and welcoming, while at the same time struggling to know how to 'do the right thing'. Some of the ethnic minority students resent being positioned as 'different' – I wonder, for example, whether I would be asked to define what, as a white woman, I would bring to a course, as Waheeda was asked to do? Rebecca expressed her resentment to her tutor that there were too many foreign students yet, at the same time, became concerned that her behaviour might be construed as racist.

This leads me tentatively to reiterate what I have said before in this series of programmes. It is not differences that are, in themselves, problematic; it is what we do with those differences and whether we use them to treat people in ways that are exclusionary. As Harrison and Peacock (forthcoming) propose: 'If home students are to develop their intercultural capabilities, opportunities need to be found for them to develop mindfulness and to challenge the taboos that surround the discussion of difference.' In tonight's programme, we have challenged those taboos; we have discussed difference openly and somewhat controversially and, in another programme [Chapter 10] we shall be offering some more practical ways for encouraging such robust dialogue through learning and teaching.

I give tonight's final word to David, as he seems to summarise succinctly what I have been striving to convey through this series of programmes:

David: I suppose if you look on it as a cultural thing, it's like you're not falling to some sort of stereotype or expectations...as I said I'm me and I don't really want to be judged as in this particular ethnic group or that. I'd rather look back and say, 'Well this is David and he's made a contribution, you know, to life.'

Sheila: Goodnight!

7

ACADEMIC ADVENTURES

This chapter recalls stories gathered through conversations with academics in three different UK universities. Two are research-intensive universities; the third one became a university in 1992, when the binary divide between polytechnics and universities in the UK was abolished.

Given that my research had developed such autoethnographic dimensions, interrogating my own values and beliefs and, in particular, my 'academic identities', I was naturally curious about the experiences of other academics. There is still very little research that focuses on the lived experiences of academics in multicultural higher education environments. Recent studies such as those by Kim (2009) and Luxon and Peelo (2009) focus on non-UK staff in British universities, while Saltmarsh and Swirski (2010) focus on similar constituencies in Australian higher education. Research that focuses on local, UK, academic staff tends to foreground responses to neoliberalism and managerialism. Exploration of academic identities, in particular the construction of those identities in higher education landscapes that are increasingly diverse – in terms of both staff and students (Hockings *et al.*, 2009) – is less common. It is within this somewhat arid landscape of previous similar studies that I had conversations with nine men and women from a range of disciplines including geography, computer science, healthcare, linguistics and education, from various countries. I did not set out to make comparisons between those disciplines, to compare the experiences of men and women or to investigate whether there were distinctive differences in experience between those from the UK and those from outside the UK. In each of the conversations, I invited the participant to share with me her/his experiences of 'working' – putting a particular focus on teaching, learning and assessment – in higher education environments that were diverse. I used the word 'diverse' because I was seeking to encourage participants to reflect on broader meanings of diversity, yet each one focused on 'cultural diversity' and 'international students' irrespective of their own background.

In each of the 'interviews', I followed principles of narrative interviewing as outlined in Chapter 4. Thus, with each 'narrator', I shared resonances from my own experiences. Such strategies resulted in collaboratively developed conversations. As the reader, you might use a range of frameworks within which to consider these conversations. You might, for example, view them through the lens of neoliberalist managerialism that may be said to have generated pedagogies that are 'closed and end-product driven' (Davies, 2009: 17) or use the notion of the sojourner, as do Luxon and Peelo (2009). As a narrative inquirer, however, I prefer not to be limited by these lenses and theoretical frameworks, and so rather than seek to extrapolate common themes or complex structural analysis, I present extracts from each conversation, together with some brief reflections of my own. One element common to all of the conversations, however, was that each narrator gave accounts of adventures in other contexts. These adventure stories of living and working in different countries were used to illustrate their experiences – emotional and intellectual – of diversity in UK higher education, and were used to explain their current behaviour, attitudes and feelings – hence the chapter's title.

(N.B. The transcripts have been edited and ellipses often indicate that part of the text has been omitted.)

Elsa

Elsa is from Austria and a lecturer in computer science at a large pre-1992 university. At the beginning of our conversation, I was interested to hear about Elsa's recollections of her early experiences of working at the university:

Elsa: I guess probably my first . . . the first experience or the first difference I noticed was that I suddenly felt I had much less freedom in what I could do in terms of the freedom relating to, you know, being independent as a teacher or as a lecturer . . . I do expect it to some extent because I knew that when I would come here I would be lecturing together with another colleague, and I was very much looking forward to that. That was something I actually wanted to try. But on the whole, you know, I was sort of used to taking over a lecture and then defining by myself what the content would be and how I would assess it, and I would do the assessments myself, I would schedule the exams myself, you know? It was very much . . . I took full responsibility from the design until the assessment of the student . . .

And here it's very different, here there's a lot of bureaucracy in terms of filling out all the forms. So it seems as though there is much more to do in order to make a change that seems appropriate from my perspective as the person knowing most about the subject here. But it feels as though there are all these hierarchies who are deemed to know more about the subject.

Elsa's responses here reflect the extent to which 'the global vista is translated via local experiences and assumptions' (Saltmarsh and Swirski, 2010: 292). In connection with this, I was curious about Elsa's colleagues – were they interested to learn from her experiences of teaching outside of the UK context?

Elsa: No. I think, on the whole, this didn't make any difference to the majority of people. Again the few colleagues I sort of really work with in terms of delivering units – they are interested and they are . . . they see the benefits of what we did. Because, I mean, at the end of the day if I'm honest, the reason why we did many things in Austria the way we did was because we realised that they are useful to get good students doing projects and dissertations and staying on. And so they are quite keen to sort of copy a couple of the things. But for other people it's like, 'Oh, you're just a European and you do things differently, and we do things differently here. Well that's European and we are English.'

I had assumed that because Elsa's first language was German that she would have taught in German in her local context. It transpired, however, that she taught undergraduate courses in German, but at Masters level she taught in English. I then assumed (again) that 'coming here and teaching in English was not so strange'. She replied:

Elsa: I think I felt quite intimidated then by suddenly realising that my English, which used to be judged as very very good in Austria, maybe wasn't that good here. Because obviously, you know, I mean, it's this thing where I see myself as a lecturer and intellectually at least as good or a little bit above my students. But then they were native English speakers and so they could sometimes easily, you know, argue with me and I would really have to say, you know, OK, I really have to think about it, because also of the language. So I think it took me a good year to actually, you know, improve my level of English that I could engage better with a cocky undergraduate.

As our conversation had turned to focusing on the differences that Elsa experienced between the higher education systems in Austria and the UK, I was interested to hear about the student populations. In the UK she worked in an international university whose students came from all over the world. Was it different or the same as in Austria?

Elsa: In Austria the international students, they come mostly from south Tyrol and speak German. [laughs]

Sheila: That's what international means, does it?

Elsa: I mean there are people from Poland, from Slovakia, who come in, so you can find that. And now I think it's getting more international because the universities make more fuss about the fact that the M-level units are typically taught in English. So, you know, you get people in, whereas before when I studied we had to speak German. Here, I don't know, I really didn't know what to expect. I think I had no expectations really about the sort of international students. I'm not even sure that I was so aware that sort of the whole MSc programme actually consists of international students...I just couldn't believe it in my first year. I was not prepared when I finally realised what was going on – I was very self-conscious anyway because of my language. But then I realised also the others might have problems, because I might not be speaking clearly enough, or, you know, whatever. And it took me a while...and I think also some help...to actually separate out, sort of, 'Well my English is not the English of a native English speaker, but then they also have a problem, it's not just my fault when they can't understand.' So, yeah, that was not nice I have to say – I did feel quite, sort of, left alone with that. Because many of my colleagues couldn't understand it, you know, they were so self-assured that you know...

Sheila: So most colleagues are British, or first-language English speakers?

Elsa: No, also rather mixed, but, you know, just...I don't know, I think sometimes I'm a little bit, maybe, more sensitive to, you know, what's going on in the classroom than they are. I mean they're just...some of them just don't care – you know they walk in, they walk out. When a student says, 'Well I can't understand it', then their position is, 'It's your fault', whereas my default position was, 'It's my fault'.

Elsa was adamant that in 'my' subject 'education', 'culture' was a 'really important thing to get to know and to sort of widen your own perspective'.

Elsa: I can see the value of having people from different countries, if possible from different backgrounds. The differences that you can see – they are important – they are part of what you're doing. But when I sort of step out of that and step back into my, sort of, maybe more mathematical computer science-y way of doing things, then it actually...it doesn't matter with what person I work, what cultural background they have...because maths is a language in itself and it's a way of doing in itself. And I'm not sure that there's a huge difference between somebody coming from a background from Austria or from Germany or from the UK in a certain field. It's the discipline that connects them. It's not the cultural background that is actually the important bit. So, you know, I'm much less enthusiastic about, you know, cultural differences and exploring them – it doesn't make a difference to me in this work...

So, what might this story tell us? Firstly, that Elsa experienced a very different 'culture' of learning, teaching and assessment, one that was much more regulated and bureaucratic from the one that she was used to (Luxon and Peelo, 2009). Secondly, her focus on her own use of English, that she was self-conscious about her language fluency, feeling that this put her at a disadvantage with 'cocky undergraduates'. Thirdly, the perceived lack of interest from her colleagues in 'her way of doing things'. The 'You're a European, we're English' comment, really troubled me as an example of the xenophobia that I referred to in the previous chapter. Finally, her comments about the discipline, distinguishing between 'mine' and hers. This belief in the disciplinary culture being more important than other definitions of culture is one that we shall see appearing in other conversations.

Julie's adventure

Julie works in a post-1992 university where she teaches on a range of courses in English Language and Communication, mainly at undergraduate level. Many of these courses are designed to support people in feeling more confident in their ability to navigate the UK higher education system. During our conversation, Julie, who is British, told me she had lived in France for many years.

Julie: In terms of diverse, I suppose you could say I've gone from teaching only international students to then teaching mature students, and then teaching a more middle-of-the-road mainstream undergraduate population. I was struck by incredibly emotionally, intellectually, psychologically – everything struck by – the divide between native-speaker English students and some of the international students I had taught previously... I was staggered by it. And so my own experiences, my own interest in internationalisation of the curriculum, came from that observation, that encounter, that moment of realising something that I did not consider to be right... OK, so I'm talking about my teacher values, my professional values.

Sheila: I'm making an assumption there that what you're referring to is a particularly dominant Western academic tradition, if I can use that term 'Western'. In other words, the way we do it here.

Julie: Yes, the way we do it here, but what I'm also saying is there is an assumption within... it's a question of people's personal histories and stories. But in terms of the actual students, it was just as if this comfort zone was being with other international students. Non-comfort zone, shut-down-completely zone, was being with other English undergraduates... But therefore, you know, what I'm actually saying is that all of this that I've done comes from personal beliefs, values and perceptions – none of it comes really from a top-down agenda.

Sheila: And you said none of that was top-down, it was about my personal beliefs... and values. So can you say something about those?

Julie: I shall try to. In terms of personal beliefs and values, I do not have them written down on a piece of paper. I do not...it's something I discover really on a daily basis. I perhaps should, and would, like to sort of write them down and think about them in that way. When I'm doing reflective work on my teaching, I sometimes do that...but no, OK, personal beliefs and values...this goes back of course to childhood – this goes back into the way I was socialised, the way I was brought up to have ideas of right and wrong, and...and, OK, more specifically, one of the values I have is that everybody should be included.

As Julie had started to talk about her teaching, I asked her whether she could tell me about the philosophical ideas that informed it. She appeared perplexed by this, responding with, 'philosophical ideas?' I modified my question to 'Well, ideas then'.

Julie: First of all, that knowledge is about a process of self-discovery and enrichment...and also in a slight, you know, bastardisation of the Socrates idea of 'Man, know thyself', I think that you know yourself through knowing other...But, however, there are all these external factors these days; you know, the student loan, the fact that students choose to live at home – they don't travel in the same way, and there's a very different...so you've only got the classroom if you're going to kind of somehow reignite this idealised...in the sense of debate being a fundamental way of ensuring that diversity is maintained rather than destroyed.

Sheila: You know, when you mentioned that divide earlier...I was really struck by that word 'divide' – I was almost visualising that in the room.

Julie: Yeah, well I suppose, listening to that, one thing I particularly picked up on was that...well, learning from another culture and what that suggests. I studied at an art school techniques for learning which I definitely still...you know, informs some of the pedagogical approaches I take...So yes, I think...and in that way a kind of different discipline culture and a different national culture. But coming back to the students in the classroom, I have many opportunities to see how perhaps students who are more used to what you might call rote learning or more used to thinking collectively – or simply not being allowed to think – some of the students from the Middle East, where if thinking is encouraged it's in one direction only – increasingly a sort of fundamentalist approach – who come here and know that they're coming here to get away from that...So I think that these people have chosen difference, they've opted for difference – they want the difference. It could be for instrumental reasons. You know it could be because an English degree back home is the only way that you've got a proper promotion opportunity or that you know rather stale ideas of the power of an English degree – I don't know how real-world they are. They could be locked into their own, you know, cultural reproduction agendas,

I'm sure. But, um... and in that sense, because they've chosen difference – they want to engage with it, they want to step outside of the norm... So I'm actually very very lucky in that I can draw on ideas, cultural identity of wider socially productive discourses, of micro-practice – everything that you want to engage students in the idea of what difference, what other-ness, what self means.

Sheila: Is that all students including local students – first-language English speakers as well?

Julie: It is, yeah, but some of them will rebel against it – of course there is resistance... you can't force them to get excited about it – of course not. They may just not see the relevance of it to their lives. And if they do see the relevance it might be, you know, going back to theoretical things, for all the wrong reasons – the exotic other... I do think that in the discourses of the working world... and there are many discourses and different ones, you know... it's everywhere – you have to understand self and other a bit. You have to... at slightly more than a kind of token level... which is already better than nothing... but try to understand, rather than stereotype or exclude... So coming back to your question about engaging with the multicultural at a local level... yeah I think that it is something I want to get them to think about, not just through an applied linguistics or a cultural studies perspective, but from this personal level... So, but learning from changing my practices – I do think I'm changing them all the time.

Julie, in particular, draws attention to the 'resistance' of some of the local students and also talks about changing her practices, 'changing them all of the time', to ensure that they are more inclusive of 'wider socially productive discourses'.

Kirsty

Kirsty works in the field of educational linguistics in a university with a large inter-national student population. She has worked in several different countries and lived in Canada for ten years. Canada was often a reference point in our conversation. A particularly powerful moment for me that emerged through our conversation was her story about a local ethnic minority student; there were resonances for me in some of the themes in the previous chapter. I invited Kirsty to begin wherever she chose to; her response was, 'I worked, I guess, the last ten years in programmes for international teachers', and took it from there:

Kirsty: I mean, what's also interesting in those settings is that the native speakers are at something of a disadvantage because they haven't learnt English as a foreign language – they've grown up speaking English... and so they don't fully understand what it's like to learn English as a foreign language in the way that the non-English-speaking teachers do. So in many of the modules that I teach they are at that disadvantage...whereas in other modules the international students seem to feel that the native speakers are at an advantage...and they don't tend to have the international experience...So it's a real learning experience for them to be on an international course with students from different countries and different educational backgrounds.

Sheila: What's your sense of how they feel about that then?

Kirsty: The local students? I think they realise how much they have to learn. They learn a lot more about what it must be like for their students, which is really good. They learn a lot more about working in a language that's not English; they're seeing how the other students do it. So it's certainly a very positive experience for them, yeah. So you get this lovely balance of, you know, each bringing different things to the group...So that's a very different cultural situation, because although this city is multicultural, you don't feel that at Masters level to the same extent as you would do in Canada – different cultures and different cultural groups and different cultural balances of power. I mean, in Canada where I was, everyone is, you know, potentially in a position of power; you don't get the same relationships between the groups. And many more people in Canada would be multilingual normally than, for instance, staff here. Most of the staff here I would say is monolingual...and in that sense monocultural.

And before that I worked in Africa for three years, I was in the Sudan for three years. Before that I was in Germany for a year, I've taught in the Ukraine, I've been to Malaysia a lot, China. So I've lived in foreign language [laughs] I know what it's like – so that really helps. The students love it when you say that you've been to their university or been to their home town – so you have that sort of trust and understanding and connection in the beginning – that definitely helps.

As Kirsty had told me that she had worked in so many different countries, I asked her about the 'kinds of ideas...ideas, values, beliefs that inform the way' she taught. Her first response was to say, 'Should be able to answer that shouldn't I'? When I said that 'it wasn't a test, I was just interested', she continued to tell me more about the students:

Kirsty: You meet them in the first week and you just think that they're not able to put together two sentences, but you know that these could be some of the students who are actually, you know, going to produce these fabulous dissertations at the end and have done this thinking that's just, you know, quite remarkable. If it's going to work – and it usually does – you know, you get that atmosphere, you get that collaboration going early on and you encourage them to set up study groups, to set up reading groups out of class...So you build those kind of networks fairly early on, and I think that's really important. I mean, they're just quite diverse – they do it on personality, I think, much more than anything academic.

Sheila: I'm struck by something you said earlier about your experience in Canada, of working in Canada, and you said the power...you mentioned something about the power, there not being so much...what was it you said, something about difference – power difference or...

Kirsty: I think because Canada is multicultural, and because...yes there are, you know, white Anglo-Canadians who, traditionally, have had more power and influence, but the people in power are not...the people of influence are not all from an Anglo background by any means. So that opens it up, but it means that it's normal to be from a different cultural background.

She then told me a story about an experience with a local British student with an ethnic.

Kirsty: For instance I had a student in here the other day who's Pakistani, local – came to university feeling very sort of self-conscious, you know, thinking that she wasn't as good as everyone else, she was going to have to work twice as hard as everybody else and developed all these kind of coping strategies very explicitly – how she was going to survive and she was going to keep going because her family expected her to. I mean just in ways that, you know, a white local student would not at all...You just feel it's not quite right, there's something not quite gelling when she's still, in this day and age, coming to university and feeling like that. ...Been through the whole education system here, yeah, and yet still feels...and there's quite a...probably about half or maybe a third of the undergraduate class that I teach would be Pakistani British, I would say. Very insecure. You really notice the difference when you have a tutorial, they're very very insecure, very sort of...looking to be directed. The white students seem to come in and just know what they're doing. It's just...it's confidence, I think. I sort of thought, OK, these are the Pakistani British who've been successful, who've got to this university, it's a good university, you know they're obviously doing well, and it shouldn't quite be like this for some of them.'

As our conversation was ending, in a similar way to Elsa, Kirsty started to reflect on different disciplines:

Kirsty: You know, I think students buy into the discipline, and they buy into the disciplinary culture and they respect what comes with that and they'll adapt to learning from whomever in whatever way...rather than someone who tries to change who they are and what they do for international students, and then treats them differently from British students. And then they're confused and . . . in a way, they want to be part of the department and part of the learning community I think really . . . And ultimately I think you know students want to be treated as people and respected in that way.

But I don't think it's necessarily essential in all fields. You know from having friends who are international students, as a student myself, you know I remember there was a whole group came from Brazil to study Biochemistry at the University I was at, and they . . . I mean they just laughed at their supervisor and they really loved him – and he hadn't a clue about Brazil but they really trusted him and respected his work and you know thought he was really brilliant. And then he would say things that showed that he totally didn't understand . . . the kind of backgrounds that they came from or what it would be like living in Brazil. And you know they didn't mind because he was honest, he was warm; he was interested in his subject area. And I think you know that's really what people want.

Kirsty's final point here reflects Elsa's comment about disciplinary cultures yet, interestingly, when I sent Elsa's extract to her for comment prior to inclusion in this chapter she replied in her email: 'It struck me that the "cultural background" in terms of "discipline" might well be influenced somewhat by the general cultural background, but I have no feeling or thoughts really about how these things could be linked. I find that an interesting question . . .'

Mike

Mike teaches geography at a post-1992 university. He is British. Mike and I had had many previous conversations about diversity in higher education. In this one, I notice how, right from the beginning, he talked about his experiences of living and working in India as a younger man and how Indian philosophies had influenced and continued to influence his life and thus his teaching.

Mike: Well it's kind of inherent . . . you know, I'm in geography so the map of the world is written in your blood somewhere . . . But having been outside and seen how other places operate . . . coming back, you become acutely aware of things about the system that people on the inside just wouldn't see . . . But the thing that really got me, of course, was working in India. And you suddenly realise that there's lots of knowledge there, which is actually excluded from any of the discourses over here – it's branded 'exotic'. And because it's exotic it's not normal, it's specialist – you don't consider it. So you find that areas of discussion and conversation and teaching and curriculum that you would consider entirely normal working out there were just considered wildly beyond the pale. And they still are, interestingly. Well, now I've become fairly senior I've felt much more confident about importing these things fairly blatantly back into teaching and the curriculum and the literature.

One of the benefits you have in my discipline in geography is that the curriculum is not very tightly defined. It's a subject that strays towards the liberal arts and these kind of things. So...there are standard courses that everybody teaches, but beyond that you're very much encouraged to develop your own ideas and your own line, based on your research directions.

But the core idea of that (William Watson Purkey) was the learning invitation, that if you're going to be a good teacher, what you do is...teachers tend to be horribly prescriptive – everybody wants to control and make them do this and bring them on and do this – it's all very active. But his approach is much more you know that you invite them, much as you would invite someone to dance and you encourage them to do their own thing...Well as I say the thing that...what it's done to me actually is changed the way I think, which is the worrying thing.

Sheila: The worrying thing?

Mike: Worrying thing, yeah. Because I'm not always conscious that I'm thinking in different patterns to the accepted norm. So you can end up with tricky situations resulting from that...What it does do, if you're operating with different objectives, or from a different set of values, then you'll formulate your arguments and topics that you select for discussion in different ways.

J. D. Phillips talks about a cosmopolitan as someone who consciously positions themselves at the borderlines between cultures and societies. I think that he's exaggerating because I think...that you have to work hard always to see yourself in these positions and often unconsciously you're at those borderlines, and you have to make the extra step to see what's the difference between where you are and where the rest of the argument is.

Those who are more...I call them 'little Englanders' – they can find it much harder going. So it's not unusual, you know, I've had lectures where people have told me this was the most tedious thing they've ever listened to, and other people thought it was wonderful, you know – in the same classroom. I think everybody has those kind of ranges...The nice thing is, because if you can create opportunities for people with these other knowledges to have their say – that's it, it's creating invitations, if you like, to bring them forward.

And in some Asian cultures it's even more complicated because, again, you can go back to India or we could talk about Japan where I see the same thing in operation. But often if you're in a group there is actually a distinct hierarchy within the group that you're looking at. And if people speak out of turn because you know someone's their senior or something of this sort, then they're in bad trouble. So you actually have to, more or less, pass it down the chain of command before you can get some of the people to speak anyway.

Of all of the people that I spoke to, Mike was probably the person who talked in most depth about the ways in which learning and teaching are culturally mediated practices. In common with most of the others, he drew on his experience of working in another country, India, to show how what he had learned in that context continued to influence his work.

Jenny

Jenny is a lecturer in Teaching English to Speakers of Other Languages (TESOL) in a post-1992 university. My conversation with Jenny, began by her recalling experiences of teaching in several other countries:

Jenny: In so many of the contexts – the classroom was a kind of peace – United Nations, which would not then replicate itself at the end of the class, you know. There would be difficulties, antipathies, political divisions, which would just be minimised, and it would vanish in the classroom – as far as possible. And I think the most evident example of that was when I was working in India and I had a group of about 40 Indian teachers and we all worked together really very interestingly. And at the end, one of them said to me, 'I'm an untouchable that converted to Christianity, but everybody knows I'm an untouchable and a lot of those people wouldn't normally sit with me or work with me. But because you're foreign and you don't know that, we all suspended our normal sort of sense of divisions and divides.'

[And in Malaysia . . .]

Yes the Muslim boys would be checking that the Muslim girls were behaving themselves. And even when they were in the UK they would sort of report back if the girls went unveiled or if they went swimming and wore bikinis . . . it would get reported back, and it would sometimes be sent back . . . Some of the Indians and Chinese students were not Muslim – they were Christian or they were Hindu – and they had to keep quiet about that, they weren't allowed really to talk openly about their religion because it's, I think, illegal to proselytise, so that makes them actually afraid to talk about it at all. So in the UK they opened out like flowers, some of these students, because they met other Hindu people, met other Christian people, they felt able to join communities and talk about their identity.

[And in China . . .]

And it's very easy to stereotype the Chinese students' experience, and they all say to us similar things, which is that the Chinese classroom is very teacher-centred and there is a tradition of passive learning. But, in fact, when I worked in China, they were the most dynamic, active, extraordinarily dedicated groups I've ever worked with – I was completely exhausted by the end of working with them. So it's easy to underestimate what's going on when you just have your own world.

They're not saying we can't do it, we don't know how to question, we're very passive learners – what they're saying is it's different in China, could you tell us, could you show us, explain to us and prepare us for what you want? I think it's a generic thing of looking at, you know, what do learners need? Are we making explicit what we expect, and is it reasonable what we expect?

Yeah, I mean, I think that it's much easier to say, well in Taiwan they don't question the teachers than to say, 'Am I doing something which makes my expectations unclear?'... And thinking, well it's far too easy to give up on them or to say, you know, well that's just their culture, and it's far harder and more... you know, much more proactive to actually say, 'How do I frame this, so that that student can make the transition from where she is to what we want, what we require?'

In this extract from our conversation, Jenny demonstrates very clearly how her experience of working in China causes her to challenge the stereotypical 'Chinese student'. As in the other conversations, I asked Jenny about the ideas that informed her work:

Jenny: Well I think the notion of education as transformation... the notion of transformational learning, that learning needs to change something in you. And the notion of freedom, like Rogers' idea of freedom... and although that in itself can be, you know, based on a very Western sense of the individual, it also has clear targets which you're asking the student to identify, to arrive at for themselves. So that doesn't mean, 'Go and do this for yourself because I've got an idea of the individual'... there's a sense of collective responsibility and accountability. I mean, I am working in a Western context, in a Western university, and I am being required to be accountable. But the best I can do is to be clear about, you know, what that means and to ask and enable students to arrive at that from where they are and in ways that they can best use in their own context.

Jenny expressed some opinions about her experiences with 'local' students:

Jenny: 'What's Sweden got to do with us? Why do I want to hear about the Brazilian system? Why can't we just have sessions just for us?' And I'm thinking, 'You listen to this, this is good for you', you know. Why should they listen to you?' So I've really seen the difference, I can immediately feel the mix when I had a strong mix of people who've never really thought about not being in their own context. That, sadly, isn't the case for all of them, but it's the case for enough of them for it to have been noticeable and then they have to work with someone from another culture and look at common values and different values. Almost invariably they come up just with common values, with things that they share – they have realised that the differences are cosmetic, the core values are the same.

I shared with Jenny an experience I had had when teaching in Hong Kong where the student group consisted of 50 per cent local Hong Kong people and 50 per cent of people from UK, North America and Australia. In spite of all of my attempts to blend students for different discussions and activities, the group remained stubbornly divided. The 'westerners' invited me to go and have coffee with them one day...

Sheila: And I said, 'Thank you, but no, I'd prefer to stay here and have some tea with the others.' And I remember feeling that was a very important statement to make.

Jenny: They would have been delighted.

Sheila: And at the end of the first day quite a number of the local people came up to me and said, 'You know there are two groups here, there are the Westerners and there are us'. And I said, 'You know I'm working really hard for that not to be the case, so you've got to help me.'

Jenny: And I think breaking rank from what looks like your peer group and joining them is a very significant act for them. I mean, when I lived in Hungary it was very hard to break into the Hungarian community because they're very much, you know, holding us at a distance. I was much more interested to engage with my Hungarian . . . But it was similarly very very hard because they didn't actually want us in . . . 'Do you not understand that collaboration is a dirty word for us?' You know it's like having an informant in the group, and they'd only recently come out of living under that sort of, you know, surveillance. And I tried to learn Hungarian and, you know, tried to come to all the meetings when they were only in Hungarian. But actually, I don't know if I succeeded because the history was too recent and too painful and they didn't trust us . . . I mean it was always interesting to know whether bringing it out in the open is going to be good, or whether it's going to just make it even messier.

Sheila: Well it is messy, isn't it? It's a messy . . . it's a messy situation I think. I mean it's different from the one you're describing with Hungary, I know, but some similarities where you've kind of got the history behind you. I find it difficult to ignore that because for me it's there in the room.

Jenny: I think one thing that is good that when you come back to your own culture you know how to make other cultures welcome, you know... So I think about when people come here, not stereotyping them, labelling them, making assumptions about where they've come from, and not judging them by their you know kind of status in the world.

My sharing of the incident in Hong Kong leads Jenny to reflect on a painful experience in Hungary and for both of us to then reflect on our cultural histories that may persuade some people to position us in particular ways. This latter point was reflected vividly in my conversation with Ronnie.

Ronnie

Ronnie describes herself as an 'educational developer'. Throughout our conversation, she recalled experiences of working in other countries; in fact, she began by recalling an incident in Fiji:

Ronnie: And I said, 'Oh come on tell me what I should be doing or not doing or what I'm doing wrong'. And the class sat there in deadly silence and then she said, 'Ronnie, we wouldn't give you any feedback because you're a white colonial, we don't give feedback to white colonials.' And learning that I was a white colonial... because I've always had the stance that I'm a liberal person and all that wasn't me, that was somebody else. But in Fiji that was me and I carried all the sins of my fathers on my shoulders, and they told me also that I would reap the wrath of that... I was a white colonial. So it changed my identity enormously and I struggled with that... I found that a really hard identity to have... they are seeing me through a different culture. They see the colour of my skin, that's the first thing they see. And that's what it is, they see the colour of your skin, and you're British. I guess in a way you try and overcome it with your personality. And also just being extra-sensitive to what you think and what you're doing... I think it makes you much more aware; I think it makes you much more aware of your own assumptions about education.

She continued to talk about 'identities':

Ronnie: I mean this whole stuff about identity nowadays. You know, there seems to be an awful lot of angst about our identity, our academic identity, our cultural identity, and all this – I mean, I hold three passports and, as I say, I've lived in four, five... whatever, six different countries, lived and worked in them. And I'm curious about my identity, but I don't angst about it, and

> I read stuff about identity and I think, 'Oh yeah, that would be interesting', you know, perhaps one day I'll sit down and sort my identity out...

Ronnie talked about some educational development work that she had conducted recently in her own university:

Ronnie: And so often staff nowadays look at me and say, 'I have no idea who my students are, like 50 per cent of them may be overseas students; I don't know where they've come from, I don't know why they're doing it'. They can't answer those questions – and even for the local students – and they don't seem to know. And I say, well it's really difficult for you to get a handle on this issue – whatever it is they're dealing with – unless you know your students...And staff seem amazed that I'd suggest that they'd hang around and spend time talking to their students, and there seemed to be a lack of knowing who their students were.

Interestingly, although in a different way from Chris in the previous chapter, Ronnie, too, brought up the issue of gender and Islam:

Ronnie: And is it OK to expect a Muslim woman to actually talk in a class in front of men? I mean, is that actually an OK expectation to have of her? But that's what we're expecting the international students to do often. They're sitting terrified in their classrooms and we're asking them to do things they feel are dangerous, they're not in their culture, you know, it's just not the way they behave, and they're very fearful – and we expect them to be able to learn and succeed in it.

Ronnie's New Zealand adventure

Ronnie: I saw this amazing thing happen once. I was doing an academic develop-ment session in New Zealand with a whole mixture of staff, but there was one Japanese lecturer in the room, and I got them to get into small groups to do things, and it was very interesting, because they shuffled their chairs around, and he was sitting there...I think there were four white people chatting away, and this Japanese guy was listening absolutely intently and, you could see, following everything. And gradually the chair shifted, and gradually they actually physically cut him out of the group because he wasn't contributing. And it was amazing to see – if you had a video you wouldn't have believed it – he was actually physically ostracised! And when there was a break I went up to him and I said, 'Oh how are you feeling? I noted that you were sort of cut out of the group', and he talked about it and he felt that, he saw that happening and he felt that happening, and he said, 'Yes, people think I'm not interested because I'm not saying anything.' And I felt really embarrassed being a teacher in that group, and yet the group totally unaware of what they'd done, totally unaware of it, yeah.

When Ronnie agreed to be interviewed by me, I had shared with her my frustration at finding people willing to be interviewed. The day after my conversation with her I received this email:

> I expect the frustration with your project is getting people to articulate what they do to change/adapt their teaching. I think it is very nuanced and a lot to do with how you relate to people, how you build confidence in them to consider that change might be possible and try and build some safety around them trying out change. Also I think it is becoming more aware how people are seeing me and add that into how I think I am coming across, and then changing my expectations of how they are going to react, and that is a continuing iterative process. Gets complicated doesn't it!

Emily's adventures

Emily teaches comparative and international education in a pre-1992 university with a large international student population. A North American by birth, she has lived and worked in other countries in addition to the UK. After a very few moments of pleasantries, she began:

Emily: I mean, for example, we've got, I think, 21 on the Masters this year, and 16 different countries . . . so it is an incredibly diverse group. And, I mean, the starting point is that I love it and I see this as a fantastic advantage and I know that there are particular challenges about that, but I absolutely love it, and . . . I like to think that the students do too . . . we're not trying in any way to promote a singular perspective or to teach skills which might be culture-bound or whatever. I mean, the starting point is that, whatever theme we're covering that week or whatever skill we're trying to work on, that we're critically unpacking this theme or skill from a comparative perspective . . . So while many of the theories, for example, that we might be covering are perhaps Western in origin, we're critiquing them all the time.

Sheila: And so they're quite happy, then, to be critiquing these ideas?

Emily: That's a good question because that's not the kind of education experiences that some of them have had in the past, sort of, you know, text is sacred in some cultures in my experience . . . But also critiquing themselves – critiquing how the theory is presented. You know there are lots and lots of different ways of approaching it.

Sheila: I was wondering what you would say informs your teaching. You know, as a teacher what kind of ideas or values would you say informed your teaching?

Emily: Gosh, um...I do take an emancipatory view of education, but broadly defined. I sometimes think that...I mean, I don't see my job purely in emancipatory terms on a minute-by-minute basis. I would describe my teaching as learner-centred, again in the broadest sense. I think that's become a term that we use very shakily and very loosely...but I try very hard to understand the people in the room I'm teaching on an individual basis and I try to read what they're getting out of things...I take feedback quite seriously. I find that if you have an interest in people, then the more diverse that group, the more interesting it is in a sense...and, you know, diversity happens...as we've said before, diversity happens on so many parameters that it's not just about cultural diversity – even in fairly mono-cultural classes there is phenomenal diversity...culture just brings a kind of additional or a different layer of diversity really.

And so I think those intercultural situations create a particular dynamic which puts people in a certain perspective in relation to each other that then, you know, makes them treat culture in a particular way...you know, the will that people have to make that work...and I think that's a phenomenal resource.

Emily talked about the 'local' student experience from her perspective:

Emily: It's a little bit difficult because they are often part-time, and that puts them in a slightly different position – they're just not around as much as the full-time students – they have so many advantages on the course in terms of language, in terms of understanding the system, in terms of, you know, the way they can access the literature and so on, that I think it does set them a little bit apart.

I had shared with Emily that I 'feel quite envious of you...because your topic is going to attract people who come with a lot of goodwill and an intention to get on with each other and to learn from each other'. She replied:

Emily: That's not to say that we've never had problems...that there have never been rifts. We have, for example, had students from Asian countries that have found it hard to accept African students on equal terms...and there's a lot of un-learning that has to happen, which is, you know, important to put everyone through, but occasionally rather painful...The single nastiest tension we've ever had to deal with...There was a really unpleasant situation a few years ago where a guy from north Cyprus was really quite ostracised by those from southern Cyprus. I've spent a little bit of time in

Cyprus and I know these things run very very deep, but as far as I'm concerned they should be leaving it at the door. I think there are a set of rules of courtesy that we all have to abide by. And so, for example, they actually put anti-Turkish slogans on the walls...I didn't understand the Greek so I don't know if it was anti-Turkish but it was basically anti-northern Cyprus, the political situation and all of that. It's just inappropriate. We can have a civilised discussion about the differ-ences...but the starting point is that you have to accept each other's points of views and be willing...to work through them and not simply have entrenched positions that you are reinforcing all the time...it's our responsibility...and, you know, I won't allow racism or inflammatory comments on my watch, basically.

But I also learn just different ways of being...just observing different ways of being and how that translates. You know, every year is another roll of the dice and you don't know what kind of combination you're going to get. And it's extraordinary to watch the intercultural dynamics and to see what sorts of strategies are going on and what's working for whom and...you know, we've got to constantly refine how we do things in the light of those sorts of observations really. And I'm constantly learning never to assume anything about anyone.

Susie

Susie is a lecturer in healthcare in a post–1992 university. In response to my reminding her that I was interested to talk with her about her 'experiences of teaching in environments that were diverse', she responded, 'I suppose that springs to my mind about my experiences with international students.' She continued:

Susie: And it was really that first intake, I think, where we had about four Indian students and realising the difficulties they had with the study, and some of them were failing. And it just made me realise, I think, about just how different a culture it was for them and how we weren't really preparing them for that. And then also talking to colleagues who were teaching those students – the same kind of issues – students were failing modules, we weren't offering any extra kind of support...And also I was a bit...not shocked, but a bit surprised by some of the attitudes of colleagues when I would talk to them about the students, and they would see them more as a hindrance rather than students that had a lot to give actually.

The other thing I found was that certainly when they first came...and it's still the same now...is that when they're with the home students they're very reluctant to speak out, Because they don't feel threatened in any way – they don't feel...I think they do feel a bit overwhelmed if they speak out in front of the home students.

Susie talked about running a workshop for her colleagues, which provided them with an opportunity to talk about how they felt about the changing environment. I asked her what their feelings were:

Susie: I think it was things like, you know, Why should we give the international students more time? You know they're here doing the same course. Aren't we discriminating or not being inclusive by doing that? Are we being unfair because we're giving them more time than the home students? And I think an assumption, too, that, well, they chose to come here, so they just have to put up with it. You know, we don't have to give them anything else.

I have found that the international students are very interested to learn what's happening from the home students – but it's not always *vice versa* – the home students will not always question . . . it's thinking about how that research is going to apply to my practice in my country – what are the different cultural values, what are the different things?

And also that whole realisation that perhaps what I was teaching was not culturally sensitive as well, and it made me look at that. And also realise that colleagues were being like that, but they weren't vindictive – they were, you know, good colleagues, so they weren't . . . they weren't vindictive colleagues, it was just that it was just . . . just they felt they couldn't cope with that, with students asking them for lots of support.

Susie, in particular, recalled her early experiences of working with international students that then led her to influencing the practices of some of her colleagues who were rather more resistant to providing support. In addition, she also reflects on the apparent parochialism of local students.

Adnan's story

Adnan is from Nigeria. He came to the UK to do his PhD, subsequently undertook a second Masters degree, and has been teaching in the UK for 12 years.

Adnan: It's quite interesting to work outside your cultural boundaries; it's a learning opportunity, because the way you do things, that's the end of it – but when you go somewhere else you take new ideas from there. But in doing so, you also discover that you have some things to offer as well. So what I'm trying to say is that there are advantages of teaching in these types of environments, both to me as a lecturer here, and my coming from other culture also have some advantages to some students too – because I've brought with me some experience other than the conventional ones they are used to . . . For instance, our administrator had to write that the students should book me through her – because the way we do back home...you are accessible any time. [laughs] You are going to your car, somebody say, 'Excuse me sir, I wanted to see you, and I have been trying to do that.' I say, 'What is it?' and then that can take 15, 20 minutes. You are already in front of your car to enter...The international students really really really need more support than people who are not used to them always think of...you see, when they leave home, some of them, because of the value they attach to education, they leave home at all costs.

Adnan talked about the difference in attitude that he perceived between him and colleagues:

Adnan: It's a function of the cultural perception of issues. People will tell you blankly that, 'I'm sorry, I cannot see you'. For instance if somebody is late for 15 minutes, some of my colleagues, they say it's late, even though I will also tell the students the reason why she must keep appointment, but I still see her if I have the time to see her. I was giving tutorial to four of them that day, and I have distributed this time in such a way that you have to be at the door as soon as somebody goes, then you come in. Then she didn't come until about 20 minutes after. Then she came and she was sweating, said, 'Oh, sorry I was trying to call'. If I say, 'Go away'...she's a new student who joined this January – so she is still acclimatising, so I said, 'Well I have some other people that are supposed to come...as soon as somebody knocks then we call it off, and then I see you some other time, but sit down', and then we continue.

Sheila: OK, but you would see her; you would give her some time. Whereas your perception is that perhaps many of your UK colleagues would say...

Adnan: They will not argue – she's late.

Adnan also referred to his discipline, public health, as being 'global':

Adnan: Yes, it calls for diversity. In fact, students...my students, they complain when they attend other courses that are purely handled by the British and people who don't perhaps have international, whatever, experience, and they are not able to draw examples round the world. And they are just using all the local terminology and examples, calling any terms which it is only people who studied here that will know it.

Sheila: So your students have complained to you about other academic staff who only draw on local examples? So when they complain to you about this, what do you do with that? Do you talk to your colleagues or what do you do?

Adnan: Yes, the feedback is presented in an appropriate manner...I have a leaflet in which I said, if somebody is going to teach in my programme I would

> tell them the constituents of the students, where they come from, and I would say it is important if you are not too much UK-centric.

Adnan then went on to talk about the way he 'organised his class':

Adnan: The way you organise your class matters. If you come in and you give everybody the impression that they are all useful to each other, they are colleagues, they will gain from each other, the diversity is a plus for you, the first day I always tell them that...when we make introductions this one says she is a GP of so many years, this one came from laboratory, this one is an administrator, this one is a director, this one...look all diverse...if you allow this opportunity to slip through your hands without making use of it, that will be bad. You've come to learn Public Health and usually public health problem is never solved by one person; it is solved by a group of people concerned. So in the real-life situation you will need to work with people. So this is opportunity for you to learn that. So learn from each other. Then they will relax and then when I group them, it's random grouping.

Sheila: So right from the beginning what you're doing there is you're celebrating the diversity. All the different kinds of diversity as you said – professional diversity, ethnic, cultural diversity...all the different experiences in the room. So right from the word 'go' you're actually saying to them, look at these opportunities that are here in this room.

So what do I conclude after hearing and storying these stories? The majority of the people I talked with have goodwill and are striving to create productive learning environments for all students. Some struggle more than others with knowing how to do that. Some have had difficult experiences, such as Emily, who described the unpleasant incident with students from Cyprus, and Ronnie and Jenny, both of whom had been marginalised and, in Ronnie's case, excluded from communities that they sought to join. Some talk about discipline variations, others comment on the importance of not differentiating between 'internationals' and 'local' students, yet others talk about the importance of acknowledging that international students may need particular kinds of support. Most, in their different ways, recalled the intransigence of local students in recognising the value of having the opportunity to learn from people from different backgrounds – academic, professional, cultural. Those from outside the UK experience a certain resistance to their traditions from their British colleagues yet find the fusion of their different experiences to be very valuable – for them and for the students. In particular, I welcomed Adnan's description of how he established the value of diversity in his student constituencies from the first moment that the groups met, as this reflects my own practice.

It may be that I was lucky because a particularly reflective group of people agreed to talk with me, but if I were to draw any conclusions from these conversations, it would be that all of the academics I spoke to welcomed the greater diversity in the higher education landscapes. None of them expressed resentment or resistance to this greater diversity or to the accompanying complexities. Some appeared to be more dedicated than others in their efforts to facilitate cultural capability, recognising that their approaches to learning and teaching were significantly culturally mediated. Two of the three people who were not from the UK commented on some unwillingness of their local colleagues to embrace their academic traditions. Such experiences reflect Kim's comment (2009: 398): 'it is not yet clear to what extent the new forms and types of transnational academic mobility have impacted on the recognition and promotion of diverse academic cultures'.

Much earlier in this book I referred to Appadurai's notion of the personal journey of internationalisation. All of these people had lived and worked in many different countries and considered these experiences to be invaluable in helping them to be more empathic towards students from different parts of the world. In other words, they had been on their own journeys of internationalisation and, in being on them, were playing their part in helping to level the playing-field. Theirs are the experiences that we need to be mindful of. Those everyday experiences of grappling with diversity, recognising 'it' and embracing it to develop learning environments that are inclusive – and much richer for being so.

8

A WHITE GIRL FROM THE NORTH COUNTRY

A pawn in a game?

He's taught in his school
From the start by the rule
That the laws are with him
To protect his white skin
To keep up his hate
So he never thinks straight
'Bout the shape that he's in
But it ain't him to blame
He's only a pawn in their game

(Bob Dylan, 'Only a Pawn in Their Game', 1963)

I have no recollection of being taught in my school that the laws were with me. Nor was I taught to hate. But along with millions of other people in the West in the 1960s, I was influenced profoundly by the singer Bob Dylan and, in more ways than one, 'grew up' with him and with his songs of protest, remaining loyal to him to this day in spite of his flirtations with other musical styles. Those were the times of the Vietnam War and of the Civil Rights Movement in the USA, times when presidents were assassinated and African-Americans could not vote; when apartheid raged in South Africa. The words of Dylan's mournful and often pessimistic songs instilled in me and raised awareness of injustices in the world – at least in the western world. Songs such as 'The Lonesome Death of Hattie Carroll', 'The Times They Are a Changin'' and, of course, 'Blowin' in the Wind' spoke to me and to others of my generation in ways that others did not. Dylan told stories through his poetry and his songs, stories that challenged what were dominant narratives of the day. He showed me that there were alternative, preferred stories that could be achieved if people worked together to challenge injustices; injustices that, in most cases, arose out of fear of difference. Difference, in particular cultural difference, is a main theme of this book. Throughout it, I am seeking to be transparent in sharing my responses to working with people whose backgrounds differ from mine. I do this not to present myself as a person whose practice is exemplary, but as someone who is struggling with the layers of complexity present in 21st-century higher education. As I have reiterated throughout this book, categories of difference can be destabilised, but we need to acknowledge how differences work in the world, usually to execute differentiated and exclusionary practices; hence this chapter.

I have proposed that words such as 'culture', 'race' and 'ethnicity', and even 'faith' often become elided in the literature and therefore, perhaps, in many people's minds. I have discussed the claims of race, culture and gender as social constructions. In my view, however, and indeed in much of my experience, sociological theorising, while fascinating, challenging and insightful, rarely scratches the surface of how, in everyday situations, many people can struggle with diversity. In this chapter, I seek to explore and confront, to 'go public' with what it means to me to be white – a nettle that I have not yet really grasped. In deciding to devote a separate chapter to such an interrogation, I am aware of the danger of being criticised for privileging whiteness and 'white culture' over the cultural and ethnic backgrounds of the majority of people that I work with and who continue to contribute so much to my learning. I might be accused of indulging in a 'self-reifying practice' (Alexander, 2004: 649), of essentialising whiteness, assuming it to be a fixed entity rather than being contingent on historical constructions (Bonnett, 2000). I am not seeking to do the latter, certainly not intentionally, but I am acutely aware that the very process of making whiteness an object of study, naming it and forcing it to be displaced from its more usual undefined yet central position, acknowledges it as a substantive presence (Watson and Scraton, 2001; Alexander, 2004).

If whiteness resists being codified and only becomes noticeable in its performance (Alexander, 2004), then in this chapter, I intend to stumble through a performance of whiteness. Rather than stand endlessly rehearsing in the wings, I am taking a few nervous steps on to the stage. I may not have built that stage, but I perform upon it and therefore influence the drama (Tatar and Bekerman, 2002). But, do I use a capital letter, and thus 'Whiteness' takes on the status of a proper noun? Or do I leave it in lower case so that it remains a common noun, but nonetheless a noun, a word used to name, to identify? I am back in my old familiar place of wrestling with dualisms, being damned if I do and damned if I don't. I shall, therefore, use 'Whiteness' and 'whiteness' interchangeably.

'Could my critique have been more liberatory? Could it have been more transformative? Could I have been more deliberate in naming my/our racism(s)' (McIntrye, 1997: 41)? The answer is 'Yes, probably' to each of those questions. In my teaching and research over the past few years, I have sustained a clumsy balance between hearing, and even colluding with, comments that were sometimes blatantly racist. In 2009, I attended a seminar by Tami Spry, a white North American Professor of Communication and Performative Studies, in which she talked about her father, a white American jazz musician. One particularly vivid story that has lingered with me was that of her father choosing, sometimes, to go alone through the front door of the motel where he and his fellow African-American musicians were staying, sometimes through the back door, as they were not permitted to use the front door. Spry proffered this powerful story as an example of what she suggested many of us do – at times collude with injustice; at others take a stand against it. This had many resonances for me. Given my stated professional position as that of an educator struggling to develop pedagogies that are respectful of a range of perspectives and experiences, this story of how I am beginning to make meaning of my whiteness, though challenging, has become compelling to tell. Being white is only one of my identities, but it is the one that I find the most difficult to define.

'Culture is not what some group has; it's what happens to you when you encounter difference.' (Agar, 1994: 22)

To my embarrassment, I began to be aware that I made assumptions about people based on their visible difference from me. In spite of my best intentions, I categorised people, subscribing, unwittingly, to imperialistic constructions of the 'other' (Said, 2003) by attributing responses and behaviours of people with cultural backgrounds different from my own – in particular those whose skin colour was different – to their cultural background. I inferred that a person speaks and behaves in particular ways because s/he is, for example, Chinese or Kenyan or Greek. I became conscious that, as a white British woman, I did not relate my attitudes and behaviours to my culture or ethnicity, my whiteness that does not have 'a clearly definable cultural terrain nor for many a desirable one' (Frankenburg, 1993: 205). Discovering this 'cultural terrain' would be 'desirable' for me, but I find it hard to define. Texts such as *The Chinese Learner* (Watkins and Biggs, 1996), *Teaching the Chinese Learner* (Watkins and Biggs, 2001) and *The Psychology of Adult Learning in Africa* (Fasokun *et al.*, 2003), all drawn on in Chapter 3, were useful in providing me with insights into philosophies and conceptualisations of learning that hold significant sway for many of the people with whom I work. But they were also seductive, alluring me into believing that behaviours, responses and interactions are a direct result of those perspectives and influences, so much more easily defined than mine. Such conclusions might be acceptable had I considered the potential relevance of cultural influence for *everyone* – including me – and in my very early encounters with international students I neglected to do so. I viewed each person as representative of a particular group, and made evaluations about that person/group, derived uncritically from my own background. The concepts, idiographic and nomothetic, are useful here as both can be used judiciously to effect and explain some greater understanding. I have come to the position where I strive to realise that it is not that either each person must be treated as an individual, unconnected to his or her cultural group(s), or that assumptions should be made based on knowledge of that particular group(s), but that both perspectives are valuable in understanding that fluid and changing nature of identities.

A danger of which I am aware is that of developing a way of talking and writing that implicitly communicates an ideological or political superiority that may alienate and 'falsely represent me as if I am less affected by my racial group membership than others' (Scheurich, 1997: 127). That is not my intention. The journey of disentangling the meanings that being white have for me mirrors all of the other journeys that I have embarked upon. Once I began to question it, as a result of particular events, other memories were stirred. I have explained my discomfort on that prosaic November evening (Prologue and Chapter 1). Subsequent conversations seemed to draw forth responses akin to those recounted by others who engage in similar critiques (Frankenberg, 1993, 2004; McIntyre, 1997; Bonnett, 2000). The 'I *am* white – what's to know?' (Bonnett, 2000: 1, original emphasis); the 'uncomfortable silences, forms of resistance, degrees of hostility and a host of other responses that many of us would prefer to avoid' (McIntyre, 1997: 73). My meanderings through the methodological literature, seeking to unravel the epistemological foundations of the methodologies I was exploring (Chapter 4), together with my challenging of fixed identities and cultures, have led me to ask a similar question to that posed in Chapter 2. If we can make choices about cultures (Sparks, 2002; Fox, 2006; Speedy, 2006), can we not make choices about whiteness, being white? If whiteness is also a historical construction, can I escape being white (Scheurich, 1997)? Do I want to escape being white?

A white girl from the North Country

> Whiteness is a location of structural advantage, of race privilege. Second, it is a 'standpoint', a place from which white people look at ourselves, at others, and at society. Third, 'whiteness' refers to a set of cultural practices that are usually unmarked and unnamed.
>
> *(Frankenburg, 1993: 1)*

Like me, Frankenburg experiences a sense of contradiction, of not being, nor of setting out to be, racist, but becoming aware of her own failure to challenge racism. Through spending time with white women, described as 'working-class women' she:

> Learned by proximity what it means to navigate through a largely hostile terrain, to deal with institutions that do not operate by one's own logic nor in one's interests, and to need those institutions to function in one's favour if one is to survive, let alone to achieve. I realised for almost the first time in my life the gulf of experience and meaning between individuals differently positioned in relation to systems of domination, and the profundity of cultural difference.
>
> *(ibid.: 4)*

Being brought up in a white, British, working class family and community in the north of England, navigating hostile terrain and being positioned differently in relation to systems of domination were very familiar to me, but not because I was white; because of social class. Even as I write this, the UK Communities Secretary, has reopened the debate in the UK about social class and race, claiming that the inequities of social class are what really need to be debated rather than the implications of race and ethnicity. This has brought forth certain responses in the media, viz. 'Yes, class is a problem but racism is still the greater evil' (Barbara Ellen, *The Observer*, 17 January 2010). In the UK, there have been several recent studies that confirm the educational underachievements of Afro-Caribbean boys and, at the same time, indicate that those who struggle most to achieve in education are 'white working class boys' (Strand and Winston, 2008).

The world in which I grew up was a different one. Passing the 11-plus examination opened the door to my small girls' secondary grammar school, which I loved, but at first provoked the taunts, bullying and accusations of snobbery from other girls in the neighbourhood. As an undergraduate student in a city across the Pennines (Leeds) with its own distinctive accent, I strove to change my Manchester elongated pronunciation of vowels and the hard 'g' on the end of words because I was teased for the way I spoke. Having listened to so many recordings of my voice over the last years I have become fond of my northern vowels and hard gs! But for many of the people with whom I work now, the way I speak is meaningless; other than many of them express their appreciation of my clarity of pronunciation. They are unaware of the baggage that accompanies a northern accent, the way it positions me with British people the moment I open my mouth. My sensitivity about my accent rose to the fore once more in my interactions with Rebecca, the white British student you met in Chapter 6. Rebecca wrote about her experiences in a learning group:

> As the course went on, I found myself becoming more impatient. One point early on in the course stands out as influencing my attitude. We were discussing Freud, and I realised that some of the non-native speakers were unable to pronounce the name correctly, pronouncing the letter 'r' as an 'l'. This flicked a switch in my brain. I was brought up in the Midlands but my father was fanatical about what he perceived as 'proper' English and drummed out of my speech the slightest hint of a regional accent until he was happy with my neutral, sub-received pronunciation speech. All this meant that the moment I heard one of the non-home students say 'Floyd' rather than 'Freud' I was lost. I think that my reaction was a combination of two things. Firstly, my childhood-imbued intolerance of 'wrong' pronunciation. Secondly, a process of completely specious reasoning that went something like this: 'If they can't even pronounce Freud's name properly, how are they going to be able to grasp the concept of psychodynamic therapy?' Intellectually, I know that these reactions are utterly indefensible. They did, however, affect the way I perceived the group... There was a sense in which my frustrations at being part of the group were like material for these stories (told to friends and family about her experiences of the course). The danger,

of which I was very conscious, was that I then started to perceive the stories as reality, which then informed my actions in the group.

I recall Rebecca telling the story of her father's obsession with drumming her regional accent out of her. I assumed that only the local students in the group would understand what she was talking about. I concur with her own words that her reasoning was specious and her reactions indefensible. 'Language barriers are often constructed in *our* minds, from the privileged position of white researchers, as social barriers which are then used to define cultural differences' (Watson and Scraton, 2001: 270). Rebecca seemed to have erected such barriers, using them to define intellectual inferiority in the 'non-home students' (Prescott and Hellsten, 2005). To what extent was she also making judgements of my intellect and me based on the way I speak? Such reflections reinforce my feelings of being an outsider – while being positioned as an insider by those members of the group for whom such 'positioned utterances' (Sparks, 2002: 116) are meaningless.

'It is easy to self-identify as white women but far more difficult to confront and alter our ways of being' (Watson and Scraton, 2001: 273). I find it difficult to 'self-identify' as a white woman; in fact I am finding it difficult to do so now. I can 'self-identify' as working-class and as a woman – but white? I no longer live in the north of England, but I still feel myself to be a northerner. What does *that* identity mean to me? It means a particular sense of humour that, I have had to learn, can be experienced as not at all humorous. It is actually a very sophisticated humour, located in a direct and sharp observation of everyday experience. The writer Alan Bennett is supreme at it and I linger, longingly, in his shadow. It means growing up in an industrial town that itself had grown up during the Industrial Revolution and had depended on the cotton picked by slaves in British colonies for its development. My paternal grandmother worked in a cotton mill and, although she died before I was born, I am fiercely proud of that identity that I have inherited. I have visited the 'heritage parks' that some of the redundant cotton mills have morphed into and have felt overcome when the spinning-machines sprang to life. In those moments I *felt* the level of noise that must have surrounded my grandmother for most of her life, and that would have surrounded me, too, had I been born earlier, or not been a clever little girl who was able to benefit from legislation that ensured that I had access to free education.

But, I rarely saw a face that was not white; the children with whom I went to primary school were all white and, like me, defined by the work of their fathers. The only 'foreigners' were white, from Poland and Lithuania, the children of refugees from the Second World War.

My earliest memory of encountering people whose skin was a different colour was a group of Pakistani men who lived close to our corner grocery shop. This was my first encounter with racism. My mother, along with everybody I knew, was a regular customer in that grocery shop, which, in north-of-England 'culture' in those days, before the emergence of the supermarket, was where everyone did his or her grocery shopping, usually on a daily basis. I recall a conversation where the other customers were being critical of the men. They reserved most of their venom, however, for the white women who were friendly with them, whom they described as 'prostitutes'. Refusing to collude in this racist tirade, my mother defended those men. They were 'people like the rest of us' and that, being people, they did not deserve to be treated any differently. I must have been eight or nine years old. I was very proud of her but I did not understand why such things were being said about the men. It seems that *my* sense of cultural and ethnic belonging is similar to that of the white women in Frankenberg's study, who saw 'ethnicity [as] more meaningful as a descriptor of others than of self' (Frankenberg, 1993: 208). The adult 'me' acknowledges that there might have been myriad reasons for the racism, including competitiveness, jealousy and economics. But, to the eight-year-old, the men were not white. This was their sin. There were stirrings of something, something not being quite right, but those stirrings were because of *their* difference. They did not cause any questioning of me as a white person.

Watson and Scraton (2001), in their study of south Asian mothers in Leeds, in the UK, raise similar questions about their own whiteness, suggesting that conducting research reflexively is a good starting point to confront the dominant position of white researchers. Their stance is another example of this unproblematised conceptualisation of reflexivity that I have referred to throughout this book, showing how, with its emphasis on the researcher, reflexivity can be another way of silencing the 'subaltern', albeit with somewhat more self-awareness (Shope, 2006). Sharing my reflections that I felt I had been engaging in imperialist and neocolonialist practices suggests that I am more aware of the potential for such behaviour. It does not follow that I have acted upon such insights. You, as the reader, only have my word that I am more likely to do so now and to challenge others who behave, in my opinion, in a discriminatory manner.

Much of Watson and Scraton's (2001) article, however, resonated with my own experiences and musings. They position themselves as white female researchers, sharing my dis-ease at the obfuscating way that many complex epistemological and methodological questions are presented (discussed in Chapter 4). Like me, they feel that these questions only 'come alive' (ibid.: 266) when explored through detailed research. Like me, they, too, recognise that there is a danger of difference being reinforced if it is only explored through the dynamics of the white researcher–black respondent position, or, in my case, the white English researcher–Chinese/ Taiwanese/Kenyan/Greek/'other' respondent position. I recognise now that, although I set out to achieve a greater understanding of difference, I rarely asked the white people in my study about their whiteness. In hindsight, I recognise how we were positioning ourselves in relation to the 'others', assuming similarity between 'us', not at all interrogating our own whiteness, our own cultural affiliations, and how we were informed by those – Chapter 9 makes some attempt to redress the balance here. In a conversation with Dau, the Kenyan woman who appears in Chapter 3, we had been discussing race. Dau told me that she had had 'white teachers', therefore there was no problem for her in my being white. I did not pursue this. Subsequently, I wanted to know how she felt about those white teachers and whether I was being elided with them because I was white? But then why should I assume that my whiteness was a problem for her because she is a black Kenyan woman? In our many conversations we discussed politics and gender issues because we shared such interests. 'As researchers we cannot assume to know when or where race ... is an issue for research participants but confronting our own whiteness can make us more sensitive to this' (ibid.: 269).

Ironically, it was not in my encounters with those people who were my research participants that this inquiry into my own whiteness began to occur (although the 'Story of Being Mild' conversation with Cheng-tsung in Chapter 5 was a mitigating factor). It was in those other everyday conversations that I had, especially with Ounkar, an Indian Sikh woman born in England, and Reena, a British Indian women (their chosen descriptors). Such experiences vindicate how, for me, 'Life and research are inseparable. They are, in many ways, one and the same' (Phillion, 2002: 538).

Reena, a part-time tutor, and I conducted recruitment interviews for a course. Following the interviews, she told me that memories and feelings about past experiences of being the only non-white person in the room had been raised for her as we were interviewing. Those memories included feeling that she was not 'good enough'; a belief that applicants would not pay attention to her because she was not white and that I would be positioned as the person with power and authority. I responded clumsily. I could not believe that she felt that way. Later, we discussed my response. I learned from her that my reaction communicated to her that I, too, had not paid attention to her, had dismissed her experience. I had denied it because I could not believe that it was 'true'; yet for her it was very true. I felt ashamed:

> It is crucial that we identify ourselves as part of racialised discourse, not so that we can become paralysed by self blame, remorse or guilt, but so that we can heighten self-awareness and live more conscious and critical lives ... thus recognising our white identity not as something static and unchanging but implicitly a part of culture, history and politics.
>
> *(Watson and Scraton, 2001: 273)*

I recall the tension of early meetings with Ounkar, whose work on her Masters dissertation I had been asked to supervise. I felt that I was being questioned closely so that she could ascertain whether I had sufficient awareness of her culture to be able to supervise her work. I had myriad feelings. I wanted to respect her ambivalence and caution yet found myself seeking to provide evidence of my cultural sensitivity and awareness; in doing so, perhaps I was not respecting her stated desire for a supervisor who shared her cultural background. Following those first edgy encounters, our relationship became a robust one. We had forthright discussions about our differences, each becoming sufficiently brave to risk asking sensitive and provocative questions of the other, to ask the other to explain their perspectives. Without such dialogue, we would have confirmed constructions of difference as immutable (Frankenburg, 1993), reproducing 'epistemological assumptions about racialised difference as an essential, absolute difference that inscribes subjectivities' (Gunaratnam, 2003: 93), and would have overlooked our many similarities.

Messy work

I like confusion and disorder, the 'messy work' (ibid.: 79) of researching difference. I like the way that Gunaratnam (ibid.) critiques the:

> Most fundamental assumption . . . that the research encounter is characterised by distance and estrangement between the researcher and the research partic- ipants which the researcher needs to 'overcome' . . . The distance of difference needs to be closed or bridged by practices – be they method- ological, linguistic and/or imaginative – that bring the researcher closer to the research participant and through this proximity can render the difference knowable. (80)

Yet I became aware that I had sought ways of closing that distance, the 'places of incommensurability' (Hall, 2000: 227). I was wary of the 'partial, incomplete and distorted' (Anderson, 1993: 50–51) responses that might arise from asking partici- pants to comment on their experiences of working with me as a white female academic. I was mindful of the allegations of those of my critics who pointed out that it would be difficult for students to challenge my hegemony (Merriam *et al.*, 2001), and I became sensitive to the concept of face (Bond, 1986, 1991). But these perspectives position whiteness as 'an uncrossable boundary' (Gunaratnam, 2003: 92). Perhaps, by trying so hard to problematise my whiteness, I neglected the 'post- colonial and multicultural realities of hybridity and hyphenated identities' (ibid.: 81). It is unlikely that even in my conversations with white local students, my cultural identity will be completely 'matched' with theirs, as I am part-Welsh, -Irish, -English and -Scottish, and those are the cultural and ethnic identities of which I am aware. I maintain that, by showing how, through my 'analyses' and 'interpretations' of the many conversations and events that took place during the research and the earlier memories that were recalled, I am reflecting on my own whiteness and indeed other differences, and I am resisting 'the apparent intransi- gence of racialised difference' (ibid.: 93), enabling us to move, albeit in a stumbling manner, towards some greater understanding of each other.

By challenging meanings ascribed to cultural difference, when there are numer- ous categories of difference such as gender, social class, sexuality, educational background, that I have specifically chosen *not* to focus on, has this obscured other differences within groups? I referred to Young's (2001) concept of transformative assimilation in Chapter 1. By focusing on the differences of *other* groups, the dominant group avoids an interrogation of its own culture. Foregrounding that very visible difference *between* groups, the differences *within* groups can be obscured, resulting in homogenising terms such as 'international students' or 'The Chinese Learner'. As Hongyu, a Chinese student pointed out to me, 'there are many differences between Chinese people as there are between white people' – 56 ethnic groupings; 'differences'.

Anderson's (1993) research influenced me when I first encountered it, because it seemed to give me permission, as a white woman, to conduct this study 'across cultures'. However, now I find myself agreeing with Gunaratnam's (2003) contention that Andersen's attempts to engage in reflexivity to address white privilege in the research process reinscribe racialised essentialisations. Thus, Andersen (1993) cannot *know* that her understandings of the lives of black women can only ever be partial, and less complete than her understandings of white women. 'Reflexivity, as making visible the social positioning of the researcher and research participant ... is not enough to understand the complexities of difference' (Gunaratnam, 2003: 94–95). The inescapable paradox of reflexivity is that 'Some of the influences arising from aspects of social identity remain beyond the reflexive grasp' (Reay, 1996: 443), a reference I made in my critique of reflexivity in Chapter 4.

Perhaps I have to settle for being 'in progress'. 'Whites, like people of color, continue to be works in progress' (Tatum, 1997: 112), to continue to recognise that there are privileges that are accorded to me because of the colour of my skin, privileges that I have not earned and do not seek.

> I don't remember
> Being taught
> That I was better
> I was taught
> That
> Under the skin
> We are all the same
> Maybe
> I have
> Though
> Been
> A pawn
> In a game?

The number of manoeuvres that a pawn can make is limited, but pawns have the potential to become equal to the most powerful piece on the chessboard. The pawn, should it move all the way to the other side of the board, can become a Queen, the most potent yet flexible piece in the game. 'Being in progress' is an apposite phrase here as I am mindful that engaging in a critique of my own whiteness in this chapter might be perceived as establishing it as an even more substantive presence, especially if, by doing so, I am now positioned as even more powerful. As I wrote in Chapter 3 rearranging chairs in a circle does not 'do away with power ... [but] displaces it and reconfigures it in different ways' (Usher and Edwards, 1994: 91). Glimpsing such grandiose possibilities, I do not care to linger.

It is time to move on. Having made some attempt in this chapter to explore my own whiteness and what I consider to be some of my own identities, I continue with these themes in the next chapter, but illustrate them rather differently – by juxtaposing conversations between people to enable them to say what is, again, often unsaid, in higher education contexts.

9
FELLOW TRAVELLERS

The fictional construction of experiences is considered to be a legitimate and persuasive form of research reporting (Clough, 2002). This chapter uses the device of fictionalised representation to orchestrate together the words from conversations with several people, extracts from my memories and reflections, to tell another story of some encounters during the research journey. It fractures different conversations, splicing words – those 'lightning-flashes' that 'open a void, a moment of silence, a question without an answer...where the world is forced to question itself' (Foucault, 1965: 287) with my thoughts and feelings and the imagined thoughts of others. I have used a different print font to represent each character; you may recognise some of the characters.

Orchestrating the voices: the polyphonic text

'Each character's sharply particularised "voice" or "discourse" articulates a recognisable social viewpoint...Orchestrated together these voices offer us a verbal image of the contentious social dialogue taking place in mid-Victorian England' (Morris, 1991, cited in Vice, 1997: 113). This reference is made to the 'Fellow Travellers' chapter in Charles Dickens' *Little Dorrit*, as an illustration of Bakhtin's (1981) concept of the polyphonic text. Character and narrator exist on the same plane, but the latter does not take precedence over the former; s/he has equal right to speak. Equality of utterance is central to the democratic, polyphonic novel. This book is not a novel, but voice is central to it and I have shared my dilemmas about equality of utterance. Inevitably, as the writer, my voice sometimes pushes out the voices of others, particularly those voices of international students that I felt were unheard (Cortazzi and Jin, 2006) and that I wanted to be heard.

There are two chapters entitled 'Fellow Travellers' in *Little Dorrit*. I have used the second one as a model for this chapter because I was impressed that Dickens did not name any of the characters in it. By that stage in the book, each one is recognisable to the reader because of the views they express. As the reader of this book, you may recognise some of the travellers, and not others, but I imagine you will conclude easily that I am the host – and the narrator. If this were to be the only chapter that you read, you would not know the identities of any of the characters. I trust, however, that I have presented the dialogue with sufficient clarity to enable you to recognise that it occurs between people with a range of backgrounds who are communicating, sometimes contentiously, about events in a multicultural environment in a northern European city. The context of the chapter enables you to remember that this is an uneven landscape of higher education in the 21st century.

There is a discomfort that I need to share at the outset. This fictionalised account has given me a vehicle to express my dismay with the racist attitudes of some of the local students. In the 'real event', I did not always challenge them about that racism, as my host self does here. I was not so brave. My braver self came to the fore during my study, and continues to become stronger. I do feel, however, that by not speaking out and confronting racist attitudes, I may have been seen to collude with them. I may have been a pawn in a game – as I explored in the previous chapter.

Ethical issues inherent in practitioner research have been noted as they have arisen throughout this book. One of my other reasons for choosing to write a chapter by fictionalised representation is that it can address some complex ethical questions, and I therefore examine some ethics of practitioner research towards the end of it.

To set the scene for the story, I would like to take you back to the dismal room on that prosaic November evening in 1999. The more observant reader will notice, however, that this evening, the tables have been moved.

Fellow travellers (with apologies to Charles Dickens)

Darkness came early, in the winter, in the northern European city. The rain was falling steadily as the travellers trudged up the hill. Some of the travellers had the pale skin of many of the local, indigenous people. Others were of Far Eastern appearance or were travellers from those countries that the local people had travelled to long ago, seeking to make their own. Each was unknown to the other, unaware that they were fellow travellers, that they were about to meet, to act and to re-act upon each other in this strange and unfamiliar landscape.

The darkness had risen to the walls of the building. It seeped right through them, adding to the gloomy feel of the bare, ill-lit room. An effort had been made to make the space welcoming. The chairs were arranged in a semicircle, and the tables, often a barrier to the sharing of travellers' tales, had been pushed to the sides of the room. As the travellers removed their coats, shaking off the rain as they did so, they took books, papers and pens from their bags in preparation for the stories they would read and write about this part of the journey. Meeting together for the first time, they were aware of their visible differences, aware that their host, the person who was to be their guide on this part of the journey was, by appearance, a local person.

The host welcomed them to his country, inviting each one to introduce themselves and to share the purpose for their journey. As each person spoke, he watched carefully, nodding to himself or frowning slightly as if making a mental note of those travellers who spoke easily and those who seemed reticent.

A younger woman introduced the traveller with whom she had been speaking. She giggled self-consciously:

'Her name is unpronounceable for us.'

The host looked uncomfortable, shifted his position slightly and encouraged her to say the name of the traveller. He then turned to her partner asking her to say her name, repeating it to her in the way that she herself had said it. Turning to the local woman, he said very calmly:

'It is not that her name is unpronounceable, more that you perhaps find it difficult to pronounce.'

An uneasy silence fell upon the room; cautious looks were exchanged. The host spoke, addressing everyone:

'There are so many different travellers making this journey. It is important that each one is heard and respected. Should you choose to use a name that differs from your given name that is your choice, but it is important that it is a choice, that you are not using an Anglo-Saxon name because you have been told that we, the local people find it difficult to pronounce your name.'

Gradually it became clear that, although he had planned the first evening's events, the host was willing to change the programme for subsequent weeks to accommodate very different requirements and expectations.

'How will he do that?' mused one of the women. 'We are all so different and the paths we want to take so varied. Surely it will not be possible to meet all of our needs on this journey?'

Suddenly, the young woman spoke again in a voice that was high-pitched and anxious:

'Why is the room set up in this way? We can't work without tables. How are we to write? How can I learn like this? I have not come here to sit in a circle and play. I have come here to learn. Perhaps you have done this for the foreigners, to make the journey easier for them but this means it will not be sufficiently challenging for me.'

The other travellers appeared ill-at-ease at this outburst. Was this the way that the local people behaved? Did she have no respect for the host who had made them welcome? In many of their countries a host was to be trusted and respected. It was the host who held the knowledge that they needed for the journey and who would impart it to them so that they could continue on their way. The arrangement of the room was unusual but many of the travellers welcomed this informality, inferring an openness from it, an invitation to communicate with each other.

A woman turned to the host:

'I am concerned for you'.

'Concerned?' he asked.

'Yes. Because if I were you and I had such a visitor as this I would feel frustrated. A Chinese traveller, even if they disagree with you, they will not say so, especially not in front of other guests. I have very bad feelings about this traveller.'

Turning to the young woman she said:

'Are you a traveller? Or perhaps you are making a different journey and have entered the wrong room?'

One of the women sitting with the group of local people spoke:

'This group of travellers is too large. There are too many people from other countries who do not speak my language.'

Turning to the others she said:

'If you don't speak my language how will you find the confidence to make this journey? I'm overawed that you feel you can make this part of the journey through a territory where the language is not your own, but I'm afraid that we lack a common language. You won't be able to speak my language in the way that I do.'

The host turned to her:

'Does that mean you feel that you'll have to be careful about the kinds of words that you use when speaking to those travellers who have already come a long distance?'

'Yes. I really enjoy using jargon in everyday life and I feel that I wouldn't be able to use any of that, because that wouldn't be fair. Because it would be excluding them and...you know it's going to be hard enough for them to make this part of the journey when the language is not their own. I feel I'm not going to be able to...to be able to express myself in a way that...'

'Because they won't understand you?'

'Yes. And it won't be fair to them. I feel I should really try to speak properly I suppose'.

Suddenly, a young man who had entered the room with the group of local people but had moved to sit with another group rose from his seat and began to speak:

'I have moved to join this group of travellers because I feel a greater closeness here than with the other Europeans. Of course, I do not know whether this has anything to do with culture or whether it is because we are all strangers in a foreign environment. Some people here tonight do not seem to want to develop relationships. I feel there's a distance between us.'

The host was concerned by these words. He felt that it was his role to ensure that any distance could be bridged. He asked him to explain what he meant.

'I was thinking that if all the experiences of the people here are to be integrated into a way of working together, then it is you, our host, and your fellow hosts that will have to change your fundamental ways of doing things.'

The host looked at him carefully, trying to understand:

'But first of all we must recognise what are our ways of doing things. It is so difficult to do that. It's not until I became a host here and I began to encounter so many different travellers with different perspectives that I started to consider my ways of hosting guests. There are many ways of being a welcoming host. Until recently my ways were those that I had learned through welcoming local people but now I realise that those ways may not be so welcoming to everyone, and for some people they may not be welcoming at all.'

Later that night...

Later that night, the host sat down by the fire to write his diary. He had written a diary every day when he was younger and was finding it helpful to do so again, especially now that he was working with so many travellers. Such visitors, although they had decided to embark on his part of the journey, seemed to want to take so many different routes. Troubled by the evening's events and lulled by the warmth of the fire, he gradually drifted off to sleep. The diary tumbled from his hand, falling open at the last entry:

It's hard not to feel disappointed by our first meeting. I was saddened because some people that I had looked forward to meeting did not arrive, and also because some people came that I had not expected. The person who seemed arrogant provoked a negative response in me, but as the evening wore on I felt that I was successful in winning her round. I suspect she will not join in with activities between meetings. I felt that those travellers who were also on other Paths had simply called in to break their journey. They hadn't really thought about what this Path might involve. I feel troubled by the young woman. I suspect that she is really very frightened of what the journey ahead might hold for her but her fear manifests itself by extreme anxiety and by rudeness. I find myself dreading the coming journey. There was so much anxiety about reading books and writing stories, even though I tried to reassure them that the stories they would write would be their stories, stories of their own lives, their own lived experiences.

Following that first evening, the host met with the travellers every week. Sometimes he would also meet with them individually and they talked together about many things. He heard stories from African countries – Kenya, Eritrea, Sudan, Uganda – from Asian countries – China, Taiwan, Hong Kong, Singapore, Japan. He listened to stories that were told by people from countries that were closer, geographically, to his own such as Greece and Malta. Occasionally, he even heard stories from people who were from his country. And he shared stories of his own. Memories of his childhood, of his family, his education, of his encounters with stories in books. Sometimes he forgot where the stories belonged, indeed whether they belonged anywhere, as they seemed to change as they were told and listened to, so that they became different stories. He heard painful stories: of the young man who hid his homosexuality from his family to protect them from shame; of the woman whose illiterate mother fought against the tribal elders so that her daughters would not be circumcised; of the young woman who could not tell her parents about the unwanted sexual advances of a family friend because of the shame that would bring to them; of the young women, marginalised because they remained unmarried, who told him of the pressure this put on them and on their families. He read stories, too, like those of Chuangtzu, the Chinese Taoist philosopher, retold by a Taiwanese woman to show how they had influenced her life:

> There are many trees in the forest.
> Most trees are huge, straight and tall
> Making them suitable for
> Constructing furniture or buildings
> One tree is
> Twisted, ugly and rough
> Making it useless and unattractive
> All of the trees
> Laugh

At this useless tree
All the trees
Are cut
And used as material
To make something
Only the 'useless' tree remains alive.

'If I were a twisted tree, could I accept myself as a twisted tree or would I always want to be the straight and useful tree? I knew that through my actions I was trying hard to become the straight one. The story was like a wise master who knew my faults well.'

Listening to all these stories he began to feel that his own stories were not so interesting, not so colourful or tragic. Then he recalled the songs, poetry and books of his childhood and adolescence. He remembered his serious childhood illness, close to death at the age of 6, and the song that helped him through that traumatic period in hospital. He knew now that the singer of that song had been a campaigner for civil rights in the USA. He learned that stories from childhood held meaning for people no matter from where they came; that even that some of those childhood myths and fairy tales that he had devoured were loved by people from other places. But perhaps the most important thing he learned was that if people listen to each other's stories, accepting them as *their* wise masters rather then seeking to impose their own wise masters upon them, then perhaps the restless world that he lived in might be a little less troubled.

Darkness came later in the spring of the year. The air was full of the promise of early summer as the travellers gathered together. Tonight was to be their final meeting. They were exchanging reflections on their experiences of the journey and hardly noticed the host as he slipped into the room by the rear door.

One of the women was speaking:

'When I first came here, I wanted to get to know the local people, to speak your language in the way that you speak it. The longer I have been here, the more I have realised that you do not want to speak to me and so I have decided to stay with people who speak my own language. We wanted to feel that you were welcoming us. You have not been entirely unfriendly but you have not tried to slow down your way of speaking, nor to avoid certain words so that we can understand more clearly. If you feel that we are excluding you, then that is your own doing. In fact, my friends laugh at me because I have tried so hard to include you in our discussions. They started to say to me "Oh X is very cooperative, Y will never show up. Why do you keep on trying to involve them? They will never show up." '

The woman, to whom she had been addressing her comments, jumped up:

> 'I want to respond to that. I met with you every week to discuss what we were going to present in our next meeting with the host. I found those meetings frustrating. You found it hard to grasp that I lived some distance away and I had a job and a family. I only came here once a week so wasn't available the rest of the week. You wanted to take far too much time to discuss the meeting. I was also aware that you were much more conscientious than I was and were reading widely around the meeting topics which I wasn't doing'.

At this point, the host signalled that he wanted to intervene. He was feeling angry with this traveller. How could she be so dismissive of her fellow travellers, especially those that had made a much longer journey? He felt sad. The woman, who had embarked on her journey with such high hopes, was feeling that those hopes had not been fulfilled.

Host: 'The other travellers...what do you imagine the other travellers thought about you?'

> 'I don't really know what you thought about me. I think you must have...I think you may have found...I don't know, the fact that we were sorting out what we would do in the next meeting, the fact that I could only be there for that particular day...I of course would have found that irritating.'

At this point she laughed.

> 'But you never gave any indication at all of being irritated. So I don't know. I did get a bit frustrated now and again but I also knew that...well I didn't sort of steamroll the group in our discussion about presentations but I did I think possibly take advantage of your tendency to defer to me, because you wanted those meetings to go on and I wanted to get it decided and leave. There was one occasion where I can remember thinking "Why don't we try that?" And I can remember thinking, "If I suggest it, they'll probably say yes." '

Until this point, the other travellers had remained silent. But now one of the local people leapt up in obvious consternation:

> 'But I have found being with these travellers a humbling experience. I think a massive amount of learning has gone on for everybody and that we've all widened our horizons through hearing everybody's different views. I got the feeling it wasn't just me that was having revelations.'

She laughed at this point as if she was slightly embarrassed to have had 'revelations'.

> 'I think it was really making us look at the sort of fundamentals we adopt, and look at them in relation to other people and other cultures. We have had such

an open dialogue and people have talked so easily. I have realised how saying one thing in one way to one person would be taken in one culture and what it would mean in a different culture. It's about being aware of who we are and being aware that we all have feelings and that we all have things that we're frightened of and we all have things that we're proud of, but we all have our differences as well. And by understanding ourselves and our similarities so that we can say the things we share but also appreciating the areas of difference will help us to be better people.'

Her outburst was echoed by that of another traveller, a young man this time:

'The most important thing I have learned through being a member of this group is that I have recognised that the way I think about things is not the only way. I felt sure that when you (turning to one of the other men) learned the ways of our culture that you would feel that they were better than yours and that you would want to adapt. Do you remember when we were discussing how we made decisions and I told you that I would never consult my parents when I was making an important decision? I can't forget that you replied that you would always consult not only your parents but also your whole family. This seemed very strange to me. I am an adult – why should I continue to talk with my parents about particular parts of my life? It was as though I wanted to convince you that our way was better. You turned to me and said, "That's very interesting. But I think I'll stick with my way."'

The host noticed that darkness had now fallen outside, a different darkness from the evening when they first met. This darkness was softer and was gradually moving the day towards its end. As they all stood, gathering their books, papers and pens preparing to depart for the final time, a man stepped out from the shadows that were descending on the room. This was a man who had become very important to all of the travellers and to the host. His quiet, gentle manner, the way he questioned himself and others had earned him the respect of everyone. Tonight he spoke directly to the host:

'The first thing I noticed about you was your pale skin, your whiteness – and I wrote about that. It was such a contrast with my yellowness. I assumed that you, a foreign host, who does not speak my language, could never understand what I might need on this part of the journey. I was wrong. We can so easily be trapped by the structures and limitations of language but I have learned that there is something beyond language. Real listening and cherishing my "being" as a traveller is far more precious than struggling to find the right words to say to each other'.

Fictionalised dialogue?

By constructing a dialogue between the characters, I have sought to give each an equal right to speak. By juxtaposing speech extracts, I have enabled the 'travellers' to speak directly to each other, and to the 'host', creating what is, at times, a confrontational and uncomfortable dialogue. This device has enabled me to use 'you', instead of 'they', and to move away from the positioning of 'us and them' (Trinh, 1989; Devos, 2003; Hellmundt and Fox, 2003; Sanderson, 2004) that I find so difficult to avoid. I have used words that have been spoken to me, but that the travellers – the students – may have found more difficult to say to each other. Attitudes, beliefs and behaviours conveyed to me have been named. I have spoken aloud my thoughts and feelings. I am thus using their refracted voices (Chase, 2005), once more, to examine my beliefs about diversity, about learning and teaching practices and to share some of my raw reflections (Clough, 2002) on my experiences of working in this environment. The host 'appears concerned', feels 'angry'; thus I can express feelings about events that I experienced as uncomfortable, and occasionally, distressing, revealing my own thoughts and perspectives about such events, without naming the protagonists. 'The "real" events may well undergo transformation, at the researcher's will, in order to tell a (particular) story – a *version* of the truth as the researcher sees it' (Clough, 2002: 18, original emphases).

This fictionalised representation allows me to do that.

It will be obvious that it is my diary that falls open in front of the fire. Here I use the literary device of flashback in time to inform the audience of the story of the present day. I am reminded in particular of Ondaatje's novel *The English Patient* (1992). The journal is symbolic in the relationship between the 'English patient' and the English woman, and is the medium through which the story of that relationship is revealed. It is used to record his archaeological expeditions and is how he acquires the identity of 'English patient'. *My* diary falling open permits the inclusion of extracts from my journal allowing my voice to dominate momentarily, and somewhat more creatively, than had I said 'An extract from my journal for that day reads...' Recording thoughts, feelings and snippets of conversations in my journal, was one of the ways in which I recorded my 'archaeological expeditions' and, subsequently, through the writing explored my identities.

Such discourse:

> Far from determining the locus in which it speaks, is avoiding the ground on which it could find support... [it] is trying to operate a decentring that leaves no privilege to any centre... it does not set out to be a recollection of the original or a memory of the truth. On the contrary, its task is to **make** differences... it is continually making **differentiations**.
>
> *(Foucault, 1972: 205–206, original emphasis)*

I had set myself a task to make differences, to risk taking roads that are less travelled, to continue to stumble over that 'slippery, uncertain ground' (Charmaz and

Mitchell, 1997: 209), avoiding ground on which I might find support. I have written this chapter because there were particular stories that I wanted to tell. I wanted to include some of the difficulties experienced by both international students, and 'host students' articulated to me and to reveal racism that can be barely below the surface. I was aware, however, that although the majority of 'fellow travellers' had agreed to participate in the research and, in most cases, were happy to be named, such consensus did not apply to every character, who 'may not necessarily be aware that they are being researched' (Costley and Gibbs, 2006: 91). Similarly, this:

> Experimentation with form can be... an expression influenced by an ideological rejection of one absolute truth or reality... Does fictionalizing data present an ethical dilemma (both for the reader and writer) rather than only a methodological choice?
>
> *(Robinson-Pant, 2005: 113)*

My rationale for this fictionalised representation is connected, inextricably, with my epistemological perspective. Even though I have not fictionalised my 'data', I accept that my experimentation with this form of re-presenting them may be unacceptable to those with strong beliefs in one 'truth', including some of those who participated in the study. My justification is that I am considering the ethical issues related to choice of form and style of the writing, in *addition* to the more usual ethical concerns. Such factors are rarely considered when discussing research ethics (Robinson-Pant, 2005), and provide another example of ethical mindfulness.

The application of the research to my practice is, as I have articulated throughout this book, an iterative process. It follows then that, 'ethics in practice' (Guillemin and Gillam, 2004: 264) is an appropriate maxim for this dimension of the research process. But 'good intent does not necessarily lead to good outcomes' (Bond and Mifsud, 2006: 249–250), and raises for me the issue of anonymity and so called 'informed consent'. Everyone that agreed to be 'interviewed' by me signed a consent form but the signed consent form as evidence of informed consent is 'perhaps of questionable value' (Guillemin and Gillam, 2004: 272). The interviews were only one part of the research process. How did I obtain consent from the people I encountered every day, students, colleagues, as well as those people such as my father, my mother, Miss and Mrs Jackson? My father is dead; it is over 40 years since I saw those Jackson teachers, and I chose not to ask my mother for her 'informed consent', making a judgement that, were she ever to read this book, she would not be unhappy about the references to her.

Throughout the book, sometimes I have used the names of the participants; sometimes I have changed them, even though they indicated that they wanted to be named. This is an example of making a judgement call about an 'ethically important moment' when 'a research participant states that he or she does not want to be assigned a pseudonym in the writing up of the research but wants to have his or her real name reported' (ibid.: 265). There are people in this book who did not want to have a pseudonym assigned, but I have assigned one because, had I used the 'real' name, those who wanted anonymity may be recognised and/or recognise themselves in the stories:

> Participants may indeed be proud to be recognised, however this needs approaching with caution. Identification of one person may lead to others being identified [who] may be harmed by being recognised. From the perspective of individual rights it might seem acceptable to take no responsibility for those not directly involved, but a more communal sense of responsibility would include the needs of these people too.
>
> *(Webb, 2006: 232)*

I have chosen to take a communal sense of responsibility and, in doing so, I have overridden the desires of some. But ownership of stories is one of the complexities of narrative inquiry. If the story is constructed collaboratively, then who 'owns' the story? Has it become a communal story of which we all have ownership? Or, indeed, do any us have ownership because the story was not *my* story or *their* story but *became* a story through those stories? In narrative inquiry, as I have explained, the research does not depend on the gathering of one form of 'data'. The 'interviews' are often considered of less importance than the noting of events, feelings, hunches, conversations in the corridor, and documents. (Clandinin and Connelly, 2000; Clough, 2002). The research depicts lived experience and, in my life, although conversations are a large and significant part of it, so, too, is my reading of the newspaper, my dreams, daydreams and reflections, my interactions with people who are (so they say) 'nothing to do with the research'.

> For example, who decides what may be disclosed about whom? What is restricted information and only disclosed outside the formal exchange, as it were 'off the record'? These are familiar problems in any qualitative research. However the nature of the narrative process means that concerns of this type may be difficult to anticipate in advance and may only become issues as they arise ... both parties need to engage reflexively in both the subject matter and the ethical challenges to create the human circumstances that enable the research to flourish and to ensure the intellectual integrity of the project.
>
> *(Bond and Mifsud, 2006: 250)*

'Narrative ethics then, position us differently... creating the space for us to imaginatively feel our way into the experiences described, whilst remaining accountable to the spirits and values of the original storytellers' (Speedy, 2007: 52). I have tried to imaginatively feel my way into experiences by the different modes of presentation. I have included dialogue so that you, the reader, can make judgments about the meanings that I have ascribed, and I have sought to ensure that the spirits and values of the original storytellers as they expressed them are embedded in the writing. But I must not forget that I, too, am an original storyteller and I, too, have striven to be accountable to my spirits and values:

> Through my own desire to explore the experiences I have shared...I realise how my biography fuelled my intuition...I, too, lead a storied life and the research relationship is part of my experiential text, whose telling and retelling creates purposes for my own future.
>
> *(Winkler, 2003: 399)*

Delamont (2009) recognises the ethical complexities of autoethnography as being 'almost impossible to write and publish ethically' because 'the other actors...will be identifiable and identified' (p. 59). In this book, I have taken care to ensure, in so far as it is possible, that those people who make an appearance have read and approved what I have written and, in many cases, added their own comments that I have included. But what about the experiences of people that I have included, but who might not know that? I have used my intellectual integrity to make a judgement call (Sparkes, 2002) at each of these ethically important moments, foregrounding those that I have identified. By striving not to 'remain bound by the ethical insights contained in any one tradition' (Evanoff, 2004: 456), I hope that there is sufficient evidence of commitment to openness and accountability in this research to enable you to trust me. The question of my trustworthiness is not, I 'trust', therefore, raised for you.

This fictionalised representation has also allowed me to experiment with methodological issues of inviting (and interpreting) others' stories (Chase, 2005). Interviewees do not necessarily reveal 'authentic', 'true', selves and speak in their 'own' voices, as if those selves and voices were not already mediated by the social and cultural contexts in which they speak (Chapter 4). The interview interaction is a 'fundamentally indeterminate' performance, and the 'complex play of conscious and unconscious thoughts, feelings, fears, power, desires and needs on the part of both interviewer and interviewee cannot be captured or categorised' (Scheurich, 1997: 73). Presenting this fictionalised account is thus another performance, one that has not only enabled 'we' talk, rather than 'us' and 'them' talk, but has also foregrounded ethical issues inherent in narrative inquiry and autoethnography in conducting research 'across cultures'.

10

DEVELOPING CULTURAL CAPABILITY IN INTERNATIONAL HIGHER EDUCATION

Glass palaces and glass cages

> Tactics are not planned in advance, nor do they serve an overall design, but they unravel as life does, with its accidents, misfortunes, boons and breaks. All of us construct and reconstruct our fragile selves, moving from glass palace to glass cage, at times feeling anxiously trapped by it, at others feeling energised and appreciated... We pursue the dream of a breakthrough – of our true worth being acknowledged – which might finally make sense of our work.
>
> *(Gabriel, 2003: 181)*

Practitioner research, like life, is fraught with 'accidents, misfortunes, boons and breaks' that cannot be imagined at the outset. That is the nature of it. But if such research is to move beyond the banal (Charmaz and Mitchell, 1997), and to be an insightful, trustworthy representation of the process in which the practitioner is enmeshed, then she needs to be transparent about each of its dimensions, showing how they are being worked with and embedded into the research process. I have sought to be transparent about these dimensions throughout this book in order to provoke readers to 'reflect critically on their own experience' (Ellis and Bochner, 2000: 748). This final chapter summarises how researching my own work as a narrative inquirer has generated insights into learning and teaching and effected changes in my own practices and those of others. The chapter begins by reflecting on the value of narrative inquiry and autoethnography in practitioner research in an international higher education landscape, moves on to gathering together some of the ways in which cultural capability may be developed in such contexts and then offers some final comments on reflexivity. Such are the tales to be told as I end this book – and, indeed, the journey (Kvale and Brinkmann, 2009).

The value of narrative inquiry

> Much educational research...has little impact in the classroom in terms of teaching and learning – either because the issues researched are too broad or that they are too theoretical. The solution is that teachers themselves, the practitioners, become the researchers. They can do this by systematically reflecting on what goes on in the classroom and, to raise these reflections to the level of objectivity, to subject them to the critical scrutiny of others. Out of such reflections, though unique to individual researchers, can come 'insightful accounts of processes which go beyond the particular story itself'.
>
> *(Pring, 1999: 6)*

From the very beginning I wanted to provide 'insightful accounts of processes that go beyond the particular story'. It would, therefore, have been disingenuous and inconsistent with narrative inquiry and autoethnography to 'plan my tactics in advance', rather than 'let them unravel as life does', by separating out the research process into the discrete elements of more conventional studies. I believed that I needed to work within a methodological approach that was sensitive to the different worldviews that I was encountering in my work. At the same time, I acknowledged the paradox of seeking to develop a conceptual framework that was grounded in those different worldviews.

In Chapter 4, I wrote about the many unexpected twists and turns of the methodological journey. Encountering the concept of epistemological racism and my subsequent critique of the Eurocentric foundations of many traditional qualitative approaches was challenging. I established narrative inquiry as the most appropriate methodology for my study, because I was investigating meanings of experiences but, at the same time, the research process itself was a series of experiences, a journey. In Chapter 1, I wrote, 'When you are preparing for a journey, you own the journey. Once you've started the journey, the journey owns you' (Shope, 2006: 165). The journey did begin to own me, entirely consistent with the concept of 'the narrative text...stressing the journey over the destination' (Ellis and Bochner, 2000: 733–5). Narrative inquiry and its allegiance to social constructionism that holds that 'our constructions are the product of social forces, either structural or interactional' (Burr, 2003: 20), fitted with the critical questioning of the epistemological foundations of many of the methodological paradigms prevalent even in qualitative research. Narrative inquiry that seeks 'to construct a different relationship between researchers and subjects and between authors and readers' (Ellis and Bochner, 2000: 733–735), reflected ways in which 'constructions' emerge through 'social forces' of relationships between the participants, between the participants and me, and between you, the reader, and me, throughout the book.

Narrative inquiry does not privilege one method of gathering data. Because the research is life as it is lived on the landscape, then inevitably other events, actions and happenings are also a part of the study and are woven into the stories. Thus, in the conversations with the many people featured throughout this book, you can 'read' how everyday events and experiences were recalled and stories told about them by each one of us. I cannot 'know' the stories that are meaningful for anyone else, and so rather than ask a series of questions, I invited participants to tell stories that were meaningful for them and I told stories that were meaningful for me. Thus I came to 'know "something" without claiming to know everything' (Richardson and St Pierre, 2005: 961), a crucial dimension of researching across cultures. Sustaining this position of the respectful and curious inquirer brought forth rich stories, stories that changed through our interactions (Ellis and Bochner, 2000) – witness the emails from Cheng-tsung. It also allowed disturbing stories of racism to emerge such as 'The story of the rotten shrimp' (Chapter 5) and those of the Fellow Travellers in Chapter 9. Constructing such dialogical experiences allowed those critical comments to be made about dimensions of working with cultural diversity in higher education that are often uncomfortable and contentious and can, therefore, remain unsaid. Such silence can make it difficult to initiate reasoned debate (Back, 2004), losing opportunities for increased understanding. I embraced those opportunities, yet, in doing so, realise that I have rendered myself vulnerable, in particular in Chapter 8.

'Postmodernism...distrusts all methods equally. No method has a privileged status' (Richardson and St Pierre, 2005: 961). More paradoxes – working within a postmodern paradigm where regimes of truth are questioned may, of course, be disrespectful to the very people to whom I was seeking to be respectful and whose conceptualisations of truth may remain firmly modernist. By positioning myself as a narrative inquirer and writing autoethnographically, I have privileged those perspectives. But I have striven not to write as a 'disembodied omniscient narrator claiming universal and atemporal general knowledge' (ibid.). Claiming that, 'I, too, lead a storied life and the research relationship is part of my experiential text' (Winkler, 2003: 399) may, however, be seen as a limitation. The telling and retelling of this experiential text may detract, at times, from the storied lives of others. But because narrative inquiry is 'a kind of conversation between theory and life or, at least between theory and the stories of life contained in the inquiry' (Clandinin and Connelly, 2000: 41), the theoretical concepts and the autoethnographical connections could not be unravelled from methodological frameworks and research strategies. For example, I re-presented at length the conversations with Cheng-tsung in order to illuminate the interactive subjectivity of those conversations in which meaningful stories were told (Chase, 2005), including those of approaches to learning and teaching. It would have been impractical to accord every conversation similar privileges; nonetheless, similar conversations have informed this book and been acknowledged respectfully. Though important, those conversations with students and academics were but one dimension of the inquiry. Other nuggets, those unanticipated narratives (Cortazzi and Jin, 2006), appeared in the most unexpected places. The 'actions, doings and happenings' (Clandinin and Connelly, 2000: 79) that included conversations at the photocopier, a chance comment in a tutorial, a difficult teaching experience, an article in the newspaper – all have played such significant roles and been integrated purposefully.

Methodological self-consciousness is, therefore, a distinctive aspect of this narrative inquiry. By the time you reached Chapter 8, you were aware, from Chapter 5, how I had glossed over another word, 'white', in addition to the word 'mild', which Cheng-tsung used to define me, and how this had effected critical reflection and writing about my own cultural affiliations. Thus, each element and dimension of the research processes is laid out in front of you. Telling the story now, in this way of braiding those elements together within the whole, the reader might be forgiven for imagining that the process was seamless. But by this stage in the book, how could you imagine that any facet of it has not been held up to the light for inspection at least a thousand times?

'Boons and breaks'

I became aware that I used the interviews to share with the participant the changes that I have made to my teaching practice, feelings about particular 'events' and my assumptions and beliefs. I spoke my thoughts aloud and, in hearing them, they became crystallised. I was aware of the perceived imbalances of power in some of the conversations, but wanted to show a symmetrical relationship between the student participants and me. This was naïve. The indeterminate play of power (Scheurich, 1997) in our discourse denoted relationships that were sometimes asymmetrical, sometimes symmetrical. Through my re-presentation of some of the conversations, I hope I have demonstrated that each one of us felt sufficiently comfortable with the other, to be able to talk about and expose assumptions, beliefs, vulnerabilities and uncertainties.

In my conversations and with the re-presentation of them, I strive to be transparent so that it is obvious where we share similar knowledge and experience. When that knowledge and experience is not shared, we make it explicit. Throughout my conversations with Cheng-tsung, for example, there are numerous points when we do not understand or think we do not understand each other, resulting, sometimes, in 'messy' dialogue. I searched out and relished the complexity of difference, but took some time to distrust the implied neatness of the conversations with those with similar ethnic and cultural backgrounds. Those conversations were as complex, if not more complex, once I began to engage in questioning that supposed neatness. I query whether our apparent sharing of knowledge and experience produces a kind of collusion, a positioning of the 'international students' as the 'other' that we fail to confront, hence Chapter 9.

I can also be criticised for seeking to understand Cheng-tsung's use of the word 'mild' (Chapter 5). Because it was not a word I would associate with myself and others would not use to describe me, I needed to understand his use of it. The attempt to find a word that, for me, better described his meaning can be construed as a colonisation of his language, perhaps seeking neatness, a wielding of my perceived 'power'. I could have accepted the word and, even though I did not like it, lived with it. I contend, however, that the conversation, triggered by his use of that word, took us to a different level of understanding. He shared with me that he felt I understood him and that 'being mild' was actually a strong connection between us. This 'uncovering and discovering' could be interpreted as a 'getting closer to' position (Gunaratnam, 2003: 102), but it was through this experience that I began to understand how my 'own positioning is produced' (ibid.).

Experiences that resonate with each other lead us to connection, but these connections are not 'contrived versions of commonality' (ibid.). I assert that Cheng-tsung and I (and others), by interrogating those 'points of commonality for the dislocations and differences that they carry', are finding 'points of alignment and orientation between us' (ibid.: 104). These are significant elements of any research encounter, but perhaps more significant when those encounters are manifestations of the cross-cultural research 'tentacles' (Chapter 4). The conceptual framework of narrative inquiry has enabled me to grasp some of those slippery tentacles and to hold on to them for sufficient time to enable the insights, summarised in the rest of this final chapter, to occur.

Insights into pedagogical theory and practice: 'flexibility, reinvention and movement'

An original aim of this study was that I might emerge with a theoretical framework of adult learning that was culturally synergistic, but it was not long before I recognised that this aim was over-ambitious (Chapter 1). I have, however, critiqued theoretical frameworks of learning and teaching in higher education, and propose that if any framework is to be inclusive, the practitioner needs to be sensitive to the assumptions inherent in its philosophical position.

I was aware of the principles that supported my own practice, but, by gaining insight into the ways in which learning and teaching are conceptualised in a diverse range of cultures, I was alerted to the cultural situatedness of those principles (Tweed and Lehman, 2002). A danger was that I began to be seduced into stereotyping, assuming that all people who shared similar cultural backgrounds would approach learning in the same way. My exposition of the dualisms in much social science thinking helped me to see that I had slipped, once more, into the 'Aristotelian principle of "either or"... which holds that every proposition must be true or false' (Al Zeera, 2001: 60). It is not that *either* each person must be treated as unconnected to his or her cultural group, *or* that assumptions should be made about individuals based on knowledge of the characteristics of their cultural group; it is that *both* can be used judiciously in order to effect greater understanding. Here is testimony to recognising and celebrating the relationship between the individual and society, the shift to a critical postmodern approach to adult learning theory that I acknowledged in Chapter 3. I have explicated the 'continual working tension between the similarities and differences of individuals, of cultures and of learners' (Flannery, 1995: 155), taken account of the situatedness and made changes to my practice based on what was emerging. Making these changes raised other questions that, in turn, were explored, and resulted in more changes. I expect this iterative process to continue indefinitely. This iteration undoubtedly makes 'research in teaching and learning more complex and less generalisable' (Malcolm and Zukas, 2001: 39), but I did not set out with the intent to generalise. My experiences may cause others to think about some of these issues. They may 'ring a bell' (Pring, 1999: 10) for you, too. By sharing my experiences – and by 'experiences' I am including conversations with students and academics, interviews and classroom events – and the learning from them – perhaps I have been able to provoke some critical reflection on *yours* (Sparkes, 2002).

Changes to teaching approaches

My extensive interrogation of research methodologies and methods has had some influence on the ways in which research methodology is taught in the Graduate School of Education. I have influenced the content and curriculum of research methodology teaching at both Masters and doctoral level and have introduced specialist sessions on narrative inquiry for Masters students. I have selected research articles that foreground intercultural communication in higher education as core readings for the Doctor of Education unit Understanding Educational Research. These articles are used to facilitate debate in multicultural groups, groups whose constituency reflects the research being critiqued. Thus I have heeded the charges of epistemological racism (Chapter 4), and acted upon the call of those (such as Stanfield, 1993 a & b, 1994; Scheurich, 1997; Ladson-Billings, 2000, 2003; Hendrix, 2001) for academics to provoke the questioning of assumptions inherent in major philosophical perspectives in social science research in their teaching of research methodology.

The changes that I have made to the ways in which I approach my own teaching are scattered throughout the book, but articulated particularly in the later chapters. The more significant changes are summarised here.

Sometimes I invite students whose first language is not English but who have a common language to speak together in the first session if they choose to do so. Such an invitation enables them to become familiar and feel confident with the discursive activities that I am reluctant to surrender in my teaching, even though I have become more aware that the philosophical ideas on which they are founded are as culturally mediated as any others. Such awareness has, however, enabled me to understand that discursive activities can be threatening for those for whom such interaction is unfamiliar and it is, therefore, important to explain my rationale for using them. In so far as is possible, I ensure that there is always a first-language English speaker in each small group to help develop other students' confidence to speak in English. I am careful in my own use of language, encouraging students to express any difficulties in understanding after the class, either face-to-face or electronically, if they do not feel brave enough to speak in front of others. At the same time, I am mindful of research (Jones, 2001; Hellsten and Prescott, 2004) that suggests that lecturers who are first-language English speakers often lower their level of language use in order to ensure that students' learning is not adversely affected. Some students can perceive this practice as contrary to their expectations of improving their English proficiency. It needs to be balanced, therefore, with encouraging them to become familiar with more complex uses of language through judiciously chosen set texts that employ a range of writing styles.

I have learned that it is unhelpful to issue a directive to read a number of articles without specifying a rationale for doing so. Several students have told me that it can take half a day to read one article. I have felt guilty at provoking such levels of anxiety, believing that it was my responsibility to find more effective ways to help them read and understand. I shared this dilemma in conversation with a Taiwanese student, inviting suggestions on how to improve this practice. Her reply was that she saw this as *her* responsibility. She had chosen to come to the UK, and therefore she needed to find a way to read the article. She added that reading it before the session gave her 'some knowledge ' and helped her to feel more confident in the class and in the discussion. (Cortazzi and Jin, 1997). She liked the discussion. She would have liked 'more classes', to have more discussion (Gil and Katsara, 1999). Difficulties with language and unfamiliarity with concepts can, however, present enormous obstacles for many students, irrespective of where they are from. A strategy that I have developed is to accompany articles or chapters with a list of questions, designed to guide students through the reading, so that they are more able to grasp the salient points. Discussing these points with others prior to the next teaching session demonstrates cognisance that, for some students, discussion is valuable but after s/he has been provided with focused opportunities to gather knowledge (Chapter 3).

I consider it important that I take responsibility for ensuring that students work in groups that I have choreographed, certainly initially. Facilitating students to work in a range of different groups from the very beginning of the course ensures that people do not have to feel embarrassed by having to choose people with whom to work. This strategy not only ensures that the more reticent students can develop their confidence to express views and opinions in smaller groups but it also models commitment to using the classroom as a space within which to develop and build on cultural capability. I have learned that in many countries, being invited to speak is important; one does not speak until invited. Issuing invitations to people to present the group's feedback is, therefore, very positive, in particular in those situations where certain students can dominate. Finally, setting small-group activities between each session encourages more contact between students and enables them to feel sufficiently prepared for the following meeting; to feel more confident to express opinions. Such activities reduce feelings of homesickness to which many students are very understandably prone (Volet and Ang, 1998) and enable intercultural understandings – and friendships – to develop.

I have resisted essentialised notions of asymmetrical relationships between students and teachers, but acknowledge that such relationships are conceptualised in diverse ways in different cultures (Carroll and Ryan, 2005; Prescott and Hellsten, 2005). I accept that I am perceived by many students as an expert and as a person with authority. Rather than seeking to dismantle such perceptions, I now respect them. I linger at the end of teaching sessions so that students have more opportunities to talk with me, to ask questions, to feel that we are developing intimate relationships (Wu, 2002).

People continue to appreciate the way I work and so, in a sense, has anything changed from what I wrote in Chapter 3? Yes. I continue to favour discursive activities, but, by explaining my rationale for using them and striving to show interest in and awareness and sensitivity to other learning paradigms, drawing on teaching strategies from those paradigms to complement my own, I place the development of cultural capability much more at the centre of my teaching. Learning is an emotional experience for me, so is teaching and so is research. I cannot assume that these practices will be emotional experiences for others, but by being respectful and genuine, supportive and empathic, I seek to ensure a climate within which everybody *feels* comfortable. They are encouraged to express themselves without fear of recrimination and to ask embarrassing questions (Palmer, 1999) as a way of developing understanding not only of the subject but also of each other.

Intercultural communication is complex. It cannot be assumed that because people look similar and share apparently similar cultural backgrounds that they will share assumptions, beliefs and values, nor can it be assumed that intercultural communication will just happen (Otten, 2000). It seems extraordinarily naïve to be writing that, but I have, in the past, made such assumptions. Egege and Kutieleh (2004) highlight the difficulties many academics encounter in understanding and working effectively with different cultural paradigms, yet working effectively within a different cultural paradigm is expected of international students. By being explicit about the diversity that is in the room and acknowledging that this is an enormous resource to us all but may also engender some difficulties, I encourage people to learn, through dialogue, about their differences and similarities. I now question more overtly my 'local culture', to dismantle dominant behaviours that may be exhibited, taking 'pedagogic control' (Wu, 2002: 389) to effect more inclusive actions.

Constructing and reconstructing fragile selves: personal insights

It seems disingenuous to present a separate section headed 'Personal insights' when so many of the insights have been personal. The journey began with an experience that then caused me to think about other experiences of my own. As a practitioner researcher, it was my own assumptions and implicit beliefs that I became curious about, as well as those of others. I have opened those assumptions and beliefs up to public viewing and criticism, sharing the beliefs that I came to (but perhaps have always held) that if I am to make sense of experiences then I have a constant need to reconceptualise. Engaging in that reconceptualising through my relationships and interactions with others is entirely consistent with narrative inquiry. But I could not have predicted the extent to which the work would give insight into the contextually specific situations of my own local context and become so autoethnographical. I tangled with the complexities of critiquing the paucity of reflexive, lived experiences in the research literature, while, at the same time, problematising reflexivity as a culturally constructed discourse in the same way as any other (Chapter 4). Questioning notions of reflection and reflexivity may make me a thorn in the flesh for those who speak unproblematically of these concepts as essential elements to developing one's own practice. I have, however, come to disagree with Erlandson (2005) and those other critics who position reflection in action as another method of controlling the practitioner, and of denying the value of her own practical skills. I do not agree that by 'thinking' about my practice and my experiences and interactions with others, I have 'been disciplined to judge and normalise [my] everyday practice with tools not from [my] own practices but from [my] discursive captors' (Erlandson, 2005: 668). Perhaps that is the glass cage that Gabriel (2003) refers to, but, for me, it is questioning myself and sharing those questions with others that moves me, occasionally, into the glass palace.

A long time ago I had an ambition to reconceptualise the meaning of becoming internationalised, defining it in Chapter 2 as a 'personal journey of deconstruction and reconstruction' (Sanderson, 2004: 16). One of the most powerful parts of the journey has been the recognition of my own shifting identities, leading to the deconstruction of my own cultural traits and affiliations and the attempted interrogation of my own 'whiteness' in Chapter 8. I feel that it is important to continue to develop a critical engagement with my own whiteness – no easy task. I have already indicated that talking about this can be difficult and uncomfortable, but such discomfort is not a reason for not doing it. Instead of treading carefully so as not to offend those of my critics who regard cultural and ethnic difference as no different from any other kind of difference, or indeed deny difference, I have become bolder, more able to situate such perspectives within their privileged paradigm of dominance and to begin to dismantle them. The jury is still out on the extent to which I have 'reconstructed' those fragile selves and become 'internationalised', but I trust I have moved away from simply stating that diversity is a 'good thing', to exploring felt modalities of diversity in everyday higher education situations. Perhaps this is where a journey such as this leads, not only towards a more inclusive approach to learning and teaching, but also towards a more radical human being.

Finally...

'Jauh Perjalanan Luas Pandangan'
    The above Bahasa Malaysia words were given to me by a Malaysian doctoral student and translate as 'The more you travel, the more you see others'. Making this journey enabled me to see others and, I venture to suggest, to enable others to see me in many ways. I have learned much from every step of it as I have striven to articulate throughout my writing.
    'We learn how to recognise emotions and feelings as forms of embodied knowledge and how to name the histories and cultural inheritances that we need to come to terms with if they are not to produce future hauntings' (Seidler, 2010: 157).

And so I come full circle. In the preface to this book, I said that one of its aims was to demonstrate the rich potential of higher education to enable greater under-standing between people. My hope is that this journey that I have recounted with all its twists and turns, its stumbling uncertainties, has shown that by embarking on a more personal journey of internationalisation in higher education, lives can be enhanced through learning and teaching strategies that celebrate diversity and are respectful and inclusive. Such strategies can challenge all of us to come to terms with our 'histories and cultural inheritances' so that fewer people are disadvantaged by particular systems, and 'future hauntings' can be prevented. 'As we learn to live sustainable and just lives so we form embodied identities that connect us to diverse others with renewed feelings for global responsibility' (ibid.: 190). Maybe the play-ing field has been levelled a little and the journey towards global citizenship begun.

REFERENCES

Agar, M. (1994) *Language Shock: Understanding the Culture of Conversation*. New York: William Morrow.

Al Zeera, Z. (2001) 'Paradigm shifts in the social sciences in the East and West', in R. Hayhoe and J. Pan (eds) *Knowledge across Cultures: A Contribution to Dialogue across Civilizations*. Hong Kong: Comparative Education Research Centre, University of Hong Kong, pp. 55–73.

Alexander, B. K. (2004) Black skin/white masks: the performative sustainability of whiteness (with apologies to Frantz Fanon). *Qualitative Inquiry*, 10 (5), 647–72.

Alexander, R. (2000) *Culture and Pedagogy: International Comparisons in Primary Education*. Oxford: Blackwell.

Altbach, P. and Knight, J. (2007) The internationalization of higher education: motivations and realities. *Journal of Studies in International Education*, 11 (3/4), 290–305.

Amstutz, D. D. (1999) Adult learning: moving toward more inclusive theories and practices. *New Directions for Adult and Continuing Education*, 82, 19–32.

Anderson, M. (1993) Studying across difference: race class and gender in qualitative research, in J. H. Stanfield II and Rutledge M. Dennis (eds) *Race and Ethnicity in Research Methods*. Newbury Park, CA: Sage, pp. 39–52.

Andrews, M. (2007) Exploring cross-cultural boundaries, in D. J.Clandin (ed.) *Handbook of Narrative Inquiry*. Thousand Oaks, CA: Sage, pp. 489–511.

Appadurai, A. (2001) (ed.) *Globalization*. Durham, NC: Duke University Press.

Asmar, C. (2003) Dissonance in diversity: differing perceptions of staff and students regarding what helps (and hinders) the learning of students from diverse backgrounds. Paper presented at the ILTHE Conference, University of Warwick, UK, 2–4 July.

Asmar, C. (2005) Internationalising students: reassessing diasporic and local student difference. *Studies in Higher Education*, 30 (3), 291–309.

Atkinson, P. (1997) Narrative turn or blind alley. *Qualitative Health Research* 7, 325–44.

Atkinson, P. and Silverman, D. (1997) Kundera's immortality: the interview society and the inventions of self. *Qualitative Inquiry*, 3, 304–25.

Back, L. (2004) Ivory towers? The academy and racism, in I. Law, D. Phillips and L. Turney (eds) *Institutional Racism in Higher Education*. Stoke-on-Trent: Trentham Books, pp. 1–13.

Bakhtin, M. M. (1981) *The Dialogic Imagination: Four Essays* (ed. C. Emerson and M. Holquist). Austin, TX: University of Texas.

Bakhtin, M. M. (1986) Response to a question from Novy Mir editorial staff, in C. Emerson and M. Holquist (eds) *Speech Genres and other Late Essays* (trans. V. W. McGee). Austin, TX: University of Texas Press.

Bauer, M. (1996) The narrative interview: comments on a technique for data collection. London School of Economics and Political Science Methodology Institute Papers in Social Research.

Benhabib, S. (1992) *Situating the Self: Gender, Community and Postmodernism in Contemporary Ethics.* Cambridge: Polity Press.

Bernal, M. (1987) *Black Athena: The Afroasiatic Roots of Classical Civilisation.* Vol. 1. London: Free Association Books.

Biggs, J. B. (2001a) Insights into teaching the Chinese learner, in D. A. Watkins and J. B. Biggs (eds). *Teaching the Chinese Learner: Psychological and Pedagogical Perspectives.* Hong Kong: Comparative Education Research Centre, University of Hong Kong, pp. 277–300.

Biggs, J. B. (2001b) Teaching across cultures, in F. Salili, C. Y. Chiu and Y. Y. Hong (eds) *Student Motivation: The Culture and Context of Learning.* New York: Kluwer Associates/Plenum, pp. 293–308.

Biggs, J. B. (2003) *Teaching for Quality Learning at University*, 2nd edn. Buckingham: SRHE/Open University.

Biggs, J. B. and Tang, C. (2007) *Teaching for Quality Learning at University*, 3rd edn. Buckingham: SRHE/Open University.

Bishop, R. (2005) Freeing ourselves from neocolonial domination in research: a Maori approach to creating knowledge, in N. K. Denzin and Y. S. Lincoln (eds) *The Sage Handbook of Qualitative Research*, 3rd edn. Thousand Oaks, CA.: Sage, pp. 109–38.

Bohanon, J. (2006) *The Talking Circle: A Perspective on Culturally Appropriate Group Work with Indigenous Peoples.* Paper presented at the 6th International Conference on Diversity in Organisations Communitiés and Nations. New Orleans, 12–15 June.

Bond, M. H. (1986) (ed.) *The Psychology of the Chinese People.* Hong Kong: OUP (China).

Bond, M. H. (1991) *Beyond the Chinese Face: Insights from Psychology.* Hong Kong: OUP (China).

Bond, T. and Mifsud, D. (2006) Narrative conversation between cultures: a novel approach to addressing an ethical concern, in S. Trahar (ed.) *Narrative Research on Learning: Comparative and International Perspectives*. Oxford: Symposium, pp. 239–51.

Bonnett, A. (2000) *White Identities: Historical and International Perspectives*. Harlow: Prentice-Hall.

Brah, A. (1996) *Cartographies of Diaspora: Contesting Identities*. London: Routledge.

Brawn, R. and Trahar, S. (2003) Supporting the learner teacher in changing higher education, in R. Sutherland, G. Claxton and A. Pollard (eds) *Learning and Teaching where Worldviews Meet*. Stoke-on-Trent: Trentham Books, pp. 245–54.

British Council (2003) *Education UK Positioning for Success*. London: British Council.

Brock-Utne, B. (2002) Stories of the Hunt – who is writing them? The importance of indigenous research in Africa based on local experience, in C. A. Odora Hoppers (ed.) *Indigenous Knowledge and the Integration of Knowledge Systems: Towards a Philosophy of Articulation*. Claremont, South Africa: New Africa Books, pp. 237–56.

Brooker, R. and Macpherson, I. (1999) Communicating the processes and outcomes of practitioner research: an opportunity for self-indulgence or a serious professional responsibility? *Educational Action Research*, 7 (2), 207–21.

Brookfield, S. D. (2005) *The Power of Critical Theory for Adult Learning and Teaching*. Maidenhead: Open University Press.

Brunner, B. B. (2006) Student perceptions of diversity on a college campus: scratching the surface to find more. *Intercultural Education*, 17 (3). 311–17.

Burr, V. (2003) *Social Constructionism*, 2nd edn. London: Routledge.

Cadman, K. (2000) 'Voices in the air': evaluations of the learning experiences of international postgraduates and their supervisors. *Teaching in Higher Education*, 5 (4), 475–91.

Caglar, A. (2006) Transdisciplinarity and transnationalism: challenges to 'Internationalization at Home', in *Internationalization at Home: A Global Perspective*. The Hague: Nuffic, pp. 33–48.

Carroll, J. and Ryan, J. (eds) (2005) *Teaching International Students: Improving Learning for All*. Abingdon: Routledge.

Caruth, C. and Keenan, T. (1995) The AIDS crisis is not over: a conversation with Gregg Borodowitz, Douglas Crimp and Laura Insky, in C. Caruth (ed.) *Trauma: Explorations in Memory*. Baltimore: Johns Hopkins University Press, pp. 256–72.

Cary, L. J. (2004) Always already colonizer/colonized: white Australian wanderings, in K. Mutuo. and B. Blue Swadener (eds) *Decolonizing Research in Cross-Cultural Contexts: Critical Personal Narratives*. Albany, NY: State University of New York Press, pp. 69–83.

Chang, H. (2008) *Autoethnography as Method*. Walnut Creek, CA: Left Coast Press.

Charmaz, K. and Mitchell, R.G. Jr (1997) The myth of silent interpretation, in R. Hertz (ed.) *Reflexivity and Voice*. Thousand Oaks, CA: Sage, pp. 193–215.

Chase, S. E. (2005) Narrative inquiry: multiple lenses, approaches, voices, in N. K. Denzin and Y. S. Lincoln (eds) *The Handbook of Qualitative Research*, 3rd edn. Thousand Oaks, Ca.: Sage, pp. 651–79.

Clandinin, D. J. and Connelly, F. M. (2000) *Narrative Inquiry: Experience and Story in Qualitative Research*. San Francisco, CA: Jossey-Bass.

Clandinin, D. J. and Roziek, J. (2007) Mapping a landscape of narrative inquiry: borderland spaces and tensions, in D. J. Clandin (ed.) *Handbook of Narrative Inquiry Mapping a Methodology*. Thousand Oaks, CA: Sage, pp. 35–75.

Claxton, G. (1996) Implicit theories of learning, in G. Claxton, T. Atkinson, M. Osborn and M. Wallace (eds) *Liberating the Learner*. London: Routledge, pp. 45–56.

Clegg, S., Parr, S. and Wan, S. (2003) Racialising discourses in higher education. *Teaching in Higher Education*, 8 (2), 155–68.

Clough, P. (2002) *Narratives and Fictions in Educational Research*. Buckingham: Open University Press.

Clough, P. and Nutbrown, C. (2007) *A Student's Guide to Methodology: Justifying Enquiry*. 2nd ed. London: Sage.

Coles, R. (1989) *The Call of Stories: Teaching and the Moral Imagination*. Boston, MA: Houghton Mifflin.

Committee on Higher Education (1963) *Higher Education: Report of the Committee appointed by the Prime Minister under the Chairmanship of Lord Robbins, 1961–63*. London: HMSO.

Conle, C. (1999) Moments of interpretation in the perception and evaluation of teaching. *Teaching and Teacher Education*, 15 (7), 801–14.

Cortazzi, M. and Jin, L. (1997) Communication for learning across cultures, in D. McNamara and R. Harris (eds) *Overseas Students in Higher Education: Issues in Teaching and Learning*. London: Routledge, pp. 76–90.

Cortazzi, M. and Jin, L. (2001) Large classes in China: 'good' teachers and interaction, in D. A. Watkins and J. B. Biggs (eds) *Teaching the Chinese Learner: Psychological and Pedagogical Perspectives*. Hong Kong: Comparative Education Research Centre, University of Hong Kong, pp. 77–98.

Cortazzi, M. and Jin, L. (2006) Asking questions, sharing stories and identity construction: sociocultural issues in narrative research, in S. Trahar (ed.) *Narrative Research on Learning: Comparative and International Perspectives*. Oxford: Symposium, pp. 27–46.

Costley, C. and Gibbs, P. (2006) Researching others: care as an ethic for practitioner researchers. *Studies in Higher Education*, 31 (1), 89–98.

Crossley, M. (1984) Strategies for curriculum change and the question of international transfer. *Journal of Curriculum Studies*, 16 (1), 75–88.

Crossley, M. (2000) Bridging cultures and traditions in the reconceptualisation of comparative and international education. *Comparative Education*, 36 (3), 319–32.

Cuccioletta, D. (2001/2002) Multiculturalism or transculturalism: towards a cosmopolitan citizenship. *London Journal of Canadian Studies*, 17, 1–11.

David, M. (2009) *Transforming Higher Education: A Feminist Perspective*. London: Institute of Education.

Davies, B. (2009) Difference and differenciation, in B. Davies and S. Gannon (eds) *Pedagogical Encounters*. New York: Peter Lang, pp. 17–30.

De Vita, G. (2001) Learning styles, culture and inclusive instruction in the multi-cultural classroom: a business and management perspective. *Innovations in Education and Teaching International,* 38 (2), 165–74.

De Vita, G. (2002) Inclusive approaches to effective communication and active participation in the multicultural classroom. *Active Learning in Higher Education,* 1 (2), 168–79.

De Vita, G. and Case, P. (2003) Rethinking the internationalisation agenda in UK higher education. *Journal of Further and Higher Education,* 27 (4), 383–98.

Delamont, S. (2009) The only honest thing: autoethnography, reflexivity and small crises in fieldwork. *Ethnography and Education,* 4 (1), 51–63.

Department for Education and Skills (2003) *The Future of Higher Education.* London: Stationery Office.

Devos, A. (2003) Academic standards, internationalisation and the discursive construction of 'The International Student'. *Higher Education Research and Development,* 22 (2), 155–66.

Dickens, C. *Little Dorrit.* London: Penguin.

Dunbar, C. (2008) Critical race theory and indigenous methodologies, in N. K. Denzin, Y. S. Lincoln and L. Tuhiwai Smith (eds) *Handbook of Critical and Indigenous Methodologies.* Thousand Oaks, CA: Sage, pp. 85–99.

Education Act 1944. London: HMSO.

Edwards, R. and Ribben, J. (1998) Living on the edges: public knowledge, private lives, personal experience, in J. Ribben, and R. Edwards (1998) *Feminist Dilemmas in Qualitative Research: Public Knowledge and Private Lives.* London: Sage, pp. 1–23.

Edwards, R. and Usher, R. (2000) *Globalisation and Pedagogy: Space, Place and Identity.* London: Routledge.

Egege, S. and Kutieleh, K. (2004) Critical thinking: teaching foreign notions to foreign students. *International Education Journal,* 4 (4), 75–85.

Ellis, C. and Bochner, A. (2000) Autoethnography, personal narrative, reflexivity: researcher as subject, in N. Denzin and Y. Lincoln (eds) *Handbook of Qualitative Research,* 2nd edn. Thousand Oaks, CA: Sage, pp. 733–68.

Entwistle, N. (2009) *Teaching for Understanding at University: Deep Approaches and Distinctive Ways of Thinking.* Basingstoke: Palgrave Macmillan.

Equality Challenge Unit (2009) *Internationalising Equality, Equalising Internationalisation: The Intersection between Internationalisation and Equality and Diversity in Higher Education: Scoping Report.*

Erlandson, P. (2005) The body disciplined: rewriting teaching competence and the doctrine of reflection. *Journal of Philosophy in Education,* 39 (4), 661–70.

Etherington, K. (2004) *Becoming a Reflexive Researcher: Using Our Selves in Research.* London: Jessica Kingsley.

Evanoff, R.J. (2004) Universalist, relativist and constructivist approaches to inter-cultural ethics. *International Journal of Intercultural Relations,* 28 (5), 439–58.

Fasokun, T., Katahoire, A. and Oduaran, A. (2005) *The Psychology of Adult Learning in Africa.* Cape Town: UNESCO/Pearson Education.

Fay, B. (1996) *Contemporary Philosophy of Social Science: A Multicultural Approach.* Malden, MA: Blackwell Publishing.

Featherstone, M. (1993) Global and local cultures, in J. Bird, B. Curtis, T. Putnam and L. Tickner (eds) *Mapping the Futures: Local Cultures, Global Change.* London: Routledge, pp. 169–187.

Flannery, D. D. (1995) Adult education and the politics of the theoretical text. In B. Kanpol and P. McLaren (eds) *Critical Multiculturalism: Uncommon Voices in a Common Struggle.* Westport, CT: Bergin and Garvey, pp. 149–63.

Foucault, M. (1965) *Madness and Civilization: a History of Insanity in the Age of Reason.* Trans. Richard Howard. New York: Vintage Books.

Foucault, M. (1972) *The Archaeology of Knowledge* (trans. A. M. Sheridan Smith). London: Tavistock.

Foucault, M. (1980) *Power/Knowledge: Selected Interviews and Other Writings 1972–1977.* Brighton: Harvester.

Fox, C. (1997) The authenticity of intercultural communication. *International Journal of Intercultural Relations,* 21 (1), 85–103.

Fox, C. (2006) Stories within stories: dissolving the boundaries in narrative research and analysis, in S. Trahar (ed.) *Narrative Research on Learning: Comparative and International Perspectives.* Oxford: Symposium Books, pp. 47–60.

Fox, C. (2008) Postcolonial dilemmas in narrative research. *Compare,* 38 (3), 335–48.

Fox, H. (1994) *Listening to the World: Cultural Issues in Academic Writing.* Urbana, IL: National Council of Teachers of English.

Frankenberg, R. (1993) *White Women, Race Matters: The Social Construction of White Women.* London: Routledge.

Frankenberg, R. (2004) On unsteady ground: crafting and engaging in the critical study of whiteness, in M. Bulmer and J. Solomos (eds) *Researching Race and Racism.* London: Routledge, pp. 104–18.

Freire, P. (1972) *Pedagogy of the Oppressed.* Harmondsworth: Penguin.

Gabriel, Y. (2003) Glass palaces and glass cages: organisations in times of flexible work, fragmented consumption and fragile selves. *Ephemera,* 3 (3), 166–184.

Gannon, S. (2009) Difference as ethical encounter, in B. Davies and S. Gannon (eds) *Pedagogical Encounters.* New York: Peter Lang, pp. 69–88.

Gergen, K. J. (1985) The social constructionist movement in modern psychology. *American Psychologist,* 40 (3), 266–75.

Gergen, K. J. (1999) *An Introduction to Social Constructionism.* Thousand Oaks, CA: Sage.

Gil, C. and Katsara, R. (1999) The experiences of Spanish and Greek students in adapting to UK higher education: the creation of new support strategies. Paper presented at the British Educational Research Association Annual Conference, University of Sussex at Brighton, 2–5 September.

Gilligan, C. (1982) *In a Different Voice: Psychological Theory and Womens' Development.* Cambridge, MA: Harvard University Press.

Giroux, H. A. (1992) *Border Crossings: Cultural Workers and the Politics of Education.* London: Routledge.

Gu, Q., Schweisfurth, M. and Day, C. (2010) Learning and growing in a 'foreign' context: intercultural experiences of international students. *Compare*, 40 (1), 7–23.

Guillemin, M. and Gillam, L. (2004) Ethics, reflexivity, and 'ethically important moments' in research. *Qualitative Inquiry*, 10 (2), 261–80.

Gunaratnam, Y. (2003) *Researching 'Race' and Ethnicity.* London: Sage.

Gustavsson, B. and Osman, A. (1997) Multicultural education and life-long learning, in S. Walters (ed.) *Globalization, Adult Education and Training: Impacts and Issues.* London: Zed Books, pp. 179–87.

Haigh, M. (2008) Internationalisation, planetary citizenship and Higher Education Inc. *Compare*, 38 (4), 427–40.

Haigh, M. (2009) Fostering cross-cultural empathy with non-western curricular structures. *Journal of Studies in International Education*, 13 (2), 271–84.

Hall, J. D. (1999) *Cultures of Inquiry: From Epistemology to Discourse in Sociohistorical Research.* Cambridge: Cambridge University Press.

Hall, S. (2000) Conclusion: the multicultural question, in B. Hesse (ed.) *Un/settled Multiculturalisms: Diasporas, Entanglements, Transruptions.* London: Zed Books, pp. 209–241.

Hallak, J. (2000) Globalisation and its impact on education, in T. Mebrahtu, M. Crossley and D. Johnson (eds) *Globalisation, Educational Transformation and Societies in Transition.* Oxford: Symposium Books, pp. 21–40.

Halliday, F. (1999) The chimera of the 'International University.' *International Affairs*, 73 (1), 99–120.

Harrison, N. and Peacock, N. (2010) Interactions in the international classroom: the UK perspective, in E. Jones (ed.) *Internationalisation and the Student Voice: Higher Education Perspectives.* London: Routledge, pp. 125–42.

Harrison, N. and Peacock, N. (forthcoming) Cultural distance, mindfulness and passive xenophobia: using Integrated Threat Theory to explore home higher education students' perspectives on 'internationalisation at home'. *British Educational Research Journal.*

Hayhoe, R. (2005) Peking University and the spirit of Chinese scholarship. *Comparative Education Review*, 45 (2), 575–83.

Hellmundt, S. and Fox, C. (2003) Linking intercultural theory with teaching and learning practice: promoting student voice through multicultural group work. *International Journal of Diversity in Organisations, Communities and Nations*, 3, 33–43.

Hellsten, M. (2008) Researching international pedagogy and the forming of new academic identities, in M. Hellsten and A. Reid (eds) *Researching International Pedagogies: Sustainable Practice for Teaching and Learning in Higher Education.* Springer, pp. 83–98.

Hellsten, M. and Prescott, A. (2004) Learning at university: the international student experience. *International Education Journal*, 5 (3), 344–351.

Helu-Thaman, K. H. (1999) Different eyes: schooling and indigenous education in Tonga, in A. L. Little and F. E. Leach (eds) *Education, Cultures and Economics:*

Dilemmas for Development. New York and London: Falmer, pp. 69–80.

Henderson, J. (2009) 'It's all about give and take, or is it?' Where, when and how do native and non-native users of English shape UK university students' representations of each other and their learning experiences? *Journal of Studies in International Education,* 13 (3), 398–409.

Hendrix, K. G. (2001) 'Mama told me...': exploring childhood lessons that laid a foundation for my 'endarkened' epistemology. *Qualitative Inquiry,* 7 (5), 559–77.

Hertz, R. (ed.) (1997) *Reflexivity and Voice.* Thousand Oaks, CA: Sage.

Hickling-Hudson, A., Matthews, J. and Woods, A. (2004) Education, postcolonialism and disruptions, in A. Hickling-Hudson, J. Matthews and A. Woods *Disrupting Preconceptions: Postcolonialism and Education.* Flaxton, Qld.: Post Pressed, pp. 1–16.

Ho, I. T. (2001) Are Chinese teachers authoritarian? in D. A. Watkins and J. B. Biggs (eds) *Teaching the Chinese Learner: Psychological and Pedagogical Perspectives.* Hong Kong: Comparative Education Research Centre, University of Hong Kong, pp. 99–114.

Hockings, C., Cooke, S., Yamashita, H., McGinty, S. and Bowl, M. (2009) 'I'm neither entertaining nor charismatic...': negotiating university teacher identity within diverse student groups. *Teaching in Higher Education,* 15 (5), 483–94.

Hofstede, G. (1980) *Culture's Consequences: International Differences in Work-Related Values.* Beverley Hills, CA: Sage.

Hofstede, G. (1986) Cultural differences in teaching and learning. *International Journal of Intercultural Relations,* 10 (3), 301–20.

Holliday, A., Hyde, M. and Kullman, J. (eds) (2004) *Intercultural Communication: An Additional Resource Book.* London: Routledge.

Honey, P. and Mumford, A. (1982) *The Manual of Learning Styles.* Maidenhead: Peter Honey.

hooks, b. (1989) *Talking Back: Thinking Feminist, Thinking Black.* Boston, MA: South End.

hooks, b. (1994) *Teaching to Transgress: Education as the Practice of Freedom.* New York: Routledge.

hooks, b. (2003) *Teaching Community: A Pedagogy of Hope.* New York: Routledge.

Horta, H. (2009) Global and national prominent universities: internationalization, competitiveness and the role of the state. *Higher Education,* 58, 387–405.

Hyland, F., Trahar, S., Anderson, J. and Dickens, A. (2008) *A Changing World: The Internationalisation Experiences of Staff and Students (Home and International) in UK Higher Education (ESCalate and LLAS report).* Retrieved on 23 February 2010 from http://escalate.ac.uk/downloads/5248.pdf

Ippolito, K. (2007) Promoting intercultural learning in a multicultural society: ideals and realities. *Teaching in Higher Education,* 12 (5), 749–63.

Jarvis, P., Holford, J. and Griffin, C. (2003) *The Theory and Practice of Learning,* 2nd edn. London: Kogan Page.

Jin, L. and Cortazzi, M. (1998) Dimensions of dialogue: large classes in China. *International Journal of Educational Research,* 29 (8), 739–61.

Jones, A. (2001) *Resistance to English Language Support*. Sydney: Centre for Professional Development, Macquarie University.

Jones, J. F. (1999) From silence to talk: cross-cultural ideas on students' participation in academic group discussion. *English for Specific Purposes*, 18 (3), 243–59.

Jones, P. (1998) Globalisation and internationalism: democratic prospects for world education. *Comparative Education*, 34 (2), 143–55.

Josselson, R. (ed.) (1996) *Ethics and Process in the Narrative Studies of Lives*, Vol. 4. London: Sage.

Josselson, R. and Lieblich, A. (2003) A framework for narrative research proposals in psychology, in R. Josselson, A. Lieblich and D. P. McAdams (eds) *Up Close and Personal: The Teaching and Learning of Narrative Research*. Washington, DC: American Psychological Association, pp. 259–74.

Josselson, R. (2006) Narrative research and the challenge of accumulating knowledge. *Narrative Inquiry*, 16 (1), 3–10.

Kahane, D. (2009) Learning about obligation, compassion, and global justice: the place of contemplative pedagogy. *New Directions for Teaching and Learning*, 118, Summer, 49–60.

Kember, D. (2001) Beliefs about knowledge and the process of teaching and learning as a factor in adjusting to study in higher education. *Studies in Higher Education*, 26 (2), 205–21.

Kember, D. and Gow, L. (1991) A challenge to the anecdotal stereotype of the Asian student. *Studies in Higher Education*, 16 (2), 117–28.

Kennedy, P. (2002) Learning cultures and learning styles: myth-understandings about adult (Hong Kong) Chinese learners. *International Journal of Lifelong Education*, 21 (5), 430–45.

Kenway, J. and Fahey, J. (2006) The research imagination in a world on the move *Globalisation, Societies and Education*, 4 (2), 261–74.

Kiley, M. (2003) Conserver, strategist or transformer: the experiences of postgraduate sojourners. *Teaching in Higher Education*, 8 (3), 345–56.

Kim, T. (2009) Transnational academic mobility, internationalization and interculturality in higher education. *Intercultural Education*, 20 (5), 395–405.

Ki-Zerbo, J. (1990) *Educate or Perish: Africa's Impasse and Prospects*. Dakar: BREDA with UCARO (UNESCO-UNICEF West Africa).

Knowles, M. (1990) *The Adult Learner: A Neglected Species*, 4th edn. London: Gulf Publishing.

Koehne, N. (2005) (Re)construction: ways international students talk about their identity. *Australian Journal of Education*, 49 (1), 104–19.

Kolb, D. A. (1984) *Experiential Learning: Experience as the Source of Learning and Development*. Englewood Cliffs, NJ: Prentice-Hall.

Kolb, D. A. (1999) *The Kolb Learning Style Inventory Version 3*. Boston, MA: Hay Resources Direct.

Kreber, C. (2009) Different perspectives on internationalization in higher education. *New Directions for Teaching and Learning*, 118, 1–14.

Kvale, S. and Brinkmann, S. (2009) *Interviews: Learning the Craft of Qualitative*

Research Interviewing, 2nd edn. Thousand Oaks, CA: Sage.

Ladson-Billings, G. (1995) Toward a theory of culturally relevant pedagogy. *American Educational Research Journal,* 32 (3), 465–91.

Ladson-Billings, G. (2000) Racialised discourses and ethnic epistemologies, in N. K. Denzin and Y. S. Lincoln (eds) *The Handbook of Qualitative Research,* 2nd edn. Thousand Oaks, CA: Sage, pp. 257–77.

Ladson-Billings, G. (2003) It's your world, I'm just trying to explain it: understanding our epistemological and methodological challenges. *Qualitative Inquiry,* 9 (1), 5–12.

Lave, J. and Wenger, E. (1991) *Situated Learning: Legitimate Peripheral Participation.* Cambridge: Cambridge University Press.

Leggo, C. (2008) The ecology of personal and professional experience: a poet's view, in M. Cahnmann-Taylor and R. Siegesmund (eds) *Arts-Based Research in Education: Foundations for Practice.* New York: Routledge, pp. 89–97.

Leonard, D. (2000) Transforming doctoral studies: competencies and artistry. *Higher Education in Europe,* XXV (2), 181–92.

Lewin, K. (1951) *Field Theory in Social Science: Selected Theoretical Papers.* D. Cartwright (ed.). New York: Harper and Row.

Li, J. (2002) A cultural model of learning: Chinese 'Heart and mind for wanting to learn'. *Journal of Cross-Cultural Psychology,* 33 (3), 248–69.

Lincoln, Y. S. and Denzin, N. K. (1994) The fifth moment, in N. K. Denzin and Y. S. Lincoln (eds) *Handbook of Qualitative Research.* Thousand Oaks, CA: Sage.

Luxon, T. and Peelo, M. (2009) Academic sojourners, teaching and internationalisation: the experience of non-UK staff in a British university. *Teaching in Higher Education,* 14 (6), 649–59.

McCoy, K. (2000) White noise – the sound of epidemic: reading/writing a climate of intelligibility around the 'crisis' difference, in E. A. St. Pierre and W. A. Pillow (eds) *Working the Ruins: Feminist Poststructural Theory and Methods in Education.* New York: Routledge, pp. 237–57.

McIntyre, A. (1997) *Making Meaning of Whiteness: Exploring Racial Identity with White Teachers.* Albany, NY: State University of New York Press.

McNamara, D. and Harris, R. (1997) (eds) *Overseas Students in Higher Education: Issues in Teaching and Learning.* London: Routledge.

Malcolm, J. and Zukas, M. (2001) Bridging pedagogic gaps: conceptual discontinuities in higher education. *Teaching in Higher Education,* 6 (1), 33–42.

Malcolm, J. and Zukas, M. (2009) Making a mess of academic work and identity *Teaching in Higher Education,* 14 (5), 495–506.

Manathunga, C. (2007) Intercultural postgraduate supervision: ethnographic journeys of identity and power, in D. Palfreyman and D. L. McBride (eds) *Learning and Teaching across Cultures in Higher Education.* Basingstoke: Palgrave Macmillan, pp. 93–113.

Maranhao, T. (1991) Reflection, dialogue and the subject. in F. Steier (ed.) *Research and Reflexivity.* London: Sage, pp. 235–49.

Marginson, S. (2000) Rethinking academic work in the global era. *Journal of Higher*

Education Policy and Management, 22 (1), 23–35.

Marginson, S. and Mollis, M. (2001) 'The door opens and the tiger leaps': theories and reflexivities of comparative education for a global millennium. *Comparative Education Review*, 45 (4), 581–615.

Marginson, S. and Van Der Wende, M. (2007) *Globalisation and Higher Education*. OECD Education Working Paper. Brussels: OECD.

Marton, F. and Saljo, R. (1984) Approaches to learning, in F. Marton, D. Hounsell and N. Entwistle (eds) *The Experience of Learning*. Edinburgh: Scottish Education Press, pp. 36–55.

Maundeni, T. (1999) African females and adjustment to studying abroad. *Gender and Education*, 11 (1), 27–42.

Maxwell, R. (ed.) (2001) *Culture Works: The Political Economy of Culture* Minneapolis, MN: University of Minnesota Press.

Merriam, S. B., Johnson-Bailey, J., Lee, M-Y., Kee, Y., Ntseane, G. and Muhamed, M. (2001) Power and positionality: negotiating insider/outsider status within and across cultures. *International Journal of Lifelong Education*, 20 (5), 403–16.

Merrick, B. (2000) Foreword, in B. Hudson and M. J. Todd (eds) *Internationalising the Curriculum in Higher Education: Reflecting on Practice*. Sheffield: Sheffield Hallam University Press, pp. xi–xiv.

Mezirow, J. (1991) *Transformative Dimensions of Adult Learning*. San Francisco, CA: Jossey-Bass.

Minnich, E. K. (2005) *Transforming Knowledge*, 2nd edn. Philadelphia, PA: Temple University Press.

Mishler, R. E. (1986) *Research Interviewing: Context and Narrative*. Cambridge, MA: Harvard University Press.

Mishler, R. E. (2004) Historians of the self: restorying lives, revising identities. *Research in Human Development*, 1 (1 and 2), 101–21.

Modood, T. (2006) Ethnicity, Muslims and higher education entry in Britain. *Teaching in Higher Education*, 11 (2) 247–50.

Mok, K-H. (2003) Globalisation and higher education restructuring in Hong Kong, Taiwan and Mainland China. *Higher Education Research and Development*, 22 (2), 117–29.

Mok, K-H. and Lee, M. L. L. (2003) Globalization or glocalization? Higher education reforms in Singapore. *Asia Pacific Journal of Education*, 23 (1), 15–42.

Montgomery, C. (2010) *Understanding the International Student Experience*. Basingstoke: Palgrave Macmillan.

Morrow, R. A. and Torres C. A. (2003) The State, social movements and educational reform, in R. F. Arnove and C. A. Torres (eds) *Comparative Education: The Dialectic of the Global and the Local*, 2nd edn. Lanham, MA: Rowman and Littlefield, pp. 92–114.

Muncey, T. (2010) *Creating Autoethnographies*. London: Sage.

Muthayan, S. (2005) *Globalization, Democratization and Knowledge Production at Three South African Universities*. Unpublished PhD dissertation, University of British Columbia.

Naples, N. (1997) A feminist revisiting of the insider/outsider debate: the 'Outsider' phenomenon in rural Iowa, in R. Hertz (ed.) *Reflexivity and Voice*. Thousand Oaks, CA: Sage, pp. 70–94.

National Committee of Inquiry into Higher Education (1997) *Higher Education in the Learning Society: 'The Dearing Report'*. London: HMSO.

Ng, K. C., Murphy, D. and Jenkins, W. (2002) The teacher's role in supporting a learner-centred learning environment: voices from a group of part-time postgraduate students in Hong Kong. *International Journal of Lifelong Education*, 21 (5), 462–73.

OECD (1999) *Quality and Internationalisation in Higher Education*. Brussels: Organisation for Economic Co-operation and Development.

Ofori-Dankwa, J. and Lane, R. W. (2000) Four approaches to cultural diversity: implications for teaching at institutions of higher education. *Teaching in Higher Education*, 5 (4), 493–9.

Ondaatje, M. (1992) *The English Patient*. London: Bloomsbury.

Otten, M. (2000) Impacts of cultural diversity at home, in P. Crowther *et al. Internationalisation at Home: A Position Paper*. European Association for International Education/Academic Cooperation Association, IAK, IESEG, Nuffic, Katholieke Hogeschool Limburg and Malmo University.

Otten, M. (2003) Intercultural learning and diversity in higher education. *Journal of Studies in International Education*, 7 (1), 12–26.

Palmer, S. (1999) In search of effective counselling across cultures, in S. Palmer and P. Laungani *Counselling in a Multicultural Society*. London: Sage, pp. 153–73.

Phillion, J. (2002) Becoming a narrative inquirer in a multicultural landscape. *Journal of Curriculum Studies*, 34 (5), 535–56.

Phillion, J. and He, M. F. (2008) Multicultural and cross-cultural narrative inquiry in educational research. *Thresholds in Education*, XXXIV (1 and 2), 2–12.

Phuong-Mai, N., Terlouw, C. and Pilot, A. (2006) Culturally appropriate pedagogy: the case of group learning in a Confucian Heritage Culture context. *Intercultural Education*, 17 (1), 1–19.

Polkinghorne, D. E. (1995) Narrative configuration in qualitative analysis, in J.A. Hatch and R. Wisniewski (eds) *Life History and Narrative*. London: Falmer Press, pp. 5–23.

Pratt, D. D., Kelly, M. and Wong, W. S. S. (1999) Chinese conceptions of 'effective teaching' in Hong Kong: towards culturally sensitive evaluation of teaching. *International Journal of Lifelong Education*, 18 (4), 241–58.

Prescott, A. and Hellsten, M. (2005) Hanging together even with non-native speakers: the international student transition experience, in P. Ninnes and M. Hellsten (eds) *Internationalizing Higher Education: Critical Explorations of Pedagogy and Policy*. Hong Kong: Comparative Education Research Centre, University of Hong Kong, pp. 75–95.

Pring, R. (1999) Reflecting on the reflective practitioners, in A-C. Chen and J. Van Maanen (eds) *The Reflective Spin: Case Studies of Teachers in Higher Education Transforming Action*. Singapore: World Scientific, pp. 3–13.

Prosser, M. and Trigwell, K. (1999) *Understanding Learning and Teaching: The Experience in Higher Education*. Buckingham: SRHE/Open University.

Rassool, N. (2004) Sustaining linguistic diversity within the global cultural economy: issues of language rights and linguistic possibilities. *Comparative Education*, 40 (2), 199–214.

Reay, D. (1996) Dealing with difficult difference: reflexivity and social class in feminist research. *Feminism and Psychology*, 6 (3), 443–56.

Richardson, L. (1994) Writing: a method of inquiry, in N. K. Denzin and Y. S. Lincoln (eds) *Handbook of Qualitative Research*. Thousand Oaks, CA: Sage, pp. 516–529.

Richardson, L. (2000) Writing: a method of inquiry, in N. K. Denzin and Y. S. Lincoln (eds) *Handbook of Qualitative Research*, 2nd edn. Thousand Oaks, CA: Sage, pp. 923–48.

Richardson, L. and St Pierre, E. A. (2005) Writing: a method of inquiry, in N. K. Denzin and Y. S. Lincoln (eds) *The Sage Handbook of Qualitative Research*, 3rd edn. Thousand Oaks, CA: Sage, pp. 959–78.

Riessman, C. K. (2004) A thrice told tale: new readings of an old story, in B. Hurwitz, T. Greenhalgh and V. Skultans (eds) *Narrative Research in Health and Illness*. London: Medical Journal Books/Blackwell, pp. 309–24.

Riessman, C. K. (2008) *Narrative Methods for the Human Sciences*. Thousand Oaks, CA: Sage.

Rizvi, F. (2000) Internationalisation of curriculum. Retrieved on 23 February 2010 from http://www.eotu.uiuc.edu/EOTUMODEL/Event/RIZVIPaperInternat RMIT.pdf

Rizvi, F. (2004) Debating globalization and education after September 11. *Comparative Education*, 40 (2), 157–71.

Robinson-Pant, A. (2005) *Cross-Cultural Perspectives on Educational Research*. Maidenhead: Open University Press.

Rogers, C. (1951) *Client-centered Therapy*. Boston, MA: Houghton Mifflin.

Rogers, C. (1994) *Freedom to Learn*, 3rd edn. Upper Saddle River, NJ: Merrill.

Ryan, J. and Viete, R. (2009) Respectful interactions: learning with international students in the English-speaking academy. *Teaching in Higher Education*, 14 (3), 303–14.

Ryen, A. (2000) Colonial methodology? Methodological challenges to cross-cultural projects collecting data by structured interviews, in C. Truman, D. M. Mertens and B. Humphries (eds) *Research and Inequality*. London: University College Press, pp. 220–35.

Said, E. (2003) *Orientalism*. London: Penguin.

Salili, F. (2001) Teacher–student interaction: attributional implications and effectiveness of teachers' evaluative feedback, in D. A. Watkins and J. B. Biggs (eds) *Teaching the Chinese Learner: Psychological and Pedagogical Perspectives*. Hong Kong: Comparative Education Research Centre, University of Hong Kong, pp. 77–98.

Saltmarsh, S. and Swirski, T. (2010) 'Pawns and prawns': international academics' observations on their transition to working in an Australian university. *Journal of*

Higher Education Policy and Management, 32 (3), 291–301.

Salvadori R. G. (1997) The difficulties of interculturalism. *European Journal of Intercultural Studies*, 8 (2), 185–91.

Sanderson, G. (2004) Existentialism, globalisation and the cultural other. *International Education Journal*, 4 (4), 1–20.

Sanderson, G. (2007) A foundation for the internationalization of the academic Self. *Journal of Studies in International Education*, 12 (3), 276–307.

Sarup, M. (1996) *Identity, Culture and the Postmodern World*. Edinburgh: Edinburgh University Press.

Scheurich, J. J. (1997) *Research Method in the Postmodern*. London: Routledge Falmer.

Scott, P. (1998) Massification, internationalization and globalization, in P. Scott (ed.). *The Globalization of Higher Education*. Buckingham: SRHE/Open University Press, pp. 108–30.

Seidler, V. J. (2010) *Embodying Identities: Culture, Differences and Social Theory*. Bristol: The Policy Press.

Shope, J. H. (2006) 'You can't cross a river without getting wet': a feminist standpoint on the dilemmas of cross-cultural research. *Qualitative Inquiry*, 12 (1), 163–84.

Skeggs, B. (2002) Techniques for telling the reflexive self, in T. May (ed.) *Qualitative Research in Action*. London: Sage, pp. 349–74.

Skelton, A. (2005) *Understanding Teaching Excellence in Higher Education: Towards a Critical Approach*. London: Routledge.

Sparkes, A. C. (2002) Autoethnography, self-indulgence or something more? in A. Bochner and C. Ellis (eds) *Ethnographically Speaking: Autoethnography, Literature and Aesthetics*. New York: Alta Mira Press, pp. 209–32.

Sparks, B. (2002) Epistemological and methodological considerations of doing cross-cultural research in adult education. *International Journal of Lifelong Education*, 21 (2), 115–29.

Sparks, B. and Butterwick, S. (2004) Culture, equity and learning, in G. Foley (ed.) *Dimensions of Adult Learning: Adult Education and Training in a Global Era*. Maidenhead: Open University Press, pp. 276–89.

Speedy, J. (2006) The Gulbarrian College Gargoyles and the narrative gaze: landscapes of the future, imaginative learning and researcher identity, in S. Trahar (ed.) *Narrative Research on Learning: Comparative and International Perspectives*. Oxford: Symposium Books, pp. 253–71.

Speedy, J. (2007) *Narrative Inquiry and Psychotherapy*. London: Palgrave.

Stanfield, J. H. (1993a) Epistemological considerations, in J. H. Stanfield II and D. M. Rutledge (eds) *Race and Ethnicity in Research Methods*. Newbury Park, CA: Sage, pp. 16–36.

Stanfield, J. H. (1993b) Methodological reflections: an introduction, in J. H. Stanfield II and D. M. Rutledge (eds) *Race and Ethnicity in Research Methods*. Newbury Park, CA: Sage, pp. 3–15.

Stanfield, J. H. (1994) Ethnic modeling in qualitative research, in N. K. Denzin and

Y. S. Lincoln (eds) *The Handbook of Qualitative Research*. Thousand Oaks, CA: Sage, pp. 175–88.

Stensaker, B., Frolich, N., Gornitzka, A. and Maassen, P. (2008) Internationalisation of higher education: the gap between national policy-making and institutional needs. *Globalisation, Societies and Education*, 6 (1), 1–11.

Storan, J. (2006) 'From exclusion to participation in English higher education', in A. Oduaran and H. S. Bhola (eds) *Widening Access to Education as Social Justice*. Dortrecht: Springer, pp. 357–68.

Strand, S. and Winston, J. (2008) Educational aspirations in inner city schools. *Educational Studies*, 34 (4), 249–67.

Stromquist, N. P. (2002) Globalization, the I, and the Other. *Current Issues in Comparative Education,* 4 (2), 87–94.

Swadener, B. B. and Mutua, K. (2008) Decolonizing performances: deconstructing the global postcolonial, in N. K. Denzin, Y. S. Lincon and L. Tuhiwai Smith (eds) *Handbook of Critical and Indigenous Methodologies*. Thousand Oaks, CA: Sage, pp. 31–43.

Tamuri, Ab. H. (2007) Islamic Education teachers' perceptions of the teaching of akhlāq in Malaysian secondary schools. *Journal of Moral Education*, 36 (3), 371–86.

Tatar, M. and Bekerman, Z. (2002) The concept of culture in the contexts and practices of professional counselling: a constructivist perspective. *Counselling Psychology Quarterly*, 15 (4), 375–84.

Tatum, B. D. (1997) *'Why Are all the Black Kids Sitting Together in the Cafeteria?' and other Conversations about Race*. New York, NY: Basic Books.

Teekens, H. (2000) Teaching and learning in the international classroom, in P. Crowther *et al. Internationalisation at Home: A Position Paper*. European Association for International Education/Academic Cooperation Association, IAK, IESEG, Nuffic, Katholieke Hogeschool Limburg and Malmo University.

Teichler, U. (2004) The changing debate on internationalisation of higher education. *Higher Education*, 48 (1), 5–26.

Teichler, U. (2009) Internationalisation of higher education: European experiences. *Asia Pacific Education Review*, 10, 93-106.

Tennant, M., McMullen, C. and Kaczynski, D. (2010) *Teaching, Learning and Research in Higher Education: A Critical Approach*. Abingdon: Routledge.

Tikly, L. (1999) Postcolonialism and comparative education. *International Review of Education*, 45 (5/6), 603–21.

Trahar, S. (1996) *Take Your Partners: A Study of the Influence of Gender on Co-training*. Unpublished MSc dissertation, University of Bristol.

Trahar, S. (2002a) Researching learning across cultures. *Counselling and Psychotherapy Research*, 2 (3), 195–200.

Trahar, S. (2002b) Towards cultural synergy in higher education. Paper presented at the Second Symposium on Teaching and Learning in Higher Education, National University of Singapore, 4–6 September.

Trahar, S. (2006) A part of the landscape: the practitioner researcher as narrative inquirer in an international higher education community, in S. Trahar (ed.)

Narrative Research on Learning: Comparative and International Perspectives. Oxford: Symposium, pp. 201–19.

Trahar, S. (2007) *Teaching and Learning: the International Higher Education Landscape. Some Theories and Working Practices.* Available to download at http://escalate.ac.uk/3559

Trahar, S. (2008) Close encounters of the cultural kind: reflections of a practitioner researcher in international higher education, in M. Hellsten and A. Reid (eds) *Researching International Pedagogies: Sustainable Practice for Teaching and Learning in Higher Education.* New York: Springer, pp. 45–61.

Trahar, S. (2009) Beyond the story itself: narrative inquiry and autoethnography in intercultural research in higher education. *Forum: Qualitative Social Research,* 10 (1), Art 30.

Trahar, S. (2010) Has everybody seen a swan? Stories from the internationalised classroom, in E. Jones (ed.) *Internationalisation and the Student Voice: Higher Education Perspectives.* Routledge: New York/Abingdon, pp. 143–55.

Trinh T. Minh-ha (1989) *Woman, Native, Other: Writing Postcoloniality and Feminism.* Bloomington, IN: Indiana University Press.

Tuhiwai Smith, L. (1999) *Decolonizing Methodologies: Research and Indigenous Peoples.* London: Zen Books.

Turner, Y. and Acker, A. (2002) *Education in the New China: Shaping Ideas at Work.* Aldershot: Ashgate.

Turner, Y. and Robson, S. (2006) *Beleaguered, Bothered and Bewildered: A Story of Academics and Internationalization.* Paper presented at the Supporting the Chinese Learner Conference, University of Portsmouth, 15–16 July.

Turner, Y. and Robson, S. (2008) *Internationalizing the University.* London: Continuum.

Turniansky, B., Tuval, S., Mansur, R., Barak, J. and Gidron, A. (2009) From the inside out: learning to understand and appreciate multiple voices through telling identities. *New Directions for Teaching and Learning,* 118, Summer, 39–47.

Tweed, R. G. and Lehman, D. R. (2002) Learning considered within a cultural context: Confucian and Socratic approaches. *American Psychologist,* February, 88–99.

Tweed, R. G. and Lehman D. R. (2003) Confucian and Socratic Learning. *American Psychologist,* February, 148–49.

Usher, R. and Edwards, R. (1994) *Postmodernism and Education: Different Voices, Different Worlds.* London: Routledge.

Vaira, M. (2004) Globalization and higher education organizational change: a framework for analysis? *Higher Education,* 48 (4), 483–510.

Vice, S. (1997) *Introducing Bakhtin.* Manchester: Manchester University Press.

Volet, S. E. (1999) Learning across cultures: appropriateness of knowledge transfer. *International Journal of Educational Research,* 31 (7), 625–43.

Volet, S. E. and Ang, G. (1998) Culturally mixed groups on international campuses: an opportunity for inter-cultural learning. *Higher Education Research and Development,* 17 (1), 5–23.

Volet, S. E. and Tan-Quigley, A. (1995) Daring to be different: unspoken agendas in interactions between international students and general staff at university. Paper presented at the International Students Advisors Network of Australia (ISANA) Conference, Fremantle, Australia.

Wachter, B. (2000) Internationalisation at home – the context. In P.Crowther *et al. Internationalisation at Home: A Position Paper.* European Association for International Education/Academic Cooperation Association, IAK, IESEG, Nuffic, Katholieke Hogeschool Limburg and Malmo University.

Wakeling, P. (2006) *The Ethnic Background of UK Postgraduates: Cause for Celebration or Cause for Concern?* Paper presented at the Society for Research into Higher Education Annual Conference, Brighton, December.

Walker, R. (1985) *Doing Research: A Handbook for Teachers.* London: Methuen.

Watkins, D. (2000) Learning and teaching: a cross-cultural perspective. *School Leadership and Management,* 20 (2), 161–73.

Watkins, D. A. and Biggs, J. B. (eds) (1996) *The Chinese Learner: Cultural, Psychological and Contextual Influences.* Hong Kong: Comparative Education Research Centre, University of Hong Kong.

Watkins, D. A. and Biggs, J. B. (2001) *Teaching the Chinese Learner: Psychological and Pedagogical Perspectives.* Hong Kong: Comparative Education Research Centre, University of Hong Kong.

Watson, B. and Scraton, S. (2001) Confronting whiteness? Researching the leisure lives of South Asian mothers. *Journal of Gender Studies,* 10 (3), 265–76.

Webb, G. (1996) *Understanding Staff Development.* Buckingham: SRHE/Open University.

Webb, S. (2006) Learning from elsewhere: ethical issues in a planned piece of narrative research in New Zealand, in S. Trahar (ed.) *Narrative Research on Learning: Comparative and International Perspectives.* Oxford: Symposium, pp. 221–38.

Welikala, T. and Watkins, C. (2008) *Improving Intercultural Learning in Higher Education: Responding to Cultural Scripts for Learning.* London: Institute of Education.

Winch, P. (1958) *The Idea of a Social Science and its Relation to Philosophy.* London: Routledge.

Winkler, G. (2003) Ethical issues in narrative research. *Educational Action Research,* 11 (3), 389–402.

Wittengstein, L. (1953) *Philosophical Investigations* (trans. Anscombe). New York: Macmillan.

Wright, S. and Lander, D. (2003) Collaborative group interactions of students from two ethnic backgrounds. *Higher Education Research and Development,* 22 (3), 237–52.

Wu, Su (2002) Filling the pot or lighting the 'fire'? Cultural variations in conceptions of pedagogy. *Teaching in Higher Education,* 7 (4), 387–95.

Yang, R. (2002) University internationalisation: its meanings, rationales and implications. *Intercultural Education,* 13 (1), 81–95.

Yang, R. (2005) Internationalizing Chinese higher education: a case study of a major comprehensive university, in P. Ninnes and M. Hellsten (eds) *Internationalizing Higher Education: Critical Explorations of Pedagogy and Policy*. Hong Kong: Comparative Education Research Centre, University of Hong Kong, pp. 97–118.

Young, I. M. (2001) Justice and the politics of difference, in S. Seidman and J. C. Alexander (eds) *The New Social Theory Reader*. London: Routledge, pp. 203–11.

INDEX